MEAT
C·O·O·K·B·O·O·K

Happy cooking!

Mitzi Ayah

MITZI AYALA

Cover photograph by Nels Shirer. Detail of Stormstown Cows by
Rebecca Shirer is taken from the book *Creature Comforts* by Marie
Shirer and Barbara Brackman, published by Wallace-Homestead
Book Company, 1986, and appears through the courtesy of the
authors.
Cover design: Geri Wolfe
Cover and Interior Layout: Anthony Jacobson

Library of Congress Catalog
Card Number 85-051024

ISBN 0-87069-459-6

Copyright © 1985
Wallace-Homestead Book Company

10 9 8 7 6 5 4 3 2 1

Published by

Wallace-Homestead Book Company
580 Waters Edge
Lombard, Illinois, 60148

One of the
ABC PUBLISHING abc
Companies

For M. Boyd Burton, Ph.D., M.S.T.A., and E.C.A.
by unanimous consent of
The Women of American Agrinet, Inc.

Contents

Acknowledgments

Unfortunately, I don't know the name of the person most responsible for this book. I met him at a convention of the National Association of Farm Broadcasters, and in the course of about three minutes, he changed my eating habits forever.

It was in 1980, and, back then, I was flirting with the idea of vegetarianism. I didn't get very far in explaining my ideas to him, though, because he said something that made me do some quick reevaluating. "Remember, Mitzi," he said, "it's either the cow or the plow." He went on to explain that when it's not economical to raise cattle, ranchers are forced to plow under the land and raise crops on it—if they want to feed their families and pay their bills. The problem is that pasture lands are usually the most fragile and easily erodible lands. When rain or wind removes the topsoil of land that's no longer protected by pasture, it takes centuries to replace what one year can carry away. The cattle industry, he convinced me, is critical for helping us preserve our soil's fertility for future generations.

That conversation was the beginning of my serious interest in meat cookery. Since then, my freezer has always had lamb or pork or beef in it from an animal raised by one of the Future Farmers of America (FFA) or one of the 4-H kids. (Incidentally, if you want to save money and help an FFA or a 4-H kid at the same time, buy one of their animals at an auction during one of your county or state fairs. They'll help you arrange to have the meat packaged and frozen, and you'll generally pay less than supermarket prices.)

There are others who contributed to this book whose names I don't know. When the great gastronome, Brillat-Savarin, said, "The discovery of a new dish does more for the happiness of mankind than the discovery of a star," he could have been speaking of the eight generations of good cooks who came up with these recipes. They all deserve mention, and maybe a star as well—if I only knew their names. Their recipes are different, special, and delicious. (I know because a lot of the beef, lamb, and pork from my freezer has been used to test these recipes.)

Some of the people who helped with this book, however, are very much known to me. Carol Ford is responsible for the organization of the book together with many of the comments on the recipes. She's also the mastermind who made sure that all deadlines were met, all references checked, and the loose ends secured. Nancy Ehrke and Carol helped select the excerpts from old issues of *The Prairie Farmer*, and Nancy typed the manuscript. Brenda Carey assisted in the assembly of the final manuscript, and we all taste-tested the recipes.

Bill Topaz and Steve Joss, from Wallace-Homestead Book Company, had the vision to recognize the legacy of fabulous recipes hidden away in the *Prairie Farmer* archives.

Introduction

Have you ever considered how much our attitude towards meat has changed over the years? Health and fitness dominate our viewpoint in the 1980s, but in mother or grandmother's time, the emphasis was quite different.

The early recipes, up through the 1950s, almost never mentioned health. Sure, meals had to be wholesome, but the big emphasis was on making mealtime an important family occasion. After that, the housewife was concerned with getting the most for her dollar, and she was concerned with making traditional meals. If you'll look at some of the early recipes, you'll see that she spent not just hours, but days on a meal. Some of the pot roast recipes in this book require up to four days' preparation time.

The 1960s and 1970s saw a major change in our eating habits. Suddenly we acquired an intense interest in health, fitness, and appearance. That's when the "Twiggy" look became fashionable. We also, for the first time, started to make large scale use of convenience foods and frozen foods. By the late 1960s, gourmet cooking was beginning to capture our imagination and cookbook authors like Julia Child or James Beard or Craig Claiborne became celebrities. Health foods became a national craze.

The 1980s have provided us with still more changes. In 1980, 25 percent of American households had a microwave oven. By 1985, this number had increased to 50 percent. The frozen food industry expanded so rapidly that by the middle of the decade, 90 percent of the kinds of foods you could find in the frozen food section of your supermarket did not exist five years before. A convenience food in the seventies might have been a frozen TV dinner that took 30 minutes to cook. The 1980s convenience food cooks in the microwave in a matter of seconds. And the pot roast that once took four days, now takes an hour with the microwave.

As Larry Booth from the Frozen Food Council of Northern California says, "By the mid-1980s, people seldom had time for the long, elaborate, time-consuming meals that used to be part of our lifestyles. Today, men and women are both working, and when they aren't working, she's attending her aerobics class and he's going bowling."

The 1980s have shown a different approach to health also. While the 1970s emphasized "health foods," the 1980s stress "healthy foods." Wheat germ and brewer's yeast lost out to fresh fruits and vegetables.

Meat has an important role in a healthy diet. It's a nutritional investment because meat is a "nutrient-dense" food, providing a large share of essential nutrients and a relatively small share of calories. For example, a three-ounce serving of lean beef supplies only 8 percent of an adult's daily calorie requirements—but 45 percent of the daily protein requirement.

There are other changes in our eating habits. The meat we buy is leaner than it used to be. Through selective breeding and scientific feeding practices, cattlemen have succeeded in producing animals that are leaner. Pork is so lean today that both Weight Watchers and Diet Workshop recommend it as part of their diets.

Another change over the years is that today's meat is subject to a higher standard of sanitation than ever before. Ground beef alone is subject to 41,000 Federal and State regulations, many of those stemming from the 200 laws and 111,000 precedent-setting court cases. In fact, the only industry more highly regulated than meat is the nuclear energy industry!

A lot has changed over the years, but the recipes that you'll find in the following pages are well worth trying. The recent ones take advantage of microwave cooking and other modern shortcuts. The older ones sometimes take longer, but we hope you'll enjoy them the way you might enjoy a family heirloom: they're part of our roots and our heritage; they're conversation pieces; they're some of the best of the past; and they're *fun*.

1
Beef Up Your Nutrition

Did you know that the nutritional value of lean beef is the same whether it comes from a steak or ground beef or pot roast—and that this knowledge can save you money? And did you know that whatever cut you buy, it's going to be leaner and have less cholesterol than it did in Grandmother's, or even Mother's time?

One of the major goals of the beef industry today is breeding leaner animals. When a particularly lean and desirable animal arises, it's now possible to propagate those traits hundreds of times faster than we ever could have done in the past. Years ago, a cow might have had half a dozen or so offspring. Today, she can easily have hundreds.

Veterinarians and other embryo transplant experts are helping the beef industry to breed leaner animals, and thanks to their efforts, the beef you'll find in the supermarkets today is much leaner than it was even five years ago.

If leanness is of particular concern, perhaps for health or diet reasons, Lois Schlickau, Past President of the American Hereford Auxillary, has some tips for you. "Choose lean cuts such as flank steak, sirloin tip, or round. These cuts have only six grams of fat per three-ounce portion. The non-lean cuts typically have eight grams of fat for the same sized portion."

Schlickau also suggests that, if we want to save money when buying beef, we should try some of the less well-known cuts. "The nutritional value of lean beef," she points out, "is the same whether it comes from a steak or ground beef or pot roast—so do try some of the lower priced cuts."

There's a good reason why the lower-priced cuts cost less. The most popular beef cuts account for only 30 percent of all the retail cuts. Since the most popular ones are in the shortest supply, and since the carcass can't be changed—there are only so many steaks and roasts available—the retailers make sure the less popular cuts sell by pricing them at lower cost per pound. You can save a lot of money by learning to prepare the less popular cuts.

Another way of getting the most for your money is taking care to store your beef in the best way. The first rule is, refrigerate it or freeze it as soon as you can after purchasing. Store it in the coldest part of your refrigerator and, if it's ground, plan to use it in two days. For other cuts, use within four days.

For longer storage, freeze it. "Be sure to overwrap the original package with freezer paper," cautions Laurena Johnson, a California cattle rancher who's active in American Agri-Women. "The problem with the original plastic wrapping," she adds, "is that it allows too much moisture to escape. You want to avoid having the meat dry out, because if it does, it's lost a lot of its special flavor and texture."

For overwrapping, you can use freezer paper or aluminum foil or a freezer bag. Be sure to seal the package tightly. Properly wrapped, and stored at 0 degrees F., beef should maintain its quality for up to twelve months. Cooked beef and ground beef don't last as long in the freezer and should be used within three months.

By the way, it's worth going to the trouble of labeling and dating your frozen beef. It's not that there's a sudden date by which the meat is no longer good—it's just that you'll find it tastier, juicier, and more palatable if you keep track of the dates and use it within the recommended time.

When you're ready to use beef from the freezer, you have the choice of three good ways to defrost it: in the refrigerator, during cooking, or in the microwave. To defrost it in the refrigerator, leave it in its original wrapping and allow an average of five hours per pound for a large roast, four hours per pound for a small roast, and two hours for a one-inch steak.

To defrost during cooking, allow one-third to one-half more cooking time for roasting. If you're broiling a steak, position the meat farther from the heat than usual so you don't end up with a charred surface and a still-frozen interior. For microwave defrosting, follow the manufacturer's directions.

Why not enlarge your repertory and try some of the favorite beef recipes from years past, or experiment with some of the new microwave ones? Either way, you'll be cooking with leaner, more nutritious beef than ever before.

Enjoy America's favorite red meat. For flavor and nutrition, you may well agree with Leo Johnson from the California Cattlemen's Association that it's the Cadillac of meats.

Beef Roasts

Roast beef—just the words make most of us hungry, as we remember Sunday dinners or special occasions of our youth. But there are almost as many ways to roast a beef as there are cooks. From the classic to the novel—we offer a collection of delicious recipes taken from the pages of *Prairie Farmer* since the turn of the century.

Here's the classic:

Standing Rib Roast Beef

1 standing rib roast of beef
salt and pepper, as needed

Sprinkle meat with salt and pepper, either before or after cooking, allowing one teaspoon of salt and one-quarter teaspoon of pepper per pound. Insert meat thermometer through fat into center of meat. Place roast, fat side up, in shallow roasting pan, with rib bones forming a rack to hold roast above the drippings.

Place in 325 degree oven and roast 22 to 26 minutes per pound for rare meat (140 degrees on meat thermometer), 26 to 30 minutes per pound for medium (160 degrees on thermometer), and 33 to 35 minutes for well done meat (170 degrees). Remove meat from oven; allow to stand in warm place for 15 to 20 minutes for easier carving. Skim fat from drippings; use remainder au jus with meat.
September 28, 1968

An excellent floor mop may be made in the following manner: Slash old stockings into strips an inch wide, forming a fringe. Stitch several thicknesses of this to a strip of cloth three inches wide and ten inches long. Machine stitching is best. Saturate this with the following ingredients: equal portions of vinegar, linseed oil and turpentine, or any good furniture polish. Fasten into a mop stick. By using this daily upon painted and hardwood floors they are kept free from dust and given a beautiful polish.
August 28, 1913

As we see over and over again when we compare the old recipes with the new, a certain brevity characterized the way cooks at the turn of the century wrote out recipes. As an example, two recipes for Roast Beef with Yorkshire Pudding follow:

Roast Beef with Yorkshire Pudding—1902

Take the roast beef from the pan, trim off part of the dripping, and put in the pan a batter made of sweet milk, baking powder and flour. Keep the roast hot, and serve, garnished with the pudding cut in squares.
November 20, 1902

Roast Beef with Yorkshire Pudding—1970s

This traditional English pudding takes the place of the usual starch served with a main dish. Serve it from the dish in which it is cooked, cut into squares. Pour juices from the roast over it. They complement this dish better than a thickened gravy would. And a special note: ingredients for Yorkshire pudding must be at room temperature or they will not puff up as they should.

1 standing rib or sirloin roast
⅞ cup all-purpose flour
½ tsp. salt
½ cup milk
½ cup water
2 eggs

Preheat oven to 550 degrees.

Place roast fat side up on rack in pan in oven. Reduce heat to 350 degrees. For medium rare, cook 20 minutes to the pound. Keep warm while making pudding.

Increase oven temperature to 400 degrees.

Sift flour and salt into a bowl. Make a well in the middle. Pour in milk and stir. Slowly pour in water. Beat eggs until fluffy, then beat them into batter. Beat until large bubbles rise to the surface. While you do this, have an ovenproof 9 x 12-inch serving dish heating. Pour into the hot dish one-quarter inch hot drippings from the beef. Pour in batter to about five-eights-inch.

Place in oven and bake 20 minutes. Reduce heat to 350 degrees and bake 15 minutes longer. Serve at once.
6 servings
December, 1974

No selection of beef roasts would be complete without Beef Wellington. Plan a simple menu around it so the Wellington can receive the primary attention it deserves. Good choices for a spring menu would be asparagus, carrots, and a green salad. Prepare Swiss Potatoes as the beef roasts. Serve individual chocolate mousses for dessert.

Beef Wellington

3½ to 4-pound beef tenderloin
3 cups all-purpose flour
1½ tsp. salt
¾ cup lard
½ to ¾ cup cold water
8 ounces liver sausage or liver pâté
1 egg, beaten

Preheat oven to 425 degrees.

Place tenderloin on a rack in an open roasting pan. Do not add water; do not cover. Place in oven and roast a total of 20 to 25 minutes for rare (depending on size of roast), 25 to 30 minutes for medium. Remove from oven and let stand 30 minutes.

Prepare pastry by sifting together flour and salt. Cut in lard to form fine, even crumbs. Add water, one tablespoon at a time, until dough just holds together. Shape into a ball. On a lightly floured board or pastry cloth roll into an 18 x 14-inch rectangle one-quarter inch thick. Spread liver sausage or pâté over surface of pastry. Place the tenderloin lengthwise, top down, in middle of pastry. Bring the long sides of the pastry up to overlap on the bottom of the beef; brush with egg to seal. Trim the ends of pastry and fold over. Brush with egg to seal.

Transfer the pastry-wrapped meat, seam side down, to a baking sheet. Cut decorative shapes from pastry trimmings and arrange on top. Brush top and sides with egg. If desired, check internal temperature by inserting meat thermometer, being sure bulb is centered in thickest part and does not rest in fat.

Return to 425 degree oven and bake for 30 minutes, or until 130 degrees for rare beef to 150 degrees for medium. Let stand 10 minutes before carving.
6 servings

The following recipe may be prepared ahead of time and reheated for 10 minutes immediately after the Wellington is removed from the oven.

Swiss Potatoes

½ cup minced onion
2 T. oil
4½ T. butter
4 eggs
½ clove garlic, mashed
2 T. minced parsley
1 cup grated Swiss cheese
¼ cup heavy cream
4 medium potatoes, peeled
salt and pepper, to taste

Preheat oven to 375 degrees.

Cook onion in oil and two tablespoons butter until transparent. Beat eggs with garlic, parsley, most of the cheese, cream, and salt and pepper. Stir in onions.

Grate potatoes. Squeeze out excess moisture with paper towels. Stir into egg mixture. Melt two tablespoons butter in a 12-inch baking dish. Pour in potato mixture. Dot with remaining butter, and sprinkle with remaining cheese.

Place in oven and bake about 30 minutes or until top is browned.
6 servings
March 15, 1975

Almost 40 years ago an enthusiastic writer for *Wisconsin Agriculturist and Farmer* did an article about New Orleans cooking. Her hint for making brown gravy is worth repeating today.

Brown Gravy

Brown gravy reached the tops in perfection in New Orleans kitchens. The trick is, of course, never to make brown gravy over a hot fire. To a tablespoonful of lard or butter melted very slowly add your meat. When the meat is brown on both sides, remove. To the grease in the pan and the meat juice add two tablespoonsful of flour, a bit at a time, letting it brown but not burn or even scorch. This is the reason for the very low heat. Next add a cupful of water, chopped onion, whatever herbs you want, some garlic salt and salt and pepper. Put back on the stove with the meat in it and cook slowly for one hour or more until the meat is tender. Then the meat and the real brown gravy will be ready to serve, and what gravy!
January 18, 1947

Corned Beef and Cabbage is a tradition in many families, and has been for generations—and for good reason. The recipe writer in 1902 will attest to its healthfulness, but we are willing to bet that you will find the modern versions easier to use. Try the New England Boiled Dinner (which must never, never boil) or, if you have a pressure cooker, the quicker Corned Beef and Cabbage—1960s. A hearty dinner featuring corned beef follows.

Corned Beef and Cabbage—1902

Corned beef and cabbage is a delicious dish, which also ranks well as a muscle and strength producer. Take a piece of corned beef which is rather fat (a plate piece is good) and having washed it, put it into cold water enough to more than cover the meat and place the kettle over a gentle heat. Boil very slowly, adding more water from time to time as needed and if very salty the water must be changed, as too much salt in any dish is bad for the kidneys. When the meat is nearly done (it requires several hours of time) add the cabbage, which has been previously cut up either in quarters or much finer, as may be preferred. It may now be boiled a little faster and served when done. Brown bread is a very palatable and valuable adjunct to this dish.
May 8, 1902.

New England Boiled Dinner

4 pounds corned beef brisket
6 medium onions
2 turnips, cubed
6 carrots, cut in half
6 potatoes, quartered
1 head of cabbage, cut in wedges

Cover corned beef with water and simmer until fork-tender. Do not boil. Allow about three or four hours. About one hour before serving time, add onions. Thirty minutes before serving, add turnips, carrots, and potatoes. Cover and continue cooking. Fifteen minutes before serving time, add cabbage. Uncover; continue cooking until all vegetables are tender.

To serve, arrange vegetables around corned beef on a warm platter.
8 to 10 servings
March 17, 1962

Corned Beef and Cabbage—1960s

4 pounds corned beef brisket
4 cups water
6 onion slices
8 cloves
12 whole black peppercorns
2 bay leaves
1 tsp. garlic salt
2 stalks celery, diced
8 carrots, quartered
1 large head green cabbage, cut in
* wedges*
8 medium potatoes, quartered

Place brisket in a 6-quart pressure cooker; add water. Press cloves into onion slices. Add onions, peppercorns, bay leaves, garlic salt, and celery to meat. Cover, set control on pressure pan and cook 45 minutes after control jiggles. Cool pan for five minutes, then reduce pressure instantly under running water. Add carrots, cabbage, and potatoes. Cover, set control and cook for eight minutes after control jiggles; reduce pressure instantly under running water.

To serve, slice meat thin; arrange on platter with vegetables.
8 to 10 servings

Horseradish Sauce

1 cup sour cream
⅓ cup prepared horseradish
2 tsp. grated lemon rind
½ tsp. salt
dash of white pepper

Blend sour cream, horseradish, lemon rind, salt, and pepper well. Chill in refrigerator until ready to serve.
Makes one cup sauce.
January 21, 1933

Pot roast has been around for a long time, with versions from simple to spicy. We found these two recipes in 1902 issues of *Wisconsin Farmer.*

Marinated Pot Roast—1902

An old housekeeper furnishes the following recipe for a pot roast of beef: Place the meat in a mixture of white wine vinegar, a dozen whole allspice, a dozen whole peppers and a half bay leaf, and leave it two days, turning the meat occasionally; then remove the beef, wipe it dry, and brown it on both sides with two sliced onions in veal suet. Put into the kettle in which the meat is to be boiled two cupfuls of spiced vinegar, with two large carrots cut in slices. When it boils add the browned meat, cover closely and cook slowly for three hours, turning occasionally, adding more vinegar as it is needed. Remove the meat; strain the vinegar in which it is cooked, add a cupful of boiling water and a little salt, and thicken with two tablespoonfuls of flour. Add the meat, and just before serving add a cupful of cream.
July 10, 1902

Pot Roast—1902

Follow this recipe for an unusually delicious pot roast. First, brown a sliced onion in plenty of drippings and then put in your beef. Brown it evenly on all sides, pour over it the contents of a quart can of tomatoes, add a bay leaf, a sliced carrot, and sufficient water to half cover the beef. Cover tightly and stew till tender. Add the seasoning when it is about half done. A good-sized pot roast will require three hours to cook. It is best to simmer gently. When it is done, remove it to a platter, and strain the gravy. Return it to the kettle, and thicken it with a little flour. Let cook for ten minutes longer, then pour it over the meat and garnish with parsley.
July 3, 1902

Beef Rolled Rump Roast with Pear-Relish

Roast

4 to 6 pound beef rolled rump roast
Salt and pepper, to season

Season meat with salt and pepper. Place the roast, fat side up on a rack in an open roasting pan. Insert roast meat thermometer so bulb reaches the center of the thickest part, being sure the bulb does not rest in fat. Do not add water. Do not cover. Roast in a 300 to 325 degree oven until the thermometer reaches 150 degrees, depending upon the desired degree of doneness. Allow 25 to 30 minutes per pound. Serve with pear-relish garnish.

Pear-Relish Garnish:

¼ cup sweet pickle relish, drained
¼ cup celery, chopped
1 tsp. pimiento, chopped and drained
1 can (16 ounces) pear halves

Combine sweet pickle relish, celery and pimiento. Chill. Place in pear halves. Serve with roast.
January 23, 1971

Boiled Pot Roast

Three and a half pounds from the round, one and a half pints of water, one level tablespoonful of salt, one tablespoonful of sliced onion, six whole cloves, one-fourth level teaspoonful nutmeg, two bay leaves, one-half level teaspoonful of white pepper, two tablespoonfuls bacon fat or lard. Place the fat in the frying pan. When hot add the meat and brown. Bring water to a boil in a stew kettle and when boiling add the meat. Also pour in any gravy which is left in the frying pan. Lower the fire or set on back of range, add the salt, onion, cloves, nutmeg, bay leaves and pepper. Cook slowly for two hours. Keep covered. The meat may be served hot or cold and the meatstock used for soup.

Horseradish Sauce for Hot Beef

One tablespoonful of butter, one level tablespoonful of browned flour, one-fourth level teaspoonful of salt, one cup of meat stock, one-half teaspoonful of chopped parsley, two tablespoonfuls horseradish. Melt the butter, add the flour and mix thoroughly. Add the salt and the meatstock. Boil three minutes. Add the parsley and horseradish. Pour the sauce around the meat.
May 11, 1916

Pan American Pot Roast

3 to 4 pound blade roast
¼ cup all-purpose flour
1½ tsp. salt
¼ tsp. pepper
2 T. cooking fat
1 T. freeze-dried or powdered instant
    coffee
1 beef bouillon cube
½ cup boiling water
1 medium onion, sliced
½ tsp. ginger
¼ tsp. coriander
4 medium sweet potatoes, pared and
    halved lengthwise
½ tsp. salt
1 can (20-ounces) sliced pineapple
2 T. chopped peanuts (optional)

Dredge meat with mixture of flour, one and a half teaspoons salt, and the pepper. Reserve the leftover flour. Brown meat in fat in a large frypan or Dutch oven and place on a rack in roasting pan or Dutch oven. Dissolve coffee and bouillon cube in boiling water. Add onion, ginger, and coriander and pour over roast. Cover tightly.

Place in a 325 degree oven and bake for one hour and fifteen minutes. Add potatoes; sprinkle with one-half teaspoon salt. Continue cooking, covered, for 45 minutes. Drain pineapple, reserving liquid. Add pineapple to pan and continue cooking, covered, for 10 minutes, or until meat and potatoes are tender. Transfer meat, potatoes, and pineapple to warm platter.

Measure liquid in pan, add reserved pineapple liquid, if necessary, to make two cups and return to pan. Blend reserved flour with one-third cup pineapple liquid, add to cooking liquid and cook, stirring constantly until thickened. Cook slowly two to three minutes.

Serve with gravy and chopped peanuts.
6 to 8 servings
May 28, 1977

While most recipes are written to be completed—from start to finish—in two or three hours—here's one that you have to begin a few days in advance. But it's worth it. Just follow the easy directions below.

German Style Pot Roast

4 pounds beef, chuck or rump
2 tsp. salt
¼ tsp. pepper
1 onion, sliced
3 bay leaves
1 tsp. peppercorns
½ tsp. allspice
2 cups vinegar
2 cups water
shortening, as needed for browning
    meat
½ cup dark seedless raisins
all-purpose flour and water, as
    needed to thicken
1 T. sugar
8 gingersnaps, rolled into fine
    crumbs

Rub meat well with salt and pepper. Place in a large bowl. Add onion, bay leaves, peppercorns, allspice, vinegar, and water. Turn meat in marinade several times. Cover. Store in the refrigerator three or four days, turning meat occasionally.

Drain meat, reserving marinade. Brown meat on all sides in shortening. Strain onion and spices from marinade. Add it to the browned meat along with three-fourths cup of the marinade. Cover and simmer three to four hours, until meat is tender, adding more marinade, as needed. Transfer meat to a serving plate. Add raisins to liquid in pan. Thicken slightly with flour mixed with a little cold water to a smooth paste. Stir in sugar and gingersnaps.

Serve sauce hot with meat.
8 to 10 servings
May 15, 1965

Hawaiian Pot Roast

*3 to 4 pound beef arm or blade pot
    roast*
3 T. lard or drippings
¼ cup soy sauce
½ cup water
¼ tsp. pepper
¼ tsp. ground ginger
1 medium onion, sliced
1 can (4 ounces) mushroom pieces
⅓ cup celery
*1 can (9 ounces) pineapple chunks,
    drained*
¼ cup water
2 T. all-purpose flour

Brown pot roast in lard or drippings. Pour off fat. Add soy sauce, one-half cup water, pepper, ginger, and onion. Cover tightly and simmer for two and one-half to three hours, or until meat is tender. Combine mushrooms, celery, pineapple and add to meat. Continue cooking for 20 to 30 minutes. Transfer meat, mushrooms, celery, and pineapple to warm platter. Mix together one-quarter cup water and flour. Add to cooking liquid and cook until thickened.

Serve gravy with pot roast.
6 to 8 servings
September 16, 1961

Pot Roast, Hungarian Style

*3 to 4 pounds beef arm or blade pot
    roast*
¼ cup all-purpose flour
1 T. salt
¼ tsp. pepper
3 T. lard
1 clove garlic, minced
1 large onion, sliced
½ cup chopped celery
¼ cup water
1 cup tomato sauce
2 T. all-purpose flour
½ cup sour cream
3 T. chopped parsley
*cooked noodles, if desired, for 8 to
    10 servings*

Coat meat with a mixture of one-quarter cup flour, salt, and pepper. Brown in lard; pour off drippings. Add garlic, onion, celery, water, and tomato sauce. Cover tightly and cook slowly for three to three and a half hours, or until meat is tender. Remove pot roast to a heated platter.

Thicken cooking liquid with two tablespoons flour; stir in sour cream and parsley. Cook only until heated through.

Serve as gravy, with noodles, if desired.
8 to 10 servings
March, 1956

When the cook is in a hurry, the microwave oven comes in handy. This hearty pot roast dinner can be ready for six to eight hungry people in less than half the time it would take to cook conventionally.

Mexican Pot Roast

3 pound boneless beef pot roast*
2 jars (12-ounces each) green chile
*   salsa, picante style***
1 can (12-ounces) beer
1 onion, sliced
1 green pepper, chopped

*Appropriate pot roasts include beef chuck, bone-in arm, or blade pot roast or boneless blade or shoulder pot roast. The pot roast should be cut 1½- to 2-inches, weighing approximately 2 to 3½ pounds. If the boneless cuts are not available, the bone-in cut can be purchased, then boned and tied.

    **Remember, salsa comes in three heat levels: mild, medium, and hot. Be sure to check the label and use according to personal preference.

    Place pot roast in a three-quart round or oval microwave-safe baking dish. Pour salsa and beer over beef; cover.

    Microwave on MEDIUM (50 percent power) for 30 minutes. Turn pot roast and stir in onion and pepper; cover. Microwave on MEDIUM 15 minutes. Let stand 15 minutes.

    Slice pot roast against the grain. Strain vegetables and spoon over meat. Serve with rice, if desired.

6 to 8 servings
California Beef Council

In roasting meat turn with a spoon instead of a fork, as the latter pierces the meat and lets the juice out.
March 3, 1904

Sauerbraten with Noodles

4 pounds beef pot roast
1 cup vinegar
1 cup water
1 large onion, sliced
2 T. sugar
2 tsp. salt
½ tsp. whole cloves
2 bay leaves
1 lemon, sliced thin
2 T. butter
3 T. all-purpose flour, divided
¼ cup raisins
½ cup gingersnap crumbs
12-ounces broad noodles

Place pot roast in a large glass or crockery bowl. In saucepan combine vinegar, water, onion, sugar, salt, cloves, and bay leaves. Heat to boiling and pour over meat. Allow to cool. Add sliced lemon, cover, and set in refrigerator. Marinate 24 to 36 hours, turning two or three times. Remove meat from marinade and drain thoroughly. Strain the marinade and reserve.

    Heat butter in a heavy kettle. Sprinkle meat with one tablespoon of the flour and brown slowly on all sides. Gradually add half of marinade, stirring constantly. Continue stirring until the browned flour and fat are blended into the liquid. Cover and simmer about two hours, until meat is tender, stirring occasionally.

    Add the remaining two tablespoons flour mixed with a little water. Add raisins, remaining marinade, about one cup water, and gingersnap crumbs. Simmer about 10 minutes to blend well. Meanwhile, cook noodles in boiling salted water until tender. Drain.

    To serve, arrange noodles on a hot platter and place meat on top. Pour a little of the gingersnap gravy over all. Serve very hot.

8 servings
December 17, 1960

Browned Stew with Noodles

1 tsp. salt
pepper, as needed
4 T. all-purpose flour
2 pounds beef roast, shoulder, or
    heel
8 small onions
8 small carrots
4 turnips, quartered
8 potatoes, quartered
noodles, as needed for 4 servings

Add salt and pepper to the flour and rub it gently into the meat. Brown the meat on both sides in a heavy pan or Dutch oven. Add enough boiling salted water to barely cover meat and cook until the meat is nearly done. Then add the vegetables and additional water, if necessary, and cook with the meat. When both vegetables and meat are done, take up the meat on a large platter. Arrange the vegetables around the meat. Then thicken the gravy. Meanwhile, cook noodles in boiling water for 15 to 20 minutes. Add to the stew gravy and send to the table in a separate dish.
February 17, 1951

Beef Steaks

There's nothing more traditional in American cooking than a thick, juicy steak. The following recipes are a dozen or so delicious ways to prepare this simple treat. But don't stop here when looking for ways to cook your steak. Many more recipes are included in the "Barbecue" section immediately following.

Porterhouse, a la Blue

3 porterhouse or T-bone steaks,
    ¾-inch thick, about 1½-pounds
    each
½ cup butter, melted
½ cup crumbled blue cheese
2 T. chopped chives
freshly ground pepper, as desired

Broil steaks to a desired degree of doneness, about seven minutes per side for medium rare. On a hot steak platter combine butter, blue cheese, and chives. Transfer steak to platter; turn several times to coat sides with mixture.

Sprinkle with freshly ground pepper and serve immediately.
6 servings
June 1, 1968

Steak Fromage

1 large beef round steak, cut ½-inch thick
¼ cup all-purpose flour
½ tsp. salt
⅛ tsp. pepper
¼ tsp. garlic salt
3 T. shortening or drippings
¾ cup water
¼ cup onion, chopped
⅓ cup cheese, grated
2 T. parsley, chopped

Remove bone and pound steak to one-quarter-inch thickness. Cut steak into six to eight pieces. Combine flour, salt, pepper and garlic salt. Dredge steak in seasoned flour. Sprinkle any remaining flour over steak. Brown in shortening or drippings. Pour off drippings. Add water and onion. Cover tightly and cook slowly one to one and one-half hours or until tender. Sprinkle cheese and parsley over meat. Cover and simmer two to three minutes or until cheese is melted.
6 servings
January 23, 1971

A slow-cooker is a valuable item in the kitchen of a busy cook. If you have one, try this recipe.

Italian Round Steak

2 pounds round steak cut in serving pieces
2 beef bouillon cubes
1 28-ounce can whole tomatoes, drained and reserve liquid
1¼ cups liquid (tomato juice plus hot water)
1 cup onion, chopped
1 clove garlic
1 tsp. salt
½ tsp. pepper
½ tsp. oregano
1½ tsp. Worcestershire sauce
¼ cup cornstarch
¼ cup cold water

Place steak pieces in a slow cooker. Dissolve bouillon cubes in liquid in a small bowl. Combine tomatoes, onion, garlic, salt, pepper, oregano, and Worcestershire sauce. Pour over steak. Add bouillon-liquid mixture. Cook on low for eight to nine hours. To thicken switch to high. Combine cornstarch and water. Stir into hot liquid and thicken.
January 1, 1977

Round Steak Spanish Style

⅓ cup all-purpose flour
1½ tsp. salt
½ tsp. garlic salt
⅛ tsp. pepper
3 pounds boneless round steak, cut 1¾-inch thick
2 T. shortening
2 cups onion, sliced
1 cup celery, sliced
1 can (8 ounces) tomato sauce
¼ cup red wine vinegar
½ cup stuffed olives, sliced

Combine flour, salt, garlic salt, and pepper. Pound seasoned flour into meat on both sides. Brown meat on both sides in hot shortening, turning once. Sprinkle remaining flour mixture over meat. Add onion, celery, tomato sauce, and vinegar. Cover; simmer until meat is tender, two to two and one-quarter hours. A small amount of water may be added to pan if needed. Sprinkle olives over meat 15 minutes before end of cooking time.
8 servings
October 25, 1969

This entree is just one of numerous dishes which can be perfectly and easily prepared with a blender. The following hints are some blender do's and don't's to streamline your meal planning.

Do's

- Add liquid before dry ingredients, unless recipe indicates otherwise.
- Cut hard or firm foods into ½- to 2-inch pieces before blending.
- Clean blender by filling half full with warm water. Add a drop of liquid detergent, cover, and blend at low speed about five seconds.
- Limit the volume to one-half the blender container's capacity when mixing thick mixtures and to two-thirds for thin or free-flowing mixtures.

Don't's

- Don't use blender as an ice crusher. Add liquid, then add ice cubes.
- Don't use to mash potatoes, whip egg whites, grind raw meat, knead or mix stiff doughs, or extract juices from fruits and vegetables.
- Don't overtax motor with extra heavy or large loads.
- Don't operate the cutting blades without the container.
- Don't operate the blender with an empty container.

Spicy Steak

2 pounds round steak, cut ½-inch thick
salt and pepper, to taste
3 T. shortening
1 8-ounce can tomato sauce
1 cup water
1 large onion, cut in pieces
½ pound fresh mushrooms or 1 4-ounce can mushrooms
1 beef bouillon cube
1 clove garlic
½ green pepper, seeded and cut up
1 T. Worcestershire sauce

Cut meat into individual portions, and sprinkle with salt and pepper. Brown meat in shortening in large skillet. Put all remaining ingredients in blender container. Cover and set to "chop" until vegetables are chopped. Pour over browned meat. Cover skillet, and cook slowly one and one-half hours or until meat is tender.
4 to 6 servings
May 25, 1974

Continental Steak Rolls with Sour Cream Sauce

1 pound tenderized round steak
(or 4 minute steaks)
¼ cup all-purpose flour
¼ tsp. salt
⅛ tsp. pepper
2 T. shortening
3 T. finely chopped mushrooms
3 T. finely chopped onion
1 can refrigerated quick crescent
rolls
1 cup sour cream
1 T. butter
½ tsp. parsley flakes
¼ tsp. salt

Preheat oven to 400 degrees.

Cut steak into four rectangular pieces. Coat with a mixture of flour, one-quarter teaspoon salt, and pepper. Brown in shortening in skillet. Drain on absorbent paper. Saute mushrooms and onions. Place one and a half tablespoons mixture on one end of browned meat; fold over other end, covering mushroom mixture. Unroll dough, leaving two triangles joined to form a rectangle. Press at perforation to seal. Place meat in center of dough. Fold up sides and ends of dough, sealing edges tightly. Place seamside down on cookie sheet.

Place in oven and bake for 10 to 12 minutes, until golden brown.

Meanwhile, prepare sauce by combining sour cream, butter, parsley, and one-quarter teaspoon salt. Heat thoroughly, but do not boil.

To serve, top hot steak rolls with sauce.
4 servings
July 12, 1969

When you're planning a special menu, remember that elegance doesn't need to be expensive. Imperial Beef Roll combines marinated round steak with a savory bread stuffing and easy-to-make sauce.

Imperial Beef Roll

1 beef round steak, about
2½ pounds

Trim meat. Cover it with plastic wrap, and flatten with flat side of meat pounder or rolling pin to about one-eighth-inch thickness, taking care not to tear meat. Peel off plastic wrap. Place in marinade.

Marinade:

½ cup soy sauce
½ cup water
½ cup dry sherry
1 T. brown sugar
2 T. lemon juice
2 T. salad oil
¼ tsp. liquid hot pepper sauce
1 clove garlic, crushed
¼ tsp. black pepper
1 T. cornstarch

Combine all ingredients except cornstarch and pour over meat in a shallow dish. Marinate, covered, in the refrigerator for at least two hours, basting occasionally with the marinade. Before stuffing, remove meat from marinade and pat dry on paper towels. Reserve marinade.

Bread stuffing:

¼ cup chopped onion
½ cup thinly sliced celery
⅔ cup water chestnuts
⅔ cup bamboo shoots
½ cup chopped canned mushrooms
⅓ cup butter
2 T. chopped parsley
⅔ cup chicken broth
⅓ cup light cream
1 tsp. salt
¼ tsp. black pepper
½ tsp. sage
¼ tsp. marjoram
¼ tsp. ground thyme
6 cups toasted white bread cubes

While meat is marinating, make the stuffing. Cook onion, celery, water chestnuts, bamboo shoots, and mushrooms in butter for three minutes. Add remaining ingredients. Spoon stuffing onto meat, spreading to within one-half-inch of edges. Roll up the meat lengthwise; secure with skewers or toothpicks and string. Place in a baking dish with reserved marinade. Cover.

Bake in 350 degree oven for one and a half hours, or until tender, basting occasionally. Place meat onto a cutting board, remove skewers and string. Cut into thick slices.

In a small saucepan, blend cornstarch with a small amount of marinade. Cook on low heat until marinade is slightly thickened. Serve as a sauce with sliced beef roll.
September 14, 1975

Oven cooking bags are a modern convenience that saves more than clean-up time and energy. They eliminate the need for pre-browning of meats, as the heat rays penetrate through oven bag film and lay down delicate appetizing browns. Stuffed flank steak is a natural for this way of cooking.

Stuffed Flank Steak in the Bag

1 T. all-purpose flour
2 pounds flank steak
salt and pepper, as desired
onion salt, as desired
celery salt, as desired
2 cups bread stuffing mix
melted butter, as needed
½ cup dry red wine
½ cup water
1 tsp. caraway seeds
parsley, as needed for garnish

Preheat oven to 350 degrees.

Shake flour in a 10-by-16-inch Brown-in-Bag, and place in a two-inch deep roasting pan. Score surface of steak. Sprinkle lightly with salt, pepper, onion salt, and celery salt. Prepare stuffing mix as directed on package, and spread stuffing on meat. Roll meat lengthwise, and lace firmly with string. Brush with melted butter. Slide stuffed roll into bag; add wine, water, and caraway seeds. Close bag and secure with twist-tie. Make six half-inch slits on top of bag.

Place in oven and bake one and a half to two hours, or until meat is tender. Snip corner of bag, pour off liquid and thicken, if desired. Transfer steak roll to platter, remove string, and slice.

To serve, garnish with parsley.
6 to 8 servings
February 8, 1979

The key words for this recipe are "quick and easy"—and tasty, as well.

Oven-Barbecued Chuck Steak

2 to 3 pound chuck steak (about 2-inches thick)
2 T. softened butter
1 lemon
1 medium-sized onion
1 cup catsup
1 T. Worcestershire sauce
¼ cup water
few drops Tabasco® sauce

Heat oven to 350 degrees.

Spread steak with softened butter. Place meat in a 13-by-9½-by-2½- inch aluminum pan. Cut lemon into thin slices and lay over top of meat. Top with thinly sliced onion rings. Mix catsup, Worcestershire, water, and Tabasco®. Pour over meat. Cover pan tightly with foil. Bake one and one-half to two hours.

4 to 5 servings
October 15, 1966

Sunday Supper Steak Sandwiches

8 sandwich steaks
butter, as needed
8 slices bread, toasted
1½ cups cooked asparagus spears
8 large tomato slices
garlic salt, to taste
pepper, to taste
8 slices American cheese

Fry individual steaks in lightly oiled pan. When just about done on the second side, remove from heat and place on toast, topping each with asparagus and a tomato slice. Season with garlic salt and pepper and add one slice of cheese to each open-faced sandwich.

Slip under broiler until cheese melts. Serve at once.

8 servings
August 7, 1965

Barbecue

The All-American Barbecue

Your success at grillside depends on building a good fire. Whether you have a portable tabletop grill, a gas or electric grill, or a stone outdoor fireplace, follow these guidelines for a great fire every time.

- Place the grill away from buildings, trees, dry grass, and shrubs. About 20 minutes before you plan to start cooking, pile charcoal briquets in a pyramid in the center of the grill base that has been lined with heavy-duty aluminum foil and covered with a shallow layer of gravel or vermiculite. The number of briquets needed will depend on the size of the grill and the amount of food to be cooked.
- Use an electric or liquid starter to get the coals going.
- The fire is ready when coals are covered with gray ash and glowing in the center. Spread coals in an even layer. Put meat on the grill and you're ready!
- During cooking, adjust heat by raising or lowering the grill, adding or removing coals, adjusting dampers or draft doors, and using windbreaks.
- Hardwood gives your meat a completely different and delicious flavor. When you use it, let the flames die down to glowing coals before putting on the meat. It's the stored heat in the coals that does the cooking. Leaping flames and meat containing fat can be a dangerous combination.
- Keep a water gun handy to put out flareups.

Barbecuing is not only a way of cooking. It's become a way of life, especially in the summertime. The enticing aroma of foods cooking over hot coals on the backyard patio or over an open campfire is hard to resist.

All-American steak has long been a barbecue favorite. Grilling steaks successfully is easy when you follow these tips:

- Be sure to select steaks at least one inch thick for grilling. A one-inch thick sirloin serves two to three people. A two-inch sirloin serves four to six.
- The fire must be started far enough in advance so that a fine gray ash has formed on the coals when cooking begins. The briquets should be spread evenly over the cooking area, leaving about one inch of space between each.
- To prevent meat from sticking, rub the grill with fat before cooking is started. Make slashes in the fat edge of the steak to prevent meat from curling during broiling. Be careful not to cut into the lean.
- One-inch steaks should be placed about three inches from the coals; two-inch steaks about five inches.
- When the steak is browned on one side, turn, season, and finish cooking on the other side. For turning, use tongs or a utility fork inserted into the fat edge. Steaks should be seasoned after they have browned.

- It's difficult to set up broiling time charts. In outdoor cookery there are many variables, such as size of piece of meat and temperature at the broiling surface of meat which may be affected by the wind, size of the firebox, and more. But you can refer to the chart below as a guideline.

Thickness of steak (inches)	Weight (lbs.)	Charcoal Broil (minutes per side)		
		Rare	Med.	Well Done
2	3-3½	8-9	10-15	19-20
1½	2½-3	6-7	8- 9	12-15
1	2½	5-6	6- 8	9-12

But don't be limited to plain steak—there's no end to the variety of good things you can do with a grill. All you need is a little imagination to turn those outdoors meals into special occasions.

The recipes that follow will get you started. As a beginning, try topping your hot barbecued steak with some new and unusual spreads.

Roquefort Cheese Spread

Cream one-third cup butter; stir in three tablespoons crumbed blue cheese. Spread on hot steak and serve.

California Steak Sauce

1 cup onion, finely chopped
1 T. butter
¼ cup dry white wine
1 T. vinegar
1 cup beef gravy (canned or
*   homemade)*
2 T. catsup
1 T. minced parsley
salt and pepper, to taste

Saute onion in butter until golden brown. Stir in wine, vinegar, beef gravy, catsup, parsley, salt, and pepper. Heat. Makes 1¾ cup.

Smoky Cheese Butter

½ cup butter
1 cup shredded aged Cheddar Cheese
dash of Tabasco® sauce
½ tsp. liquid smoke
½ tsp. fines herbes* or bouquet garni

Combine butter, cheese, Tabasco®, liquid smoke, and herbs and whip until light and fluffy.

*Equal amounts of chives, tarragon, parsley, and chervil, all finely chopped.
Makes 1¼ cup spread.

Smoky Sauce

1 cup tomato sauce
¼ cup cooking oil or butter
3 T. wine vinegar
⅓ cup green onions, finely chopped
1 T. sugar
1 tsp. salt
dash of black pepper
½ tsp. liquid smoke, as desired

Combine tomato sauce, oil or butter, vinegar, green onions, sugar, salt, pepper, and liquid smoke. Heat.
Makes 1½ cups sauce.

Sesame Seed Steak Spread

½ stick (¼ cup) butter or margarine
1 tsp. garlic powder
2 tsp. sesame seeds

Combine butter, garlic powder, and sesame seeds. Stir to thoroughly combine ingredients. Let stand about 30 minutes to attain a good garlic flavor.

Spread on hot broiled steak before serving.
July 10, 1971

Peppery Steak Sizzle

1 3-pound sirloin steak, 1½-inches
  thick
2 tsp. whole peppercorns
1 cup mayonnaise
1 cup Italian salad dressing
salt, as desired

Slash edges of steak to prevent curling and trim excess fat. Crush peppercorns coarsely. Mix pepper with mayonnaise and salad dressing. Spread half the mixture over top of steak. Place steak coated side down in a shallow pan. Spread remaining mixture over steak. Let stand at room temperature for two hours or in refrigerator overnight.

Prepare barbecue. When coals are gray, place steak eight inches above coals and grill for 10-12 minutes per side for well done. Sprinkle steak with salt before cutting into thin slices.
July 2, 1977

Broiled Sirloin Steaks with Flaming Fruit Sauce

sirloin steaks, cut 1 to 2-inches thick
salt and pepper, as desired
1 can (16-ounces) sliced peaches
1 can (16-ounces) dark sweet
  cherries, drained
1 can (11-ounces) mandarin oranges,
  drained
1 T. lemon juice
1 tsp. vanilla
1 tsp. almond extract
½ cup sugar
2 T. butter or margarine
sugar cubes soaked in lemon extract

Place steaks on the hot grill; steaks cut one inch thick should be placed two to three inches from the heat; steaks cut two inches thick, three to five inches from the heat.

When one side is browned, turn, season cooked side, finish cooking on second side and season. Steaks cut one inch thick require approximately 10 to 12 minutes for rare, 12 to 16 minutes for medium. Steaks cut two inches thick require approximately 16 to 18 minutes for rare, 20 to 30 minutes for medium.

Meanwhile, prepare sauce by draining peaches, reserving one-half cup syrup. Combine peaches and reserved syrup with cherries, mandarin oranges, lemon juice, vanilla, and almond extract in a saucepan. Sprinkle with sugar and dot with butter. Heat slowly on grill.

Just before serving, top with sugar cubes and ignite.

July 24, 1976

Charcoal Broiled Herb-Garlic Sirloin Steak

1 large sirloin steak
⅓ cup salad oil
⅓ red wine vinegar
2 cloves garlic, crushed
1 tsp. basil
½ tsp. salt
½ tsp. pepper

Trim excess fat from steak, and slash fat edge at one inch intervals. Place steak in a dish or pan large enough to allow steak to remain flat. Combine oil, vinegar, garlic, basil, salt, and pepper; mix and pour over steak. Cover. Chill two to three hours, turning several times.

Start charcoal fire 30 to 40 minutes ahead of time. Rub hot grill with a bit of beef fat trimmed from edge of steak. Broil one and one-half to two-inch steaks five to six inches above a bed of glowing coals covered with gray ash or place one-inch steaks on a rack four and one-half to five inches above coals. Broil first side; turn with tongs and brush with marinade, if desired. Broil second side. To check steak for degree of doneness, cut a small slash with a sharp knife in center of steak and examine color.

Plan for one-half to three-quarters of a pound of steak per person with the bone-in.

August 22, 1972

Flank Steak with Zesty Barbecue Sauce

¼ cup chopped green pepper
¼ cup chopped onion
1 medium clove garlic, minced
2 T. salad oil
1 can condensed tomato soup
¼ cup water
2 T. brown sugar
2 T. vinegar
1 tsp. Worcestershire sauce
dash Tabasco® sauce
1 2-pound flank steak

Prepare barbecue grill.

In a saucepan, cook green pepper, onion, and garlic in oil until vegetables are tender. Add tomato soup, water, brown sugar, vinegar, Worcestershire, and Tabasco®. Simmer about 10 minutes, stirring now and then. Makes about two cups sauce.

Score flank steak. Place steak on grill about four inches above the coals. Cook about six minutes on each side, or until desired doneness, brushing often with sauce.

Heat remaining sauce and serve with meat.

June 20, 1964

Barbecued Round Steak En Brochette

2 pounds round steak, 1½-inch thick
6 carrots, cut in 2-inch pieces
4 zucchini, cut in 1-inch pieces
1 jar (10 ounces) whole onions
Barbecue sauce (your favorite)

Prepare barbecue.

Chill or partially freeze round steak to make cutting easier. Slice steak into strips one-quarter-inch wide. Cook carrots until almost tender. Cook zucchini two minutes. Thread on four 14-inch metal skewers strips of steak (accordion-style): two pieces carrot, two pieces zucchini and two onions. Thread remaining vegetables alternately on two 14-inch metal skewers. Grill or broil four inches from coals. Broil three to four minutes on each side. Brush with barbecue sauce. Continue turning and brushing with barbecue sauce until broiled to desired doneness.
4 to 6 servings
May 17, 1975

To complement these grilled kabobs, include:

Roast Ears of Corn

Turn back the husks and strip out the silk. Lay back the husks and tie in place. Dip in cold, salty water (¼ cup salt to a quart of water). Place ears on grill over hot coals. Cook 10 to 15 minutes, turning the ears with tongs until the husks are dry and browned. Serve with butter, pepper and salt.

Alternatively, instead of roasting corn in the husks they can be removed, the ears brushed with butter and sprinkled with pepper and salt. Then ears can be wrapped in foil and cooked over the hot coals.

Toasting sticks can be used in place of forks. Use sweet woods—apple, poplar, basswood, maple, or cherry. Peel and sharpen at one end.
July 2, 1960

Herb Beef Kabobs

¼ cup onion, finely chopped
½ cup lemon juice
¼ cup salad oil
½ tsp. salt
¼ tsp. celery salt
¼ tsp. pepper
½ tsp. oregano
½ tsp. thyme
1 clove garlic, finely chopped
2 pounds beef sirloin tip cut into
    1½-inch cubes
8 eggplant wedges, cut 2 inches in
    length
4 small cooked onions
4 12-inch skewers
4 cherry tomatoes

Combine onion, lemon juice, salad oil, salt, celery salt, pepper, oregano, thyme, and garlic. Pour marinade over meat. Cover tightly and refrigerate overnight.

Prepare barbecue grill. Pour off marinade and reserve. Thread each skewer with meat, eggplant, meat, onion, meat, eggplant, and meat. Brush with marinade. Place on grill three to four inches from heat. Cook 10 to 12 minutes or until done. Place cherry tomato on each skewer about two minutes before meat is done.

Heat French bread along the edge of the grill to serve as an accompaniment to the kabobs.
4 servings
April 25, 1971

Roast beef on the outdoor grill is an easy way to keep the kitchen cool and at the same time present a special dinner.

Grilled Beef Roast

If your grill does not have a hood, make your own out of aluminum foil. Tear off long sheets of foil and mold over the grill, letting the ends drop down one foot. Cover the grill completely, overlapping the foil. Seal with tape. Turn up bottom edges all around about two inches and fold firmly. Leave a small opening in the top that can be opened and closed for draft. Remove cover, and prepare the fire.

Meanwhile, make a foil pan about one inch larger all around than the roast. Tear off heavy duty aluminum foil; fold to make double thick, turn up edges and miter corner to make it firm. Place this pan beside the fire under the place where the roast will rest.

1 roast of beef (a standing rib, a
  boned and rolled rib, or a top
  sirloin roast)
salt and pepper, to taste
1 can beef consomme
½ cup tomato juice
1 clove garlic, crushed
¼ tsp. freshly ground pepper
1 T. Worcestershire sauce

Season the roast with salt and pepper, and place on grill. Insert a meat thermometer in the thickest part. Place the hood over the grill, making sure the damper is open. Press the foil to the side of the grill all around. Let the meat roast for 45 minutes, or longer. Listen and smell to judge the cooking.

Combine consomme, tomato juice, garlic, pepper, and Worcestershire. Lift hood and baste. Add damp hickory chips and a few charcoal briquets, if needed. Again cover and continue roasting, basting once or twice more, adding more hickory and briquets, if needed. Roast will be done when the meat thermometer registers 140 degrees for rare, 160 for medium, and 170 for well-done.

Remove roast to carving board or platter. Slip foil pan with drippings onto a cookie sheet for support. Combine drippings with any remaining basting juice. Skim off excess fat, simmer until slightly reduced, add additional seasonings, if needed, and serve with the roast.
June 1962

Short Ribs

Beef short ribs are the basis for delicious and hearty meals. Allow about one pound of uncooked ribs for every two servings and trim the excess fat from the bones before cooking.

Sweet-Sour Short Ribs

2½ to 3 pounds short ribs, cut in
    serving pieces
salt, pepper, all-purpose flour, lard,
    as needed
1 cup onions, sliced
1 clove garlic, sliced
1½ cups hot water
1 small bay leaf
3 T. brown sugar
⅓ cup catsup
¼ cup vinegar
½ tsp. salt
2 T. all-purpose flour and water, as
    needed for thickening
hot, buttered noodles, as needed for
    4 to 6 servings

Trim excess fat from ribs. Sprinkle with salt and pepper and roll in flour. Brown well on all sides in a large skillet in several tablespoons hot lard. Remove to a Dutch oven or other heavy utensil. Add onions and garlic to fat in skillet and cook until lightly browned; add to short ribs. Combine water, bay leaf, brown sugar, catsup, vinegar, and one-half teaspoon salt and pour over ribs. Cover and cook over low heat until tender, two and a half to three hours.

Remove ribs to serving dish and keep in a warm place. Pour off most of fat from gravy, stir in two tablespoons flour and enough water to dilute to strength desired. Cook until thickened.

Serve short ribs on hot buttered noodles topped with sauce.
4 to 6 servings
January 19, 1957

Braised Short Ribs

1 T. salt
2 tsp. ground black pepper
2 cups all-purpose flour
4 pounds short ribs of beef
shortening, as needed
1 T. salt
1 T. Worcestershire sauce
½ tsp. ground black pepper
¼ tsp. Tabasco® sauce
2 bay leaves
½ tsp. basil
½ tsp. marjoram
1 clove of garlic, sliced
1 medium onion, sliced
6 carrots, peeled and cut in pieces
2 cups small white onions, peeled
all-purpose flour and water, as
    needed for thickening

Mix one tablespoon salt, two teaspoons pepper, and two cups flour in a large paper bag. Add short ribs and shake to coat well. Brown ribs on all sides in a little melted shortening in a large heavy kettle or Dutch oven. Add salt, Worcestershire, one-half teaspoon pepper, Tabasco®, bay leaves, basil, marjoram, garlic, sliced onion, and enough water to cover ribs. Simmer covered until tender, about two hours.

Add carrots and small white onions during last 20 minutes of cooking time. Remove ribs and vegetables to a casserole. Remove fat from broth left in kettle. Thicken broth by adding two tablespoons flour mixed with one-quarter cup water for each pint of broth. Cook, stirring until mixture thickens. Pour over ribs and keep hot in a 350 degree oven until serving time.
6 to 8 servings
May 3, 1969

Barbecue style short ribs can be served on hot cooked rice or noodles, or served with mashed potatoes on the side. The menu could include buttered peas, a tossed green salad, crusty rolls, and fruit for dessert.

Barbecue Style Short Ribs

2½ to 3 pounds short ribs
2 T. vegetable oil
12 oz. tomato puree
1 cup water
1 cup chopped onion
¼ cup brown sugar
1 T. prepared mustard
1¼ tsp. salt
⅛ tsp. pepper

Cut beef into serving-size pieces and trim off excess fat. Brown short ribs on all sides in oil in heavy skillet; pour off excess fat. Combine remaining ingredients and pour over ribs. Cover and simmer one and a half to two hours or until meat is tender.
4 servings
September 1969

Short Ribs on Fruited Rice

Ribs:

8 pieces (4 pounds) beef short ribs
⅓ cup prepared mustard
⅓ cup molasses or syrup
¼ cup cider or wine vinegar
¼ cup Worcestershire sauce
¼ tsp. hot sauce
2 T. minced onion
½ tsp. salt
½ cup water

Fruited Rice:

13½ oz. pineapple tidbits
¼ cup reserved basting sauce
1 cup water
1 T. butter or margarine
2 cups precooked rice
2 T. minced parsley
1 T. minced chives, optional

Preheat oven to 400 degrees.

Place short ribs, fat side up, in a shallow baking pan. Mix mustard and molasses. Stir in cider or vinegar, Worcestershire, hot sauce, onion, and salt. Reserve one-quarter cup sauce for rice. Brush short ribs with spice sauce.

Place in oven to brown, about 40 minutes, brushing ribs with sauce three times during browning. Brush ribs with remaining sauce and add water. Cover pan with foil, crimping foil securely to edges of pan; return to oven and cook until ribs are very tender, about 30 minutes.

To prepare fruited rice, drain pineapple tidbits; pour syrup into measuring cup and add water as needed to make ¾ cup liquid. Combine pineapple syrup, short rib basting sauce, one cup water and butter in saucepan with close-fitting cover; bring to a boil. Stir in rice; cover and remove from heat. Let stand five minutes. Stir in pineapple tidbits, parsley, and chives. Cover and heat slowly until warm enough to serve.

To serve, arrange ribs on fruited rice; skim fat from pan and pour drippings over ribs.
6 servings
September 1964

Soups and Stews and Casseroles and More

Oriental Steak Strips

2 pounds beef round steak, cut
*   1-inch thick*
2 T. shortening
water, as needed
⅓ cup soy sauce
2 tsp. sugar
¼ tsp. pepper
1 clove garlic, minced
3 carrots
2 green peppers, cut in 1-inch squares
8 green onions, cut in 1½-inch pieces
½ pound mushrooms, halved
1 can (8 ounces) water chestnuts,
*   halved*
2 T. cornstarch
¼ cup water
cooked rice, as needed

Cut round steak in strips one-eighth-inch thick or thinner and three to four-inches long. Brown strips in shortening in a large frying pan. Pour off drippings, measure, and add water to make one cup. Combine soy sauce, sugar, pepper, and garlic and add to meat. Cover tightly and cook slowly 45 minutes. Using a vegetable parer, cut carrots lengthwise into thin strips and cut strips in half. Add carrots, green peppers, onions, mushrooms, and water chestnuts to meat, cover, and continue cooking 15 minutes. Combine cornstarch and water and use to thicken cooking liquid.

Serve with cooked rice.
6 to 8 servings
January 17, 1976

Curried Steak

2 pounds beef round steak, cut
*   ½- to ¾-inch thick*
3 T. all-purpose flour
1 tsp. salt
⅛ tsp. pepper
2 T. shortening or drippings
1 tsp. curry powder
1 small onion, chopped
1 clove garlic, crushed
¾ cup water
1 can (15 ounces) tomato sauce
2 tsp. lemon juice
1 cup rice
1 package (10-ounces) frozen peas

Cut round steak in strips one-eighth-inch thick and two to three inches long. Combine flour, salt, and pepper. Dredge beef strips. Brown in shortening in a large frying pan. Pour off drippings. Sprinkle curry powder over meat and stir in onion and garlic. Add water, cover tightly, and cook slowly 30 minutes, stirring occasionally. Stir tomato sauce and lemon juice into beef mixture and continue cooking, covered, 30 minutes, or until meat is tender. Cook rice and peas according to package directions, and drain.

To serve, place curried beef and peas over rice.
6 servings
January 17, 1976

32

Spicy Steak and Rice Supper

1½ pound round or sirloin steak (1
　　inch thick), cut in thin strips
1 large green pepper, sliced
1 large onion, sliced
marinade (recipe given below)
3 medium tomatoes, peeled and cut
　　into wedges
1 T. butter or oil
2 T. cornstarch
3 cups hot cooked rice

Combine meat, pepper, onion and marinade. Refrigerate several hours or overnight, stirring occasionally. Add tomatoes
an hour before cooking. Drain meat and
vegetables (saving marinade) and brown in
oil over high heat. Mix cornstarch with
marinade and add to meat. Cook five to 10
minutes longer. Serve over hot, fluffy rice.
6 servings

Marinade

2 T. brown sugar
1 tsp. dry mustard
½ tsp. ginger
½ tsp. garlic powder
1 tsp. salt
2 T. vegetable oil
1 T. vinegar
6 T. soy sauce
¾ cup water

Mix all ingredients thoroughly and use to
marinate meat and vegetables in recipe
above.
November 10, 1973

Sukiyaki

1 pound beef sirloin steak, cubed
1 T. salad oil
3 small onions
1 small bunch carrots
1 stalk celery
1 pound green beans
1 bunch green onions
2 green peppers
¾ cup Chinese cabbage or cauliflower
1 cup soy sauce
1 T. sugar
6 cups hot cooked rice

Brown the meat in salad oil. Cut vegetables
into small pieces. Arrange vegetables over
meat in a casserole in the following order:
onions, carrots, celery, green beans, green
onions, green pepper, cabbage, or cauliflower. Cover tightly and steam until
vegetables are about half done. Add soy
sauce and sugar and continue steaming
until vegetables are tender, but not mushy.
Serve over hot rice with additional soy
sauce.
6 substantial servings
August 12, 1967

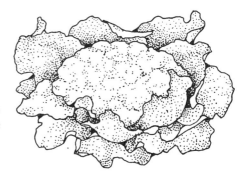

Sukiyaki Hawaiian Style

2 T. shortening
1 cup celery, diagonally sliced
1 cup onion, thinly sliced
1 clove garlic, finely minced
1 pound sirloin, cut ½-inch thick,
    thinly sliced
1 cup mushrooms, sliced
10 ounces asparagus, cut, cooked,
    and drained
½ cup water
1 T. soy sauce
1 T. cornstarch
1 tsp. salt
1 beef bouillon cube, optional
½ tsp. sugar
¼ tsp. ginger
hot rice, as needed for 4 servings
    (optional)

Heat shortening in heavy pan. Add celery, onion and garlic; stir and fry over high heat one minute. Add meat; stir and fry one minute. Add mushrooms; stir and fry one minute. Add asparagus; heat one minute. Blend together water, soy sauce, cornstarch, salt, bouillon cube, sugar, and ginger. Add to meat mixture. Cook and stir until sauce thickens.

Serve plain or with hot seasoned rice.
4 servings
November 13, 1971

Ginger Beef with Raisin Sauce

1½ pounds tender beef steak
2 T. all-purpose flour
1½ tsp. powdered ginger
1 tsp. paprika
1 tsp. seasoned or garlic salt
3 T. oil
⅓ cup dark or golden raisins
2 T. butter or margarine
1 tsp. soy sauce
3 T. catsup
½ cup bouillon or water
hot cooked rice, as needed for 4 to
    6 servings

Cut the steak into thin strips. Dredge in flour mixed with ginger, paprika and salt. Brown quickly in heated oil; remove meat from pan and keep hot. Add remaining ingredients to pan in which meat was cooked. Stir to gather up all the rich brown pan drippings. Bring to a boil; simmer two to three minutes. Add steak strips and heat briefly.

Serve with rice.
4 to 6 servings
January 17, 1970

Two variations on the "Stroganoff" theme follow.

Beef Stroganoff

1 pound round steak, cut in ¾-inch
    cubes
¼ cup all-purpose flour
1 tsp. salt
⅛ tsp. pepper
2 T. shortening
½ cup onion, chopped
1 clove garlic, minced
1 can (4 ounces) mushrooms
1 can (10½ ounces) condensed toma-
    to soup or consomme
1 T. Worcestershire sauce
1 cup sour cream
hot cooked rice, noodles, or spaghetti,
    as needed for 4 servings

Combine flour, salt and pepper; roll meat in mixture. Melt shortening in skillet, then add meat, browning all sides. Add onion, garlic, and drained mushrooms; saute until partially tender. Add tomato soup and Worcestershire sauce. Cook until meat is tender; spoon off excess fat. Stir in sour cream. Heat at low simmer, but do not boil.

Serve over rice, noodles, or spaghetti.
4 servings.
January 8, 1966

34

Serendipity Beef

5 T. soy sauce
1 T. cornstarch
1 tsp. sugar
salt, to taste
2 T. sherry, optional
1 pound top round beef, thinly sliced
1 package (10 ounces) frozen string
  beans, julienne cut
4 T. cooking oil
2 cups hot buttered rice

At least one hour ahead, prepare marinade of soy sauce, cornstarch, sugar, salt and sherry. Slice beef in one-quarter-inch strips and marinate at room temperature for about an hour. (Beef slices easily when frozen slightly.) In saucepan, cook frozen beans as directed, less one minute, taking care not to overcook. Drain. While beans cook, heat oil in wok or large frying pan. When hot, add beef for a few seconds, turning frequently with fork. Add beans to beef and stir-fry until beef is cooked, about three minutes.

Serve over hot buttered rice.
2 servings
September 2, 1972

Entertaining on a budget? This recipe serves 19 to 20 with just two pounds of meat. The meat-vegetable sauce is simmered and served buffet style from the same pot.

Beef-Oriental Sandwiches

2 pounds thinly cut round or flank
  steak, cut diagonally into strips
  2-inches long and 1½-inch wide
oil, as needed for browning
2 tsp. salt
2 T. soy sauce
3 cups water
¼ cup cornstarch
2 cups onions, thinly sliced
1 cup green pepper, diced
3 cups fresh small tomato wedges
sandwich buns, as needed

Preheat slow cooker or large pot on stove.

Add just enough oil to quickly brown half the meat. Push meat to side of pot and brown remaining half, about three minutes per pound. Remove from heat. To meat in pot, add salt, soy sauce and one and one-half cups water. Cover and let simmer for one hour (No. 5 setting on slow cooker). In small bowl combine cornstarch with remaining one and one-half cups cold water. Stir slowly into meat mixture. Add onions, green pepper and tomato wedges. Cover and simmer for one hour. (No. 4 setting on slow cooker). Turn down heat (No. 3 setting) and keep warm for serving. Serve about one-quarter cup meat mixture in sandwich bun.
18 to 20 servings
May 18, 1974

Fondue is a simple, carefree way to eat. It brings people together and gives them something to share—the fun of cooking at the table. Fondue can fit into any part of the menu—appetizer, entree, or dessert.

Here are a few helpful hints to assure a successful meat fondue.

Peanut and salad oils are best to use for cooking meat. Heat oil in a saucepan on the stove and then pour into fondue pot. Oil that is hot enough for cooking must be handled with care. Keep the fondue pot over canned heat or an alcohol flame to keep it hot. Never leave the pot of hot oil unattended. Four people can cook adequately with one fondue pot, but more than four people reduces the temperature of the oil and slows the cooking process. Tender steaks such as tenderloin and sirloin are best for fondue, but less tender cuts can be used, especially if they are marinated.

Fondue Bourguignonne

½ cup clarified butter*
1½ cups salad oil
1 tsp. salt
beef tenderloin or well-trimmed sirloin,
    cut in ¾-inch cubes

*Place butter in a cup and stand the cup in hot water. When the butter is melted, pour off the butter and discard the milky sediment in the cup.

In a fondue pot heat oil and butter on top of range to 400 degrees. Add salt. Transfer to fondue burner over high heat. Have meat at room temperature. With long-handled forks spear pieces of meat and cook to desired doneness. Allow one-third to one-half pound of meat per person.

Note: pork or chicken cubes or shrimp may be substituted for beef.

Serve with one of the following sauces:

Mustard Sour Cream Sauce:

¾ cup sour cream
¼ cup salad dressing
2 T. prepared mustard
1 tsp. prepared horseradish
2 dashes hot pepper sauce

Combine all ingredients. Mix well. Cover and chill. Serve cold.

Horseradish–Sour Cream Sauce:

½ cup sour cream
½ tsp. prepared horseradish

Blend together.
January 22, 1968

Old Fashioned Beef Stew

2 pounds beef stew meat
3 tsp. salt
pepper, to taste
5 T. all-purpose flour
2 T. lard
3 cups water
1 bay leaf
4 cloves
2 T. celery leaves, chopped
2 sprigs parsley
12 small white onions
6 medium carrots
3 potatoes, halved
½ cup cold water

Cut beef in one and one-half-inch pieces. Blend together one teaspoon of the salt, pepper, and three tablespoons flour; roll meat in the flour mixture. Melt lard in heavy kettle, brown the meat on all sides. Add water, bay leaf, cloves, celery leaves, parsley, and one teaspoon salt.

Cover and simmer until meat is tender. Then add remaining salt, onions, carrots, and potatoes; cover and cook 20 minutes. Blend together two tablespoons flour and one-half cup cold water. Add small amount of liquid from stew. Pour into stew stirring and cooking until thickened.
September 18, 1954

36

Country Style Beef Stew

4 slices bacon
2 pounds boneless beef for stew,
*   cut in 1½-inch cubes*
2 tsp. salt
¼ tsp. pepper
½ tsp. marjoram
1 clove garlic, minced
2 cups water
4 medium potatoes, halved
6 medium carrots, halved
6 small onions
1 small turnip, quartered
3 T. all-purpose flour

Cut bacon into one-inch pieces; cook until lightly browned. Remove bacon pieces; brown beef in drippings. Add bacon, salt, pepper, marjoram, garlic, and water. Cover tightly and cook slowly two hours. Add vegetables; cook an additional 45 minutes or until meat is tender and vegetables are done. Transfer meat and vegetables to serving platter. Add water to cooking liquid to make two cups. Blend flour with a small amount of water and liquid from stew. Pour into pan, stirring and cooking till thickened.
6 servings
March 22, 1969

Black Forest Beef Stew

1½ pounds beef cubes (1½-inch size)
2 T. butter or margarine
1 can (10¾ ounces) condensed
*   tomato soup*
½ cup water
4 small carrots, cut into 1-inch pieces
1 T. parsley, chopped
½ tsp. Worcestershire sauce
⅛ tsp. caraway seed
1 small head cabbage (about 1 pound),
*   cut into 4 wedges*

In large heavy pan, brown meat in butter. Add soup and water. Cover, cook over low heat one and one-half hours. Stir now and then. Add carrots, parsley, Worcestershire sauce, and caraway seed; place cabbage on top. Cover, cook one hour more or until vegetables are tender. Stir now and then.
4 servings
January 15, 1972

An excellent recipe for a party of 12.

Beef Burgundy

⅔ cup all-purpose flour
1 T. salt
½ tsp. pepper
4 pounds beef chuck, cut in 1-inch
*   pieces*
3 T. shortening
2 beef bouillon cubes
1 cup boiling water
2 cups burgundy wine
¾ tsp. thyme
1 bay leaf
1 clove garlic, crushed
4 large carrots
12 small onions
1 pound fresh mushrooms, sliced
2 T. snipped parsley

Combine flour, salt and pepper. Dredge meat, reserving any leftover flour. Lightly brown meat (a third at a time), in shortening in Dutch oven. Pour off drippings. Sprinkle reserved flour over meat. Crush bouillon cubes. Dissolve in boiling water. Add bouillon, burgundy, thyme, bay leaf and garlic to meat. Cover tightly and cook in a 325 degree oven for 45 minutes. Cut carrots in pieces two inches long and cut each in two to four strips. Stir carrots and onions into meat and cook, covered, one hour. Remove bay leaf, stir in mushrooms and continue cooking 15 minutes or until meat and vegetables are tender. Sprinkle with snipped parsley.
12 servings
January 17, 1976

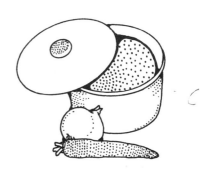

From 1900, a recipe calling for beef cut in "uniform pieces the size of a hand."

Rolled Beef

Trim slices of round steak in thin uniform pieces about the size of a hand. Force the trimmings through a meat chopper, add to them a slice of soaked bread squeezed dry and season palatably with salt, pepper, onion juice, and a little butter. Spread this mixture on the slices of meat, roll up tightly, and tie with twine. Fry out some breakfast bacon in a skillet, add the meat rolls and brown well on all sides. Add enough hot water or stock to half cover them; cover closely, simmer until tender, adding water if necessary from time to time, letting it cook down towards the last to about a cupful. Thicken the gravy and add seasoning if necessary. Remove twine from the meat, arrange on a platter garnished with parsley and pour around the gravy.
October 11, 1900

Hungarian Goulash And Noodles

¼ cup all-purpose flour
2 tsp. salt
¼ tsp. pepper
¼ tsp. thyme
2 pounds beef chuck, cubed
¾ cup butter
1 cup onions, sliced
1 can (13½ ounces) tomato juice
2 T. sugar
2 T. paprika
½ cup sour cream
12 ounces enriched durum wide
  noodles
butter, as needed

Combine flour, salt, pepper and thyme: use to flour meat. Brown in three-quarters cup butter; add onions and cook until golden brown. Stir in tomato juice, sugar, and paprika. Simmer one and one-half hours or until meat is tender. Stir in sour cream; bring to serving temperature. Do not boil.

Cook noodles in boiling, salted water until tender, yet firm, about five minutes. Toss with butter.

Serve noodles topped with meat and sauce.
6 servings
October 11, 1969

Alpine Goulash with Noodles

2½ pounds boneless round steak,
  cut into 1½-inch cubes
2 T. beef drippings or shortening
3 cups onion, coarsely chopped
1 clove garlic, minced
1 can (8 ounces) tomato sauce
2 T. brown sugar
1 T. paprika
1½ tsp. salt
1 tsp. caraway seed
1 tsp. dill seed
1 tsp. Worcestershire sauce
¼ tsp. pepper
½ pint (1 cup) sour cream, optional
hot buttered and seasoned cooked
  noodles

Brown meat well on all sides in hot drippings or shortening. Turn beef cubes as needed to brown evenly. Add onion, garlic, tomato sauce, sugar, paprika, salt, caraway seed, dill seed, Worcestershire sauce, and pepper; mix carefully. Cover and cook slowly until beef cubes are tender, about two and one-half hours. If desired, stir sour cream into mixture just before serving.

Serve on noodles.
October 25, 1969

Mexican Chili Con Carne

4 T. all-purpose flour
2 T. chili powder
2 cloves garlic, minced
2 pounds beef, cut in ½-inch cubes
2 T. suet, chopped
4 T. butter
2 onions, chopped fine
⅓ cup celery, chopped
2 T. parsley, minced
1 T. salt
water, as needed to cover meat
3 cups cooked red or kidney beans
1 small can tomato paste
½ tsp. oregano

Combine flour, chili powder, and garlic, and mix well in a large bowl. Add the meat, and mix thoroughly with hands until meat is coated, and all flour is absorbed. Melt suet and butter in a large skillet. Add the onion, celery, and parsley and brown lightly. Add salt. Add the meat; mix well, and simmer for 20 minutes, stirring frequently. Now gradually add water stirring constantly.

Simmer slowly for about one hour, or until the meat is very tender. Now add the beans, and mix. Simmer for five minutes. Stir in tomato paste and oregano and simmer for five minutes more.
October 2, 1954

This stew bakes in the oven for five hours—assemble the ingredients and you're ready for an afternoon outdoors.

Stew While Gardening

2 pounds stewing beef, cubed
3 medium carrots, sliced
2 onions, chopped
3 potatoes, peeled and quartered
cooked or frozen peas or any
*   leftover vegetables*
10½-ounce can condensed tomato soup
½ soup can of water
1 tsp. salt
sprinkle of pepper
1 bay leaf
¼ cup sweet or sour pickle juice or
*   cooking wine*

Combine beef, carrots, onions, potatoes, vegetables, tomato soup, water, salt, pepper, bay leaf and pickle juice or wine in a large casserole with lid. You need not brown the meat first. Mix ingredients, cover, and bake in a 275 degree oven for five hours.
May 10, 1969

Another recipe for the microwave.

Beef Mushroom Stew

*1½ pounds boneless beef chuck,
  cut into 1½-inch cubes*
*1 envelope beef-flavored onion soup
  mix*
2 cups water
¾ pound new potatoes, quartered
2 carrots, sliced
4 ounces mushrooms, quartered
½ cup dry red wine
3 T. all-purpose flour

Place beef cubes in three-quart round or
oval microwave-safe baking dish. Mix soup
and water in two-cup glass measuring cup.
Microwave soup on HIGH (100 percent
power) three minutes. Stir and pour over
beef; cover. Microwave on MEDIUM (50
percent power) one hour. Add potatoes and
carrots; cover. Microwave on MEDIUM 15
minutes or until beef is tender. Mix wine
and flour; stir into beef mixture. Add
mushrooms and cover. Microwave at
MEDIUM five minutes; stir and cover. Let
stand 10 minutes.
6 servings
California Beef Council

Meat Supper Pie

4 cups mashed potatoes
1 egg
salt and pepper, to taste
2 cups meat gravy
¼ tsp. sage
1½ to 2 cups cooked beef, cubed
1 cup cooked carrots, diced
1 cup cooked onion, sliced
1 cup cooked peas

Preheat oven to 375 degrees.
  Combine mashed potatoes and egg; beat
well. Season with salt and pepper. Combine gravy, meat, carrots, onion, and peas;
season with sage and pepper. Spread half
of potatoes in bottom and sides of nine-inch
pie plate; cover with meat mixture. Top
with remaining potatoes.
  Place in oven and bake for 30 minutes.
6 servings
July 20, 1946

40

If you're looking for tasty meals which can
be prepared ahead of time and frozen, why
not follow the example of the TV dinner
processors? This is one of the best cooking ahead routines. And assembling the
family's favorite meat, vegetables, and
accompaniments in one package ready for
the oven is so easy. Try these dinners on
your grill, too. Simply adjust the size of the
portions to fit your family's appetite!

Beef Dinner

onion, chopped
butter or margarine
chunks of tender beef
fresh tomatoes
potatoes, cut into chunks
fresh or frozen green beans
salt and pepper

Preheat oven to 375 degrees.
  Saute onion in melted butter until tender
but not browned. Brown beef chunks. Peel
and slice tomatoes in large wedges. For
each dinner serving, place on a large square
of heavy duty foil a serving of beef chunks,
about one tablespoon onion, one-half cup
potatoes, one-half cup green bean pieces,
one-half cup tomato. Season each serving
well with salt, pepper and other favorite
seasonings. Bring two sides of foil up over
food, double sealing edges lightly on top of
package. Double-fold each end of package.
Refrigerate or freeze.
  To cook, place on a cookie sheet and
bake one hour if only chilled; one and one-
quarter hours if frozen. Cook same length
of time on outdoor grill. Do not turn. To
serve, place on dinner plate and let each
person open his own package.
June 1976

Quantity cooking...if you're elected to feed a crowd of 25 people, try the recipes collected below. A steaming onion soup, followed by a tasty beef casserole and salad, is topped off with a fruit shortcake dessert. Accompany it with hot bread and butter.

Onion Soup

6 quarts boiling water
10 T. beef soup base
2 T. cornstarch
1 pint cold water
¾ cup shortening
4 pounds onions, thinly sliced
½ tsp. pepper

Boil water and stir in beef soup base. Stir cornstarch into cold water and add to stock. Melt shortening and saute onions slowly until browned. Add pepper. Stir into hot stock. Simmer for 10 to 20 minutes.
25 servings

Beef Casserole

10 pounds beef (chuck or round)
   cut in 2-inch cubes
2 cups all-purpose flour
3 T. salt
2 tsp. pepper
1½ cups (3 sticks) butter or margarine
4 carrots, diced
4 onions, sliced
1 quart tomato juice
4 bay leaves
2½ pounds rice
¼ pound butter or margarine

Dredge beef in flour seasoned with salt and pepper. Melt one and one-half cups butter or margarine in large heavy skillet. Add beef and brown well on all sides. Transfer to a large Dutch oven or heavy saucepan. Add carrots, onions, tomato juice and bay leaves.

Cover and simmer over low heat about one and one-half hours, or until tender. Cook rice as directed on package; add remaining butter.

To serve, spoon beef over rice.
25 servings

Cottage Cheese-Nut Salad

3 pounds cottage cheese
2 cups stuffed olives, chopped
2 cups pecans
3 heads lettuce, shredded
1½ cups French dressing

Mix cottage cheese with olives. Make into small balls using a scant tablespoon of the cheese and olive mixture to each ball. Chop pecans and roll each ball in nuts. For each salad, arrange three balls of the cottage cheese-olive mixture on a bed of lettuce. Top each salad with two teaspoons dressing.
25 servings

Molded Peach Shortcake

18 slices pound cake
5 packages peach gelatin
5 cups boiling water
4 packages frozen peach slices
2 cups heavy cream, whipped
3 8-inch-square pans

Fit pound cake slices tightly into bottom of pans. Dissolve gelatin in boiling water. Add frozen peaches and let stand until thawed and gelatin slightly thickened, stirring occasionally. Break peaches into bite-size pieces. Fold whipped cream into gelatin mixture. Pour over pound cake slices. Chill until firm.
25 servings
June 19, 1965

A classic of American cookery, from 1911:

Pot Pie

A meat pot pie is all right if made right. Try this plan: line a jar or deep dripping pan with nice biscuit dough, rolled out half-inch thick. Have your meat cooked tender and sliced and have sliced potatoes stewed rarely done. Put a layer of meat in the crust and then a layer of potatoes, season with salt, pepper, and a bit of butter. Repeat these layers until the pan is half filled, dredge with flour, pour in the broth in which the meat was cooked, cover with a top crust and bake thoroughly. Ham, beef, mutton or any lean meat may be used, or leftovers from stews and roasts, the gravy being thinned and added in place of broth or stock.

July 20, 1911

Found under the heading "Good Things to Eat" in a 1915 newspaper was "Beefsteak Pie (French Style)."

Beefsteak Pie (French Style)

Take a nice piece of beef, rump or sirloin, cut in small slices; slice also a little raw ham; put both in a frying pan, with some butter and small quantity chopped onions; let them simmer together a short time on the fire or in the oven; add a little flour and enough stock to make sauce; salt, pepper, chopped parsley and a little Worcestershire sauce as seasoning; add also a few slices potatoes and cook together for about twenty minutes; put this into a pie dish, with a few slices of hard-boiled eggs on the top and cover with a layer of common pie paste. Bake from fifteen to twenty minutes in a well-heated oven. All dark meat pies can be treated precisely in the same way. If poultry, leave the potatoes out.

November 10, 1915

Company Meat Pie

2 pounds stewing beef
4 cups water
2 tsp. salt
½ tsp. sugar
¼ tsp. paprika
⅛ tsp. pepper
1 bay leaf, size of a dime
1 T. catsup
1 tsp. Worcestershire sauce
1 cup onion, chopped
¼ cup celery, chopped
6 T. all-purpose flour
water, as needed for gravy
biscuit dough for top of meat pie

Brown the beef and add water, salt, sugar, paprika, pepper, bay leaf, catsup, Worcestershire sauce, onion and celery. Simmer until meat is tender, about one and one-half hours. Lift the meat out of the broth into a casserole or baking dish. Discard the bay leaf and make gravy of the broth. You should have about three cups which will take the flour mixed with a little water to make a paste.

Preheat oven to 425 degrees.

When the gravy is thick, taste for seasoning and add more salt if needed. Pour the gravy over the meat, enough to just cover it.

Set casserole in the oven and let it heat to bubbling while you make a rich biscuit dough. Roll about one-half inch thick and cut a piece the size of the casserole. Set it gently on top of the meat and gravy.

Brush the top with milk and bake at 425 degrees until crust is brown.

October 19, 1957

The idea for these complete meals, including potatoes, vegetables, and meat wrapped in a jacket of extra-rich biscuit dough, was borrowed from the industrious and thrifty Welsh. Each pasty (pronounced pas'ty, with a short "a") is a hearty meal in itself.

As the introduction to this recipe, written in late 1943, said, "One pasty will satisfy the hunger of the busiest hero of the production line."

Meat and Vegetable Pasties

Filling:

1 T. shortening
½ pound beef (or lamb), cubed
2 cups diced potatoes
1½ cups diced carrots
1 cup diced celery and leaves
chopped onions to flavor
1 T. salt
¼ tsp. pepper

Brown meat in shortening. Remove from heat. Add diced raw vegetables, salt, and pepper. Mix thoroughly.

Dough:

4 cups sifted all-purpose flour
4 tsp. baking powder
1½ tsp. salt
¾ cup shortening
1¾ to 2 cups milk

Preheat oven to 375 degrees.

Sift together flour, baking powder, and salt. Cut or rub in shortening. Add milk to make a soft dough. Turn out on lightly floured board and knead gently one-half minute. Roll out one-fourth-inch thick.

Cut into eight-inch rounds. On half of each round put one cup filling. Fold other half of round over filling, sealing edge firmly with finger tips or fork. Place on ungreased baking sheet.

Bake in oven 50 to 60 minutes. Serve hot with Tomato Sauce.

Tomato Sauce:

2½ cups tomatoes with juice
1 onion, chopped
½ tsp. salt
¼ tsp. pepper
3 T. butter
3 T. all-purpose flour

Cook tomatoes five minutes with onion, salt, and pepper. Melt butter and stir in flour. Gradually add tomatoes and stir until mixture thickens. Cook about three minutes longer, stirring occasionally.
6 large pasties with 2 cups sauce
October 16, 1943

Country Kettle Soup

¼ cup butter or margarine
⅓ cup green onions, sliced
2 pounds beef stew meat or round steak, cubed
2 cups potatoes, diced
1 cup carrots, sliced
1 cup celery, diagonally cut
1 tsp. salt
½ tsp. Italian herb seasoning
¼ tsp. garlic salt
1 13¾-ounce can chicken broth

Melt butter in an electric kettle at 300 degrees or in large pot. Add onions; saute until crisply tender. Stir in meat; brown thoroughly. Reduce heat to simmer. Stir in potatoes, carrots, celery, salt, Italian seasoning, garlic salt, and broth. Cover; cook one and one-half hours or until meat and vegetables are tender.
6 to 8 servings
May 4, 1974

A delightful 1925 recipe that includes a lesson in nutrition as well.

Aunt Elizabeth's Vegetable Soup

2 pounds brisket or short ribs
¼ cup pearl barley
1 carrot
½ turnip
2 small onions
1 big potato
2 quarts water
½ cup diced celery, if liked
¼ cup minced cabbage, if liked
salt, to taste

Cover the meat with cold water and simmer gently in a covered pan till tender. This should be done the day before serving. Let meat stand overnight in a cold place. In the morning remove the cake of grease which has formed on top of the soup. Remove all bones, fat and leave only the meat in the pot. An hour before serving, add the pearl barley. Cut all the vegetables the size of a kernel of corn and add to soup 20 minutes before serving.

This is a splendid way to give children their vegetables. Most housekeepers cook their vegetables in lots of water, then pour off the water which contains the valuable minerals and vitamins. By cooking vegetables in soup, all these essential minerals and vitamins are saved.
November 19, 1925

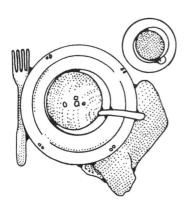

If you really want to start "from scratch," as they did in the early part of the century, here is the soup for you.

Creole Soup

Two pounds shin beef (meat and bone), one and one-half quarts of water. Cut the meat from the bone into small pieces. Crack the bone and soak one hour in cold water. Bring to a boil slowly and when boiling, place in cooker for five to seven hours. When cooked, strain and set away to cool. The cake of fat which forms on top when stock is cold seals the stock and keeps out air and germs, and should not be removed until soup is to be made. Then fat is removed and stock heated, and any seasonings or additions desired are put in. To one quart of this stock, or one quart of water in which chicken has been cooked, add one quart of canned soup mixture and two tablespoonfuls of rice or barley, bring to a boil and cook in cooker two to three hours. This will make a delightful soup.
December 24, 1915

Great for snacks!

Beef Jerky

1 beef flank steak, well-trimmed
½ cup soy sauce
garlic salt, as desired
lemon pepper, as desired

Cut steak lengthwise with the grain, no more than one-quarter-inch thick. Toss with soy sauce. Arrange beef strips in a single layer on a wire rack; place on a baking sheet. Sprinkle with garlic salt and lemon pepper. Place a second rack over the beef and flip over; remove top rack (or turn over by hand). Sprinkle again with seasonings.

Place in a 150 to 175 degree oven and bake overnight, 10 to 12 hours. Remove, and store in a covered container. Jerky should not be crisp.
February 19, 1972

Often your favorite foods, nicely packaged and wrapped, make great gifts. Here is one for seasoning salt that works well. Enclose with it a small card explaining that it can be used in salad dressings, on meat and poultry, in casseroles, or over hot cooked vegetables.

Seasoning Salt

¾ cup parsley flakes
¼ cup crushed basil leaves
3 T. salt
1 T. paprika
1 T. garlic powder

Crumble parsley flakes and basil leaves together in a bowl. Stir in salt, paprika, and garlic powder. Store in tightly covered container.
1⅓ cups seasoning
December, 1977

"Didn't They Eat Meat, Before?"

One of the most frequent complaints about meat rationing is this: "Why does it take more meat for a man in the army? These men were here in civilian life all the time, and didn't need so much."

One answer is that Uncle Sam takes better care of his men than they took of themselves as far as diet is concerned. And here are comparative figures showing what a man eats when he's a civilian and what he eats when he's in the army:

The average yearly per man consumption of meat in civilian life is 172 pounds: in the armed forces, 306 pounds, a 77.9 per cent increase.

In civilian life it takes 86,000 tons per million men; in the armed forces, 163,000 tons per million men.
February 6, 1943

Leftovers

If you are fortunate enough to have leftovers from your beef roasts, look through the following recipes for some excellent ways to use that meat. You may even be tempted to cook an especially large roast the next time, just to be sure there'll be plenty left over.

Croquettes of Cold Roast Beef

Chop into tiny bits enough lean roast beef to make two cupfuls. Cook together in a saucepan a tablespoonful of butter and two of flour, and when these are blended pour upon them two cups of milk, to which you have added a pinch of baking soda. Stir to a smooth sauce then add the minced beef and remove from the range. Beat in a few drops of onion juice, a dash each of paprika and nutmeg, and salt to taste. Set aside until very cold, then mould into small croquettes. Roll each croquette in beaten egg, then in cracker dust. Set all in a cool place for two hours, then fry in deep boiling fat. Drain free of grease in a hot colander.
September 20, 1900

Tomato Beef

Sprinkle small pieces of beef cut from the remains of a roast with salt, pepper, and flour. Put a layer of meat in a baking dish, over it put a layer of canned tomatoes or sliced fresh tomatoes. Scatter bits of butter over it. Cover with a layer of beef, then tomato. Make the top layer of buttered crumbs. Bake slowly for one hour.
October 30, 1902

An excellent appetizer:

Beef Logs

Beef logs can be made ahead and refrigerated. Spread slices of roast beef with softened cream cheese mixed with finely chopped chives or onion. Roll up, jelly-roll fashion, and chill. Slice before serving. Serve as "on-pick" appetizers.
December, 1977

You can make a festive luncheon from leftover roast beef.

Luncheon Beef Rolls

Cut thin slices of roast beef sirloin tip. Form into rolls. Fasten each with a wooden pick on which olives and radishes have been skewered. Place on a bed of lettuce and serve with assorted meat spreads. Each spread yields approximately one cup.

Mustard Spread: Blend three-quarters cup prepared mustard and one-quarter cup mayonnaise. Sprinkle one-half to one teaspoon dill weed over top.

Horseradish-Sour Cream Spread: Blend one cup sour cream and one tablespoon prepared horseradish. Stir in one to two tablespoons chopped green onion, if desired.

Catsup Spread: Stir two to three tablespoons chopped pickles into one cup catsup.
October 28, 1972

When there's leftover corned beef in the kitchen, try an old favorite, Red Flannel Hash. Or, substitute any cooked beef for corned beef and add a teaspoon of salt to the recipe.

Red Flannel Hash

3 cups chopped cooked corned beef
2 cups coarsely chopped cooked
*   poatatoes*
1 cup chopped cooked beets
1 small onion, finely chopped
2 T. minced parsley
½ tsp. salt
⅛ tsp. pepper
1 can (5½-ounces) evaporated milk
2 T. shortening

Combine beef, potatoes, beets, onion, parsley, salt, and pepper. Stir in evaporated milk. Heat shortening in a large frying pan. Place beef mixture in pan, pressing down firmly. Cook, uncovered, pressing together and turning for 15 to 20 minutes. Press together and cook slowly for five minutes or until crust forms on bottom. Loosen hash from pan with a turner and invert on platter to serve.
4 servings
January 17, 1976

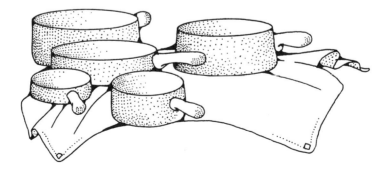

Julienne Beef Garden Salad

¾ cup cooked salad dressing
¾ cup sour cream
½ cup crumbled blue cheese
¼ cup milk
⅛ tsp. garlic powder
1 to 1½ pounds cooked beef, cut in
    julienne strips
salt, to taste
½ small head lettuce
¼ pound fresh mushrooms, sliced
1 cup thinly sliced celery
½ cucumber, sliced
½ cup halved pitted ripe olives
⅓ cup sliced green onions
12 cherry tomatoes, halved

Combine salad dressing, sour cream, blue
cheese, milk, and garlic powder. Cover and
refrigerate at least one hour. Salt meat as
desired. Tear lettuce into bite sized pieces
and combine with beef strips, mushrooms,
celery, cucumber, olives, and green onions
in large salad bowl. Cover and refrigerate
until ready to serve.

To serve, add tomatoes and toss lightly.
Add the blue cheese dressing.
6 servings
August 27, 1977

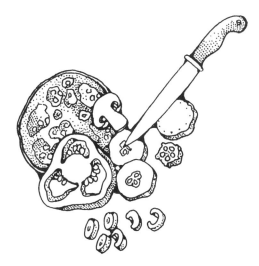

Roast Beef Macaroni Salad

1 T. salt
3 quarts boiling water
2 cups elbow macaroni
2 cups diced cooked roast beef
1 medium tomato, diced
½ cup sliced sweet gherkins
¼ cup sliced green onions
¾ cup creamy French dressing
2 T. sweet pickle liquid

Add salt to rapidly boiling water. Gradually
add macaroni so water continues to boil.
Cook, uncovered, stirring occasionally until
tender. Drain in colander. Rinse with cold
water; drain again. Combine with roast
beef, tomato, gherkins, onions, French
dressing, and pickle liquid. Toss and chill.

Serve in lettuce cups, if desired.
6 servings
May 11, 1968

Second-day beef gives a first-rate perfor-
mance when used in these Italian
sandwiches.

Italian Beef Sandwiches

1 can (10½ ounces) beef consomme
½ cup catsup
1 medium onion, cut crosswise in slices
1 small green pepper, cut in strips
¼ cup water
1 clove garlic, minced
¼ tsp. leaf oregano
1 pound thinly sliced cooked roast beef
6 large rolls, halved

Combine consomme, catsup, onion, green
pepper, water, garlic, and oregano in a large
saucepan or frypan and heat to boiling. Add
beef, cover tightly, and cook slowly for 25
to 30 minutes. Drain and reserve cooking
liquid; dip cut surfaces of bottom halves of
rolls in the liquid. Place hot beef and
vegetables on bottom halves. Dip cut surfaces of roll top in reserved liquid and place
on top of sandwiches.

Serve hot.
6 servings
April 9, 1977

Beef Chart

WHOLESALE CUTS OF BEEF AND THEIR BONE STRUCTURE

APPROXIMATE YIELDS*

FOREQUARTER	PERCENT
Chuck (5 ribs)	26
Rib (7 ribs)	9
Shank	4
Brisket	5
Short Plate	8
	52

HINDQUARTER	
Round	23
Sirloin	9
Short Loin	8
Flank	5
Kidney, Suet and Hanging Tender	3
	48
Total	100

*No allowance for cutting shrink

CHUCK RIB SHORT LOIN SIRLOIN ROUND
FORE SHANK BRISKET SHORT PLATE FLANK

RETAIL CUTS OF BEEF AND WHERE THEY COME FROM

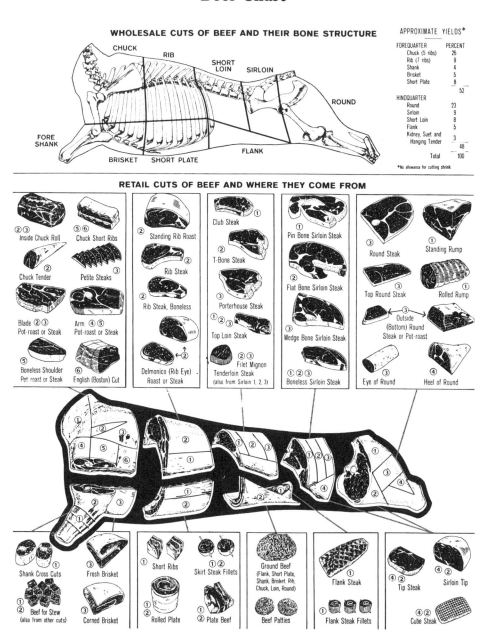

Inside Chuck Roll ②③ — Chuck Short Ribs ⑤⑥ — Chuck Tender ② — Petite Steaks ③ — Blade ②③ Pot-roast or Steak — Arm ④⑤ Pot-roast or Steak — Boneless Shoulder Pot-roast or Steak ⑤ — English (Boston) Cut ⑥

Standing Rib Roast ② — Rib Steak ② — Rib Steak, Boneless ② — Delmonico (Rib Eye) Roast or Steak ③

Club Steak ① — T-Bone Steak ② — Porterhouse Steak ③ — Top Loin Steak ①②③ — Filet Mignon Tenderloin Steak ②③ (also from Sirloin 1, 2, 3)

Pin Bone Sirloin Steak ① — Flat Bone Sirloin Steak ② — Wedge Bone Sirloin Steak ③ — Boneless Sirloin Steak ①②③

Round Steak ③ — Standing Rump ① — Top Round Steak ③ — Rolled Rump ① — Outside (Bottom) Round Steak or Pot-roast ③ — Eye of Round ③ — Heel of Round ④

Shank Cross Cuts ① — Fresh Brisket ③ — Beef for Stew ①② (also from other cuts) — Corned Brisket ③

Short Ribs ① — Skirt Steak Fillets ①② — Rolled Plate ① — Plate Beef ②

Ground Beef (Flank, Short Plate, Shank, Brisket, Rib, Chuck, Loin, Round) — Beef Patties ①

Flank Steak ① — Flank Steak Fillets ①

Tip Steak ④② — Sirloin Tip ④② — Cube Steak ④②

Reprinted through the courtesy of
The National Live Stock and Meat Board
444 No. Michigan Avenue
Chicago, Illinois 60611

Supper Sandwich

4 slices bread
butter, as needed
4 slices cooked beef, cut ¼-inch thick
1 package (3-ounces) cream cheese
1 T. blue cheese, crumbled
1 tsp. mustard
1 T. finely chopped onion
1 tsp. chopped parsley

Preheat oven to 450 degrees.
   Toast bread on one side. Butter untoasted side. Place meat on buttered side. Cream together cream cheese, blue cheese, mustard, and onion. Place two tablespoons of the mixture on each sandwich and spread within one-half-inch of edge of toast. Sprinkle parsley on top.
   Bake in oven for eight to 10 minutes.
4 servings
July 1, 1961

Beef Pie with Potato Crust

Slice very thin enough cold roast beef to half fill your baking dish. Place the beef, any leftover gravy, a large tablespoon of butter, a small onion, sliced, and salt and pepper together in a stewing pan; cover with water and dredge with flour to thicken the gravy. Cover and simmer gently until gravy is reduced and rather thick. Have mashed potatoes prepared in usual way. Put the meat and gravy in the baking dish and cover with a thick crust of the potatoes. Brush with beaten egg and bake in a quick oven long enough to brown the crust. A few spoonfuls of leftover tomatoes or a spoonful of Worcestershire sauce may be added to the stew for variety.
March 28, 1901

Meat and potatoes have been popular together for a long time. This meat loaf, from a 1909 publication, is a good example of the combination.

Meat Loaf

Butter a long cake tin and line it with mashed potatoes about an inch thick. Chop some cold roast beef rather coarse; season it with salt, pepper, a little onion juice and moisten it with gravy. Fill the center with this meat and cover with mashed potato. Bake in hot oven for half an hour and turn out on long platter. It will look like a crusted loaf, and may be cut in neat slices for supper.
January 14, 1909

2

Game
Or,
How To Cook Your Moose

If you're used to cooking the kinds of meats you find in the supermarkets, you can feel equally comfortable cooking game; the principles are similar. For the tougher cuts, use moist heat, such as stewing or braising, and for the tender cuts, you will want to use a dry heat method, such as roasting or broiling.

The fact is, a lot of game recipes are interchangeable with domestic animal recipes. You can use rabbit or squirrel in most chicken recipes, and you can use bear in most pork recipes.

As for venison, Dolly DeChambeau, a National Rifle Association member and an avid cook, says: "Cook venison the way you do beef. Venison that requires special soaking, treating, or saucing is inferior meat which has been improperly killed, dressed or handled—and if you keep a dog you will know exactly what to do with such meat."

The principle for cooking wild game may be the same as for cooking supermarket meats, but, as Hugh Galbreath, manager of DuPont's wildlife management demonstration area, Remington Farms, points out, "Don't expect the taste to be the same. Flavors vary between the different species and even between deer of the same species, depending on what the animal's been eating. A white tail deer that's been browsing on woody vegetation yields a different taste from one that's been eating a farmer's corn crop."

In other words, don't expect that your venison is going to taste like beef or even like the venison you ate at your neighbor's last week. The flavors will vary, but that's part of the attraction, once you've developed a taste for it.

If you're a hunter yourself, there are a couple of things you can do to insure that your game would pass Dolly DeChambeau's quality test. Dr. George York, from the University of California's Cooperative Extension, says, "To maintain the quality of your freshly killed game, the most important thing is to get it eviscerated quickly. You want to get rid of the entrails since they can be the entry point for bacteria." Dr. York goes on to explain that avoiding spoilage organisms is also the reason for making sure to bleed game. "Unlike muscle tissue, blood isn't protected by membranes and any time you have pockets of blood, you have a terrific medium for bacteria."

Bacteria is also the reason that Dr. York recommends chilling freshly killed game as soon as possible. "Bacteria grows slowly at temperatures below 40 degrees so your meat will stay in better condition for longer if you can chill it quickly."

Although it's true that cooking game is much like cooking meat from domestic species, here are a few specific suggestions. Deer tends to have little fat, and benefits from being treated like veal, which also has little fat. For tougher cuts, if you're not using moist heat, you might try treating the meat as you would veal scallops. Just slice thinly—a quarter of an inch—across the grain and cook it rapidly so that you don't toughen the tissue.

Moose meat, should you ever encounter it, is unlike any other antlered species and tends to be fatty. Treat it more like pork.

Bear, like moose, is fatty, but also tends to be tough. Marinate it for 24 hours before cooking and then it's ready to be interchanged with pork recipes. One thing to keep in mind about bear—and it happens very rarely—is that bear, like pork, can harbor trichina. Fortunately, trichinosis can be entirely prevented by cooking the meat to an internal temperature above 140 degrees. As long as you don't go in for rare bear, you never need to worry.

The leg muscles of venison tend to be tough, but if you grind them they can make wonderful venison burgers. Or you could try George York's Venison Jerky.

To make jerky, cut into strips a quarter to a half-inch wide, sprinkle with salt (three-quarter teaspoon per pound of meat), coarse ground pepper and garlic powder (one teaspoon per pound of each, or to tatse). Mix thoroughly and let stand in the refrigerator overnight. Place strips on racks and dry in the oven at 140 degrees with the oven door slightly ajar or in a home dehydrator set at 140 degrees. It takes four to five hours to dry. Take strips out of heat and allow to cool to room temperature before testing. When dried enough it should be chewy without a raw meat flavor. It should not be brittle.

Cooking game is an adventure, but it's a fun adventure rather than a perilous one, if you know the principles and when you have a guide. You already know the principles now, and the recipes that follow can serve as a time-tested guide.

Fried Rabbit

Probably the most popular way of preparing rabbit is to fry it, especially if it is young and tender. Soak it or not, as you wish, but cut up the pieces much as you would cut up a chicken. Roll each piece in a mixture of seasoned flour and fry in piping-hot fat. Serve with gravy made in the pan where the rabbit has been fried.
November 3, 1951

Rabbit/Lagos Stefado

2 young rabbits, 6 to 7 pounds
1 cup red wine vinegar
8 whole cloves
2 large onions, sliced paper thin
3 to 4 bay leaves, depending how fresh
3 to 4 cinnamon sticks, depending
    how fresh
6 garlic cloves, minced
2 tsp. allspice
pepper, to taste
2 T. butter
2 cups white wine
16 ounces tomato sauce
32 small onions
butter, as needed for sauteing onions

Cut rabbits into serving pieces. Combine vinegar, cloves, onion, bay leaves, cinnamon sticks, garlic, allspice and pepper. Put rabbit in bowl and pour marinade over it. Make sure all of the rabbit is covered. Marinate 24 hours. Drain rabbit, saving marinade. In a skillet, sear pieces on all sides in two tablespoons butter. Remove rabbit from pan and place in a baking dish. Combine marinade with tomato sauce and wine. Pour over rabbit. Saute small onions in butter. Pour onions around the rabbit. Cover tightly.

Bake in a 350-degree oven for one and one-half hours.
6 to 8 servings
Lynne Scalapino Thompson, 1982

The comment accompanying this 1922 recipe was right to the point—"Very good."

Rabbit in Tomato Sauce

1 large rabbit, cut in serving pieces
oil or shortening, as needed to
    brown meat
2 T. butter
3 T. all-purpose flour
1 large onion, chopped
1½ cups tomato pulp and juice
½ tsp. pepper
2 tsp. salt
3 cups boiling water

Dip rabbit pieces in flour, brown in a little oil or shortening. Put the butter in a deep iron skillet or a roasting pan, and stir in the flour. Add the chopped onion, tomato, salt, pepper, and water, and cook for five minutes. When boiling, add the rabbit. Cover and simmer for one hour.
4 servings
January 4, 1923

Rabbit Baked in Milk

⅓ cup all-purpose flour
1 tsp. salt
1 tsp. sage
1 rabbit, cut in pieces for frying
3 T. shortening
3 strips bacon
thin white sauce, as needed

Mix flour, salt, and sage in a bowl. Thoroughly coat the rabbit pieces with this mixture. In a skillet, brown rabbit in shortening on all sides. Place meat in a casserole and lay bacon strips on top. Pour white sauce over and around the rabbit. Bake in a 350-degree oven for two hours, or until the meat is tender.
4 servings
November 3, 1951

Hassenpfeffer

2½ to 3 pound rabbit
½ cup vinegar
2 cups water
2 tsp. salt
¼ tsp. pepper
½ tsp. whole cloves
2 tsp. sugar
4 bay leaves
1 onion, sliced
3 T. all-purpose flour
shortening, as needed to brown meat
all-purpose flour, as needed to
    thicken sauce

Cut the rabbit in serving pieces. Combine the vinegar, water, salt, pepper, cloves, sugar, bay leaves, and onion together. Place the rabbit in a glass or enameled ware bowl. Pour the pickling mixture over it. Let stand in the refrigerator for eight to 12 hours. Turn the pieces occasionally so they will absorb the flavor evenly.

Remove the rabbit pieces. Save the liquid and onion but discard the bay leaves and cloves. Roll the pieces in flour. Brown in a frying pan in hot shortening. Pour the pickling mixture over the rabbit and cook over low heat until tender, about one hour. Thicken the sauce in which the rabbit has been cooked with flour and pour over the rabbit.
4 to 6 servings
February 6, 1954

Deviled Rabbit

1 rabbit, cut into serving pieces
salt, pepper, and paprika, to taste
2 T. all-purpose flour
½ cup shortening, melted
1 cup hot water
2 tsp. Worcestershire sauce
2 tsp. catsup
1½ tsp. dry mustard

Season cut up rabbit with salt, pepper, and paprika and roll in the flour. Brown well in the hot shortening and remove from the pan. Add remaining flour to fat in pan and stir till smooth. Add hot water, Worcestershire sauce, catsup and mustard and mix well. Put rabbit in covered casserole and pour the sauce over it. Bake, uncovered, for one hour to one and one-half hours or until tender.
4 to 6 servings
January 9, 1971

Creole Rabbit

2 medium-sized onions, sliced
1 clove garlic, finely chopped
1 T. parsley, chopped
3 T. butter
3½ cups tomato juice (No. 2½ can)
¼ tsp. Worcestershire sauce, if desired
1 young rabbit, cut into serving pieces
¼ cup milk
¾ cup sifted all-purpose flour
1 tsp. salt
¼ tsp. pepper
shortening, as needed for browning

Preheat oven to 375 degrees.

Cook onion, garlic, and parsley in butter until golden brown. Add tomato juice and Worcestershire. Boil gently 15 minutes. Dip rabbit in milk, then in flour, salt and pepper sifted together. Brown rabbit lightly in the shortening. Place pieces in a baking pan and add the tomato mixture.

Cover and bake for one and one-half hours or until tender. Uncover and bake 30 minutes longer to brown.
4 servings
September 15, 1951

Rabbit in Batter

Make a frying batter with half pound of flour, a small cup of tepid water in which is melted two tablespoons of cooking oil, lard or butter, and salt, and the yolks of two eggs. Let stand for an hour, then beat in the whites of the eggs. Disjoint and bone the rabbit; cut into cutlets, dip in this batter and fry.
December 1, 1922

Rabbit was a popular meat in the early part of the century. Cooks found a seemingly limitless number of ways to prepare it. Some of their recipes follow, beginning with two versions of Rabbit Pie.

Rabbit Pot Pie

Boil rabbit meat until very tender. Remove meat from broth and boil broth down to one-half. Pick the meat from bones in as large pieces as possible. Thicken stock with one tablespoon flour to every cup of broth and pour over meat. Add two teaspoons salt and a little pepper. Line the sides of a baking dish with crust, add the meat mixture, cover with crust and bake in a hot oven 30 minutes.

Pie Crust for Rabbit Pie:

The crust may be made in two ways—one as pie paste and the other as rich biscuit dough.

Pie paste:

1 cup all-purpose flour
4 T. shortening
2 T. water
¼ tsp. salt

Mix and roll as ordinary pie dough.

Rich biscuit dough:

1 cup all-purpose flour
2 tsp. baking powder
¼ tsp. salt
2 T. shortening
½ cup milk

Sift together the flour, baking powder, and salt. Cut in the shortening and add milk to make a soft dough. Roll on board to one-half inch thickness and cover baking dish. This dough may also be cut as biscuits and these put on top of meat mixtures in baking dish.
January 4, 1923

From 1900 we find a recipe for sauteed rabbit alongside one for a good sauce to serve with it.

Panned Rabbit

Clean and cut in halves. Place in a baking pan, spread with butter, dust with pepper and salt and bake in a quick oven one hour, basting frequently. When done, lay on a heated dish. Add a tablespoonful of browned flour to the gravy in the pan; mix well; add half a pint of boiling water; stir, season with salt and pepper and pour over the rabbit.

Bread Sauce for Game

Sift a pint of bread crumbs, put two-thirds of a pint of milk in a saucepan, add a little grated onion, set on the stove, season with cayenne pepper, salt and a little nutmeg, let come to a boil; add half the bread crumbs. Fry the remainder in butter until brown.
December 6, 1900

Here's an excellent sauce to serve with wild game.

Hot Orange Sauce

¼ cup all-purpose flour
½ tsp. salt
¼ cup butter, melted
1⅓ cup brown stock
1 cup orange juice
grated rind of 1 orange

Add flour and salt to butter, stirring until well-browned. Slowly add stock. Just before serving, add orange juice and rind.
November 2, 1963

In 1919, *The Wisconsin Farmer* asked its readers for their favorite way of preparing the "cotton tails" and, in turn, offered them this very good recipe.

Rabbit Sausage

After skinning the rabbit soak the meat overnight in salt water. In the morning cut meat from the bones and run through a food chopper. For the meat of one rabbit add:

2 slices onion, chopped
3 T. bread crumbs
¾ tsp. salt
⅛ tsp. pepper
dash of cayenne
1 egg

Make into patties and fry slowly in bacon drippings. A good-sized rabbit should make a dozen to 15 patties.
December 19, 1919

Roast Haunch of Venison

1 6-pound haunch of venison, shank
*   bone removed*
equal parts vinegar and oil mixture,
*   as needed to cover roast*
1 large onion, sliced
1 clove garlic, crushed
1 bay leaf
3 juniper berries
6 strips fat bacon
boiled pureed chestnuts, if desired as
*   an accompaniment*

Combine vinegar and oil mixture with onion, garlic, bay leaf, and juniper berries. Place meat in a large bowl and marinate in the vinegar and oil mixture overnight.

Preheat oven to 450 degrees.

Remove meat from marinade and skewer and tie into a compact shape. Strain and reserve the marinade. Insert a thermometer in the thickest portion of muscle and place the meat on a rack in an open roasting pan. Place the bacon strips on top of meat.

Roast meat 20 minutes. Reduce the oven temperature to 325 degrees and cook 15 to 18 minutes per pound to an internal temperature of 140 degrees for very rare; 150 degrees for medium well done. While the meat is roasting, baste occasionally with the marinade.

Serve with boiled pureed chestnuts.
10 to 12 servings
January 9, 1971

Two very different marinades for venison, but, in our opinion, equally good.

Orange Marinade for Venison

equal parts vinegar and salad oil,
*   as needed to cover roast*
1 bay leaf
6 peppercorns
½ tsp. salt
dash cinnamon
½ red pepper, sliced
juice of one orange
4 to 5 pound venison roast

In a large bowl combine vinegar and oil mixture with bay leaf, peppercorns, salt, cinnamon, red pepper, and orange juice. Carefully wash and dry the venison and place it in this solution and refrigerate for 48 hours. Remove from marinade and roast to desired doneness.
6 to 8 servings
January 9, 1971

Herb Marinade for Venison

1 cup beef broth
1 tsp. salt
1 T. pickling spice
½ tsp. celery seeds
½ tsp. each of basil, marjoram,
*   thyme, and sage*
1 bay leaf
3 peppercorns, crushed
3 whole allspice, crushed
2 T. lemon juice
¼ cup vinegar

Combine beef broth, salt, pickling spice, celery seeds, basil, marjoram, thyme, sage, bay leaf, peppercorns, allspice, lemon juice, and vinegar. Put meat in glass or crockery bowl and cover with marinade. Cover; refrigerate from 10 to 12 hours. Remove meat, drain and cook as desired.
November 2, 1963

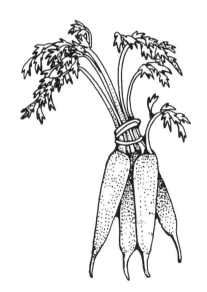

Venison Steak

4 venison round steaks, 8- to 9-ounces
*   each, cut ½- to ¾-inch thick*
2 carrots, sliced
2 onions, sliced
1 clove garlic, chopped
⅛ tsp. thyme
2 bay leaves
⅓ tsp. freshly ground pepper
small pinch of ground cloves
1 cup mild vinegar (¾ cup cider
*   vinegar of 5 percent acidity mixed*
*   with ¼ cup water)*
½ cup olive oil
shortening, as needed for frying

Place steaks in an enamel, glass, or earthenware bowl. Add carrots, onions, garlic, thyme, bay leaves, pepper, cloves, vinegar and olive oil, and let stand in refrigerator 24 hours. Turn meat several times.

Remove steaks and dry, reserving the marinade. Saute steaks in shallow, hot shortening until brown on both sides. The steaks should be rare. Serve on a hot platter.
4 servings
January 9, 1971

Some good, general directions.

Venison, Moose, or Elk Steaks and Chops

If these are from young animals, they need no marinating. To cook your steaks or chops, heat a heavy skillet until quite hot. Add half butter and half oil. Saute the meat, turning it frequently to brown on both sides without charring. Salt and pepper to taste. If you like, flame the meat with cognac just before serving. Steaks and chops from young animals may be cooked in the same manner as beef steaks or lamb chops: broiled, grilled, or sauteed. When broiling or cooking on an outdoor grill, cook quickly, and do not overcook. Game will become tough or dry with long broiling or frying. Salt and pepper to taste.
October 26, 1968

This is a dish that seems to improve after being frozen or stored in refrigerator overnight.

Venison Hot-Dish

1 large onion, sliced
2 ounces butter
3 pounds venison stew meat, cubed
*   to 1-inch squares*
2½ cups water
salt, to taste
1 bay leaf
3 peppercorns
3 large carrots, cut up
1 pound potatoes, cut up
2 tomatoes, cut up
½ green pepper, sliced
1 parsnip, cut up
1 package frozen peas
1 T. all-purpose flour
¼ cup water

Saute onion in butter until transparent. Add cubed meat and brown. Add two and a half cups water and bring to boil. Salt to taste. Simmer five minutes. Add bay leaf and peppercorns, and simmer until meat is tender. Add carrots, potatoes, tomatoes, green pepper, parsnip, and peas, and cook until vegetables are done.

Mix flour with one-quarter cup water. Remove pot from heat; stir in flour and water mixture. Return to heat and simmer until thickened, about five minutes.
10 to 12 servings
January 9, 1971

This is an excellent main dish to serve with red cabbage cooked with apples, and buttered noodles or boiled new potatoes covered with sour cream.

Venison Goulash

2 pounds venison (any cut), cut into
*   1½-inch cubes*
3 T. all-purpose flour
3 T. bacon drippings
1 large onion, sliced or chopped fine
2 cloves garlic, chopped
1 T. paprika
¼ cup wine vinegar
1 quart boiling water or stock
salt, to taste
1 small can tomato paste
1 cup sour cream (optional)

Roll the meat in the flour, pressing the flour into the cubes. Melt the drippings in a skillet, add the onion and garlic and cook until browned. Add the meat and brown well. Add paprika, wine vinegar, boiling water or stock, salt, and tomato paste. Stir well, cover, and simmer gently until the meat is tender, two to three hours, adding more stock, water, or wine vinegar if necessary.

Just before serving, stir in the sour cream.
6 servings
January 9, 1971

This recipe from the early 1960s called for cooking in a pressure cooker. Since the pressure cooker isn't a standard item in kitchens today, improvise by cooking the meat until tender in any heavy-duty casserole.

Paprika Cream Schnitzel

1 pound deer round, cut in cubes
½ cup water
3 or 4 slices bacon, finely cut
2 T. onion, chopped
1 clove garlic, chopped
1 tsp. salt
1 tsp. paprika
½ cup tomato juice
1 cup sour cream
chopped parsley, as desired

Place deer meat and water in a pressure pan and cook about 30 minutes at 10 pounds pressure. Fry bacon until crisp, add cooked meat, onion, garlic, and cook until brown. Add salt, paprika, tomato juice, and sour cream. Simmer this mixture gently until the sauce is thick. Sprinkle with parsley just before serving.

4 servings
November 11, 1963

Venison, Hunter's Style

salt and pepper, to taste
3 pounds venison, cut in 2-inch cubes
2 T. butter
1 onion, chopped
½ cup cubed ham, minced
1 clove garlic, minced
2 bay leaves
2 strips thyme, crushed
1 T. all-purpose flour
2 cups warm water
1 quart consomme
½ pound fresh mushrooms, chopped
grated peel of 1 lemon

Generously salt and pepper venison cubes. Heat butter in skillet and brown venison slowly. When almost done, add onion; brown slightly. Then add ham, garlic, bay leaves and thyme. Stir and simmer for two minutes. Add flour and cook a few minutes longer.

Add warm water and let cool to a good simmer. Add consomme and cook slowly for one hour. Season again according to taste; then add mushrooms and lemon peel. Let cook 30 minutes longer.

Serve on a very hot plate.

8 servings
November 27, 1971

Venison Salami

8 pounds venison
2 pounds pork fat
6 T. salt
1⅔ cups ice water
2 cups dried milk solids
1 T. pepper (white or black)
2 tsp. cracked pepper
5 cloves garlic, chopped Or 1 T.
    garlic powder
⅓ cup dry red wine
2 T. corn syrup
½ tsp. of cure (Prague powder®,
    Morton's Tender Quick®, or
    similar preparations) Or ¼ tsp.
    sodium or potassium nitrate

Chill meat and pork fat. Grind venison through a three-sixteenth or one-eighth-inch plate. Cut pork fat into three-quarter to one-inch cubes.

In a mixer or tub, add the meat and fat to all the other ingredients. Mix until all the ingredients are evenly distributed. Pack down tightly, cover with plastic wrap or butcher paper, and place in a refrigerator at 38 to 40 degrees for two to three days.

Remove from the refrigerator and regrind the cold mixture through the same sized plate. Stuff the sausage into hog casing of medium, English medium, wide, or special wide, ranging from 32 to 44 millimeters. The sausage should be linked in lengths of 10 to 12 inches.

The sausage can be cooked, smoked and cooked, or dried.

To cook, place the salami in smokehouse or oven set at 130 degrees for 30 minutes to dry surface. Raise temperature to 150 degrees and cook for one hour. Raise temperature to 160 degrees during the next hour, and bring final temperature to 165 degrees. Cook until internal temperature of meat is 152 to 154 degrees. Remove, rinse in cold water, and refrigerate.

To smoke, follow same initial step as in cooked. Apply smoke after the first thirty minutes and continue for two hours.

To dry, after stuffing, cure the salami by holding at 65 to 70 degrees for three days with a relative humidity of 70 to 80 percent.

Then store at 40 to 50 degrees with a relative humidity of 60 to 65 percent for 80 to 90 days or until it has lost a quarter of its original weight.
George York

Nibbles can be used for cocktail hors d'oeuvres or an evening snack for the family.

Venison Nibbles

venison steak, cut into strips 3
    inches by 1 inch, as needed
salt and pepper, to taste
1 egg, beaten
cracker crumbs, as needed
shortening or oil, as needed for deep
    frying

Preheat deep fat fryer to 365 degrees.

Season venison strips with salt and pepper. Dip in egg and then in cracker crumbs. Fry in very hot, deep oil just like french fries until golden brown.
October 22, 1977

A writer and cook in 1900 had this to say about squirrel.

Squirrels in many districts are such a pest that hunting them is a matter of self preservation. Fortunately, when well-skinned and properly prepared, they make good eating. One nice way of cooking squirrel is to smother in onions. Allow one quart of peeled white onions for three small squirrels jointed; cover with water and simmer until the onions and meat are both tender, seasoning when half done; lift out the nicest joints, saving the remainder for soup, and lay on a hot dish while you remove the onions with a skimmer. Mince these fine and heat very hot with butter the size of an egg, a tablespoonful of flour, one of cream, and salt and pepper to taste. Spread this puree smoothly over the meat, and send a gravy boat of the broth thickened and colored like a brown sauce, to the table with it.
February 1, 1900

One Dish Squirrel

1 squirrel
salt and pepper, as needed
all-purpose flour, as needed
vegetable oil, as needed
1 cup onion, diced
6 small potatoes, cubed
1 medium can tomatoes

Cut squirrel meat into serving-sized pieces. Sprinkle with salt, pepper, and flour. Fry in oil until lightly browned. Layer squirrel, onion, and potatoes in casserole dish. Cover with tomatoes. Bake covered in a 350-degree oven for one and one-half hours.
4 servings
October 26, 1963

A recipe published during the game-hunting season of 1905 went like this.

Squirrel Stew

Skin, dress, and place for one hour in salted water, to which a little vinegar has been added. Wipe dry, place in a saucepan, cover with sweet milk and stew thirty minutes. Season to taste and serve with small squares of toasted bread.
November 16, 1905

Serve this tasty stew with hot squares of buttered cornbread.

Brunswick Stew

3 squirrels, cut in serving pieces
3 quarts of water
¼ cup bacon, diced
⅛ tsp. cayenne
2 tsp. salt
¼ tsp. black pepper
1 cup onion, chopped
2 cans (1 pound, 3 ounces each)
* tomatoes, drained*
2 cups potatoes, diced
2 cups lima beans, fresh or frozen

Place squirrel pieces in a large kettle. Add water. Bring slowly to boil, reduce heat, and simmer one and one-half to two hours or until squirrel is tender, skimming surface occasionally. Remove meat from bones and return to liquid. Add bacon, cayenne, salt, pepper, onion, tomatoes, potatoes, and lima beans. Cook one hour.
6 to 8 servings
November 19, 1960

3

Ground Beef—America's Favorite Choice

What meat appears most frequently as the main dish in America's kitchens? The answer, almost without competition, is ground beef. Forty percent of the beef consumed in the United States comes to us in ground form.

The lean-to-fat ratio is an important factor in selecting ground beef. To give you a benchmark idea of what constitutes "leanness," remember, a piece of beef with absolutely no visible fat is 3 to 4 percent fat. (You're unlikely ever to find ground beef that's as lean as this in your supermarket—unless you ask for it specially—because most people would find it too dry when it's cooked.) The ground beef sold in supermarkets generally ranges from about 10 to 30 percent fat. If the label says, "Extra Lean," it's approximately 15 percent fat. "Lean Ground Beef" is approximately 23 percent fat, and "Regular Ground Beef," by government standards, cannot be more than 30 percent fat. In practice, it's usually 27 percent fat.

Virtually all the popular ground beef dishes can be prepared with ground beef that falls in the 10 to 30 percent fat category. Go by your preferences, your diet requirements, and the price.

When considering price, keep in mind that the price of ground beef increases as the percentage of fat decreases. If you're dieting, it's also worth knowing that according to Dr. Burdette Breidenstein, Director of Research and Nutrition Information for the National Livestock and Meat Board, the caloric difference between a regular grind four-ounce patty and an extra lean, four-ounce patty, after cooking, is only 24 calories.

Cooking makes a big difference in calories, especially in the case of regular ground beef. As Breidenstein explains, "The more you cook regular ground beef, the more you reduce the fatty part and thus the caloric content." In the case of extra lean ground beef, cooking doesn't make as much difference in calories. Even though in both cases a four-ounce patty will be reduced to a three-ounce patty after cooking, with the extra lean you're losing water rather than fat.

When it comes to family preference on the degree of leanness, Susan Steeleman, from the California Beef Council, says that the following are popular choices for the different grinds:

- Regular ground beef (no more than 30 percent fat) for hamburgers), Sloppy Joe's, chili and spaghetti sauce.
- Lean ground beef (approximately 23 percent fat) for meat loaf, meat balls, Salisbury steak, Tamale pie, and beef and noodles or rice.
- Extra-lean ground beef (approximately 15 percent fat) for low-calorie diets and in combination dishes.

When thinking about family preferences, keep in mind that generally, an entree prepared from 30 percent fat ground beef will be juicier than one made from, say, 10 percent fat.

When you've chosen the degree of leanness that you want, next check for freshness. Packaged ground beef should be bright reddish pink. You've probably noticed that it's often red on the outside and a dull, grayish brown on the inside. This comes about because of the pigment responsible for the red color in meat, oxymyoglobin, a substance found in all warm-blooded animals. When oxymyoglobin comes in contact with air, it combines with oxygen to produce the red color called the "bloom." The inside of the meat doesn't have the red color because it hasn't come in contact with oxygen.

Before buying, check to make sure the package isn't torn. While you're at it, feel the package to make sure it's cold. Most important, in Susan Steeleman's view, make beef one of your last purchases before leaving the store. Then get it home quickly and refrigerate it or freeze it immediately. These steps are important to preserve the freshness of the meat and extend its storage life.

Ground beef will retain its quality for a day or two if you keep it in the coldest part of your refrigerator. Says Doctor Breidenstein, "If your refrigerator is down to 35 degrees—most are at 40 degrees or more—it could last a week. But if you have kids around opening the refrigerator, or if you're not keeping it very cold, then—we're talking optimum—it's best to freeze it if you won't be using it in a couple of days."

To freeze ground beef, wrap it tightly in moisture-resistant material such as aluminum foil, freezer paper, or a plastic freezer bag. It's a good idea to date it also. For best flavor, texture and juiciness, use it within three to four months. If you've had ground beef in your feezer longer than this, it's still edible, but it won't be as good.

Mary Martin from the American Hereford Auxiliary is someone who uses a lot of ground beef in her cooking. "When we put a new side of beef in the freezer it always looks like we have more hamburger than we can ever eat. Yet we always seem to run out of hamburger first because it is the most flexible form of meat there is."

Since hamburger is so popular and flexible—and economical too—try some of the special recipes we've collected from eight generations of hamburger cookery.

Let's begin with one of Mary Martin's favorites.

Gertrude's Savory Beef Pie

1 pound lean ground beef
½ tsp. garlic salt
¼ cup finely chopped green onions
¼ cup finely chopped celery
¼ cup finely chopped bell pepper
1 cup finely sliced water chestnuts
1 cup sour cream
1 cup shredded Old English cheese
1 cup mayonnaise
1 8-ounce can crescent rolls or biscuits
2 medium tomatoes, thinly sliced
prepared Picante sauce, as desired

Preheat oven to 375 degrees.

In a skillet, brown ground beef and garlic salt until crumbly and light brown. Drain. Add green onion, celery, green pepper, and water chestnuts. In a small bowl, combine sour cream, cheese, and mayonnaise.

Separate dough into portions and place in an ungreased glass pie pan, press over bottom and up sides to form a crust. Spoon meat mixture evenly over crust. Arrange tomato slices over meat mixture, overlapping to cover. Spread sour cream mixture over the filling.

Bake for 25 to 30 minutes, or until crust is golden brown. Cool five minutes before serving.

Cut in wedges to serve with Picante sauce.
6 servings

Beany Beefburgers

1 pound ground beef
1 tsp. chili powder
1 tsp. salt
dash of pepper
1 can (11¼ ounces) condensed bean
* with bacon soup*
¼ cup chili sauce
¼ cup water
6 slices mild cheese
6 hamburger buns, split and toasted

Combine beef, chili powder, salt and pepper. Shape into six burgers. Brown in skillet; pour off drippings. Stir in soup, chili sauce and water. Cover and cook over low heat for five minutes; top with cheese and cook five minutes more. Serve on buns.
6 servings
July 17, 1965

Teriyaki Burgers

10 slices canned pineapple
⅓ cup soy sauce
1 tsp. ginger
1 tsp. sugar
¼ tsp. garlic powder
¼ tsp. salt
2 T. onion, chopped
2 pounds ground beef
6 to 8 hamburger buns, if desired
mustard, catsup, relish, as desired
* for garnish*

Drain pineapple, reserving syrup. Combine soy sauce, ginger, sugar, garlic powder, and salt to make teriyaki sauce. Add three tablespoons of this mixture, one-quarter cup of the reserved pineapple syrup and onion to the meat. Mix thoroughly. Form into six to eight patties and cook in skillet. When meat is turned, dip a pineapple slice into the teriyaki sauce. Then place on hamburger while second side is cooking.

Serve plain or on toasted hamburger buns with mustard, catsup or relish.
6 to 8 servings
February 13, 1971

Blueburger Steaks

2 pounds ground beef
1 egg
¼ cup coarse dry bread crumbs
½ tsp. hot pepper sauce
½ cup blue cheese, crumbled (about
*   3 ounces)*
2 T. butter
2 T. all-purpose flour
1 4-ounce can mushrooms, liquid
*   drained and saved*
1 beef bouillon cube
boiling water, as needed

Mix beef, egg, crumbs, and hot pepper sauce lightly. Form into twelve patties. Crumble blue cheese on six patties. Top with remaining patties. Pressing edges together, seal in the cheese. Brown on both sides in butter. Remove meat and blend in flour. Combine mushroom liquid, bouillon cube and enough boiling water to make two cups. Add to pan and cook until thickened and smooth. Add mushrooms and heat five minutes. Return blueburgers to gravy and heat thoroughly.
6 servings
August 2, 1969

Pizza Burgers

1 pound ground beef
½ cup grated Parmesan cheese
¼ cup onion, chopped
¼ cup tomato paste
1 tsp. garlic salt
½ tsp. leaf oregano, crushed
½ tsp. salt
dash pepper
6 to 8 pieces thickly sliced round
*   white bread, toasted*
chopped salami, to taste
1½ cups American cheese, shredded

In medium bowl, combine beef, Parmesan cheese, onion, tomato paste, garlic salt, oregano, salt, and pepper. Spread meat mixture on bread, being careful to bring meat out to edges. Sprinkle with desired amount of chopped salami.

Broil, six inches from heat, for eight minutes or to desired doneness. Sprinkle generously with cheese and desired amount of chopped salami and continue broiling until cheese is melted.
6 to 8 servings
July 13, 1974

When it's time to fire up the barbecue and cook outdoors, the cook will be looking for variations on the theme of plain-barbecued-hamburgers-on-a-bun. Here's a good alternative.

Beef Patty Melt

12 slices rye bread
butter, as needed
2 pounds ground beef
12 slices (¾ to 1 ounce each) Swiss
*   or Colby cheese*
salt and pepper, to taste
¾ cup Thousand Island dressing

Prepare barbecue grill.

Spread bread with butter and place, spread side down, on hot baking sheet on grill or on grill top. Toast until golden brown on one side. Wrap to keep warm. Divide ground beef into six equal portions and shape into oval patties (the size of bread slices) about one-half inch thick.

Place on grill and broil at moderate temperature 15 to 17 minutes, until almost desired doneness, turning occasionally. Season with salt and pepper.

To assemble sandwiches, place one cheese slice on untoasted side of each slice of bread, spread each cheese slice with one tablespoon dressing, place patties on half the spread slices of bread and top with remaining slices, prepared side down. Wrap each sandwich in 12- by 17-inch piece of heavy duty aluminum foil, folding edges to seal. Heat packets on grill, five minutes on each side.
6 servings
May 28, 1977

Another for the barbecue grill:

Beezer

Horseradish Dip:

¾ cup sour cream
1 T. horseradish
½ tsp. French onion soup mix
¼ tsp. garlic salt

Sandwiches:

12 slices enriched Russian rye bread
butter, softened, as needed
1½ pounds ground beef
6 slices (¾ ounce each) mild
    cheddar cheese
6 slices (¾ ounce each) Swiss cheese

Prepare barbecue grill.

Make Horseradish Dip by combining sour cream, horseradish, soup mix, and garlic salt. Refrigerate to let flavors develop.

To prepare sandwiches, butter bread. Shape ground beef into six patties, and grill until done. On the unbuttered side of six slices bread, place one slice cheddar cheese, a beef patty and one slice of Swiss cheese. Close sandwiches with remaining bread slices, buttered side out. Grill on both sides until golden brown and cheese is melted.

Serve each sandwich with small dish of Horseradish Dip, about two tablespoons.
6 servings
August 10, 1974

Mexican Sandwiches

1 pound ground beef, chuck or round
1 cup onion, coarsely chopped
1 T. shortening
1 T. all-purpose flour
1½ tsp. chili powder
1½ tsp. oregano
1 tsp. salt
¼ tsp. cinnamon
3 to 4 dashes hot red pepper sauce
1 can (8¼ ounces) tomatoes
¼ cup chili sauce
¼ cup sliced ripe olives
8 tortillas or hamburger buns
1½ cups grated cheese or sour cream

Cook beef and onion in shortening until meat is brown in color and crumbly. Blend in flour and seasonings. Add tomatoes, chili sauce and olives. Mix. Cover, cook slowly to thicken and blend flavors, about 20 minutes.

To serve, spoon about one-third cup meat mixture onto crisp hot tortillas or toasted buns. Top with cheese or sour cream.
8 servings
January 13, 1973

Fiesta Tacos

Filling:

1 pound ground beef
¼ cup onion, chopped
1 7-ounce can Mexicorn, drained
1 8-ounce can tomato sauce
1 T. sugar
½ tsp. oregano
⅛ tsp. chili powder
½ tsp. ground cumin
½ tsp. salt
dash garlic salt

Tacos:

10 to 15 small taco shells
shredded lettuce
shredded cheese
finely chopped tomato
chopped onion
prepared Taco sauce

To prepare filling, brown ground beef with onion; drain. Stir in corn and tomato sauce; add sugar, oregano, chili powder, cumin, salt, and garlic salt. Simmer about 15 to 20 minutes until sauce is absorbed.

Makes 3 cups filling.

Prepare tacos by filling each taco shell with meat filling. Garnish with lettuce, cheese, tomato, and onion. Add extra zest with taco sauce—use sparingly!
10 to 15 tacos
January 27, 1973

It's a simple case of saving time when you prepare this basic barbecued hamburger mixture. Freeze what you don't use the first day; then, at your convenience, thaw out portions to use in many different and tasty ways. Lots of ideas follow below.

Double-Up Barbecued Hamburger Mix

4 medium onions, chopped
3 cloves garlic, finely chopped
2 cups celery tops, chopped
¼ cup shortening
4 pounds ground beef
4 tsp. salt
½ tsp. pepper
3 T. Worcestershire sauce
2 12-ounce bottles catsup

Pan fry the onion, garlic, and celery in shortening in large kettle. Add ground beef and stir; cook until all redness of meat disappears. Add salt, pepper, Worcestershire sauce, and catsup. Simmer 20 minutes. Skim off excess fat.

Makes 10 cups.

To Freeze: Cool quickly. Spoon mixture into five one-pint containers. Seal. Label with name and date. Freeze at zero degrees or lower. Do not stack containers until thoroughly frozen.

To Thaw: Place container in hot water or under running hot water just long enough to allow mixture to slip out of container.

Barbecued Buns: Heat mix slowly in a skillet or chafing dish. Spoon into hot buttered buns allowing one-quarter cup mix for each bun. Pass mustard, pickles and onion.

Hot Stuffed Rolls: Let mix thaw in refrigerator. Add some shredded cheese, if desired. Spoon generously into hollowed-out French rolls. Wrap rolls individually in aluminum foil and heat for 30 minutes in 350 degree oven or on a picnic grill.

Mock Pizza: Let mix thaw in refrigerator. Spoon generously over lightly toasted English muffins. Cover with sliced or shredded Italian or American cheese and sprinkle with chopped parsley. Broil until heated through and cheese melts. Makes 6 servings.

Spaghetti Sauce: Heat mix in a saucepan or skillet. Add dash of cayenne pepper and garlic salt, if desired. Serve on hot cooked spaghetti and top with grated Parmesan cheese.

Quick Chili Con Carne: Heat mix in skillet with an equal measure of canned red kidney beans. Season with chili powder. May 27, 1972

Beating rugs on the grass beats the dust out and in again. Beating the larger rugs on a line is better, but the process generally fills the lungs of the housewife with dust. If an old-fashioned spiral spring bed spring can be secured, use it for holding rugs to be cleaned. Lay them on the springs and beat vigorously. The dust will drop down through the springs and will neither fly back into the rug nor blow into the lungs of the beater.
May 6, 1915

Here is an alternative to the traditional recipe for pasties. It uses ground beef and features a white sauce, conveniently made from soup.

Cornish Beef Pasties

Filling:

¼ cup onion, finely chopped
1 T. butter or margarine
1 pound ground beef
½ cup (2 ounce can) mushroom
   pieces and stems, drained
½ cup extra sharp cheddar cheese,
   grated
1 tsp. Worcestershire sauce
½ tsp. salt
dash pepper
⅓ cup catsup

Crust:

2 cups all-purpose flour, sifted
¾ tsp. salt
¼ tsp. thyme
¼ tsp. marjoram
¼ cup shredded wheat biscuits,
   crushed
1 egg, beaten
¼ cup soft butter or margarine
½ cup warm milk

Sauce:

⅓ cup milk
1 can cream of mushroom or celery
   soup

Preheat oven to 400 degrees.

Cook onion in butter until clear. Add ground beef. Cook thoroughly. Drain. Add mushrooms, cheese, Worcestershire, salt, pepper, and catsup. Mix well. To make the crust, sift together flour, salt, thyme, and marjoram. Stir in cereal crumbs. Add egg, butter, and milk. Mix until smooth. Knead several times on a floured board. Divide dough into two equal parts. Roll each very thin. Cut from each two six-inch circles. Place a heaping one-quarter cup of filling on one half of each circle. Cut slots for steam to escape in other half. Fold dough over filling. Bring edges together and seal.

Bake on cookie sheet 20 minutes or until brown.

To prepare sauce, combine milk and soup; heat. Serve over hot pasties.
4 large servings
May 2, 1964

Hamburger Picnic Pie

2 pounds ground beef
½ cup onion, chopped
1 can (10¾ ounces) condensed
   tomato soup
1 T. parsley flakes
2 tsp. Worcestershire sauce
1 tsp. salt
¼ tsp. garlic salt
⅛ tsp. pepper
pastry for 2 double crust pies

Preheat oven to 425 degrees.

In a skillet, brown beef and cook onion until tender. Drain. Remove from heat and add soup, parsley, Worcestershire, salt, garlic salt, and pepper. Pour into two pastry-lined pie plates (throw-away aluminum ones for quick cleanup). Cover meat with top crusts, seal edges, slit tops and decorate with scraps of pastry rolled and cut into pretty shapes.

Bake for 30 minutes.

This is delicious eaten cold in the hand. It may also be served hot.
8 generous servings
August 9, 1969

Cheese Tamale Pie

3 cups water
1 cup yellow corn meal
1 tsp. salt
1 cup milk
1 pound ground beef
½ cup onion, chopped
1 tsp. salt
1 tsp. chili powder
1 tsp. basil
¼ tsp. garlic salt
⅛ tsp. pepper
2 cups (1 pound can) kernel corn
1½ cups (10½ ounce can) tomato puree
½ cup ripe olives, sliced
½ cup Parmesan cheese, grated
2 cups Cheddar cheese, diced

In top of double boiler bring water to a boil. Combine corn meal, salt, and milk and stir slowly into water. Cook, stirring constantly, until mixture boils. Place over simmering water, cover, and cook 15 minutes, stirring occasionally. Meanwhile, in a large skillet brown beef and onion. Stir in salt, chili powder, basil, garlic salt, and pepper. Add corn and tomato puree; simmer 10 minutes. Stir in olives and Parmesan cheese. Add Cheddar cheese to corn meal mixture; mix well. Line a buttered baking dish with two-thirds of the Cheddar-corn meal mixture. Fill with meat mixture. Top with remaining corn meal.

Bake in a 350 degree oven for one hour.
8 to 10 servings
May 21, 1966

Golden Rice Hamburger Pie

Filling:

1 pound ground beef
¾ cup onion, chopped
¾ cup celery, chopped
½ cup green pepper, chopped
⅔ cup tomato sauce or catsup
1 tsp. salt
¼ tsp. black pepper

Crust:

2 cups rice, cooked
1 T. prepared mustard
2 eggs, beaten

Preheat oven to 375 degrees.

Brown ground beef slightly and drain off excess liquids. Add onions, celery, green pepper, and catsup. Mix well. Place in one and one-half-quart baking dish. Blend rice, mustard, and eggs and spread over meat. Cover and bake for 30 minutes.
6 servings
August 9, 1975

With the aid of a microwave you can be ready to serve a hearty casserole to six hungry people in less than a half-hour.

Beef Macaroni Casserole

1 pound ground beef
1 onion, chopped
1 green pepper, chopped
1 clove garlic, finely chopped
1 jar (32 ounces) spaghetti sauce
1½ cups uncooked elbow macaroni
1 tsp. oregano leaves
1½ cups mozzarella cheese

Crumble beef into a microwave-safe plastic colander; place colander in microwave-safe dish. Stir in onion, pepper, and garlic. Microwave on HIGH (100 percent power) five minutes, stirring once during cooking. Stir beef mixture and remaining ingredients, reserving two tablespoons of the cheese. Pour into three-quart round micro-safe dish; cover. Microwave on MEDIUM (50 percent power) 16 minutes. Stir and sprinkle top with remaining cheese. Microwave on MEDIUM three minutes.
6 servings
California Beef Council

Trappers Steak and Spaghetti

¾ pound ground chuck
¼ cup dried bread crumbs
½ tsp. salt
⅛ tsp. pepper
1 T. butter
1 can (4 ounces) mushroom stems
   and pieces
1 tsp. instant minced onion
1 cup carrots, sliced
1 T. capers
2 tsp. dried parsley flakes
1 cup apple cider
1 T. flour
¾ tsp. salt
⅛ tsp. pepper
⅛ tsp. ground cloves
8 ounces spaghetti

Set out a two-quart casserole. Combine beef, bread crumbs, one-half teaspoon salt, and one-eighth teaspoon pepper; form into four to six patties. In a large skillet melt butter and brown the meat patties on both sides. Remove from pan and reserve.

Drain mushrooms and reserve liquid and add onion to liquid. Put mushrooms, carrots, capers, and parsley through a food grinder or blender. Turn out in a skillet. Stir in cider and onion mixture, flour, three-quarters teaspoon salt, one-eighth teaspoon pepper, and cloves; cook, stirring constantly, until mixture boils.

Reduce heat and return meat to skillet, cover, and simmer for 15 minutes. Meanwhile cook spaghetti in boiling, salted water until tender but firm. Drain.

To serve, turn spaghetti into casserole, pour sauce over, and arrange meat patties on top.
4 to 6 servings
September 18, 1965

One criteria for a great party dish is that it can be prepared ahead of time. In the case of Stuffed Manicotti, all the preparation, except baking, can be done early in the day. Prepare and then refrigerate. If you take the casserole from the refrigerator to oven, allow an additional five to 10 minutes for baking.

Stuffed Manicotti

1 clove garlic, crushed
2 T. oil
2 cans (8 ounces each) tomato sauce
1 T. dehydrated minced onion
1 T. all-purpose flour
1 tsp. salt
2 tsp. oregano
2 tsp. basil
1 tsp. sugar
¼ tsp. pepper
2½ cups water
1 can (4 ounces) mushrooms, stems
   and pieces, drained
1 pound ground beef
½ cup onion, chopped
1 pound Ricotta cheese
12 enriched manicotti shells
1 cup Mozzarella cheese, shredded

Preheat oven to 400 degrees.

Brown garlic in hot oil. Add tomato sauce. Stir in onion, flour, salt, oregano, one teaspoon basil, sugar, and pepper. Add water and mushrooms. Bring mixture to a boil. Reduce heat and simmer, uncovered for 25 minutes. Brown ground beef and onions; pour off excess liquids. Stir in Ricotta cheese and remaining basil. Stuff shells with meat mixture. Arrange in a 9x13x2-inch casserole. Pour sauce over manicotti, making sure all shells are covered. Cover, and refrigerate, if desired.

Bake for 45 to 50 minutes. Remove cover and sprinkle with Mozzarella cheese. Return to oven for five minutes or until cheese melts.
6 servings
August 28, 1978

Easy Italian Lasagne

8 ounces thin lasagne or wide noodles
1 pound ground chuck
1 can (15 ounces) tomato sauce
2 tsp. sugar
1 tsp. salt
¼ tsp. garlic salt
¼ tsp. pepper
1 carton (16 ounces) cottage cheese
2 cups (16 ounces) Mozzarella
cheese, shredded
½ cup sour cream
½ cup green onions, sliced, with tops
½ cup green pepper, chopped
⅓ cup grated Parmesan cheese

Preheat oven to 375 degrees.

Cook lasagne noodles according to package directions; drain. In skillet cook ground chuck until brown; drain off excess drippings. Stir in tomato sauce, sugar, salt, garlic salt, and pepper. Remove from heat. Combine cottage cheese, Mozzarella cheese, sour cream, green onion, and green pepper. Spread half of noodles in 13x9x2-inch buttered baking dish. Moisten noodles with some of the meat sauce. Cover with cheese mixture; top with remaining noodles, then meat sauce. Sprinkle with Parmesan cheese.

Bake, covered, for 40 minutes. Allow to stand 10 to 15 minutes before serving.
12 servings
September 27, 1966

Chili Con Carne

⅔ onion, chopped
1 clove garlic, sliced
4 T. bacon drippings
1 pound ground beef
4 cups kidney beans, cooked
⅔ cup green pepper
4 cups cooked or canned tomatoes
2 bay leaves, crushed
4 tsp. sugar
2 T. chili powder, to taste
salt and pepper, to taste

Brown onion and garlic in drippings. Add meat and cook slowly a few minutes, stirring occasionally. Add kidney beans, green pepper, tomatoes, bay leaves, sugar, and chili powder. Season with salt and pepper and simmer until meat is tender and flavors are blended, about an hour.
8 servings
December 5, 1953

Baked Bean Barbecue

1 pound ground beef
¼ green pepper, finely chopped
1 medium onion, chopped
½ cup celery, thinly sliced
1 8-ounce can tomato sauce
½ cup water
2 T. vinegar
1 clove garlic, chopped
1 tsp. dry mustard
½ tsp. oregano
½ tsp. ginger
1 T. brown sugar
1 tsp. salt
4 cans baked beans
1 cup, sharp cheddar cheese,
shredded

Crumble ground beef into a cold skillet. Cook over moderate heat until the pink color disappears. Add green pepper, onion, and celery. Cook about five minutes or until the vegetables are limp but not browned.

Stir in tomato sauce, water, vinegar, garlic, mustard, oregano, ginger, brown sugar, and salt. Bring to a boil, reduce heat and simmer five to 10 minutes. While the sauce is simmering, place beans in a casserole dish. Spoon hot meat sauce over beans.

Bake in 350 degree oven about 20 minutes. Sprinkle cheese over top and return to oven until it melts. Serve hot.
6 servings
July 7, 1963

Creole Beef with Macaroni

1 pound ground beef
3 T. shortening
1 T. onion, chopped
½ cup celery, chopped
2 T. all-purpose flour
2 cups canned tomatoes
½ tsp. chili powder
1 tsp. salt
1 tsp. Worcestershire sauce
1 cup water
cooked macaroni, as needed for 6
* servings*

Brown beef in two tablespoons of shortening. In another pan, brown onion and celery in one tablespoon shortening. Add flour; stir well. Add tomatoes to make a sauce. Add chili powder, salt, Worcestershire sauce, the browned meat, and water. Cook slowly 10 minutes.

Serve on hot, cooked macaroni.
6 servings
March 19, 1949

A quick and hearty one-dish meal—with only one pan to wash afterwards.

Mexicali Rice

1 pound ground beef
1 medium onion, thinly sliced
½ medium green pepper, diced
2 cups enriched precooked rice
¼ cup bacon drippings or butter
2 cans tomatoes
1 tsp. salt
dash of pepper
½ tsp. prepared mustard, if desired

Saute beef, onion, green pepper, and rice in bacon drippings in skillet until lightly browned, stirring constantly. Add tomatoes, salt, pepper, and mustard; mix well. Bring to boil. Reduce heat and simmer, uncovered, for five minutes.
6 servings
November 9, 1968

Beef and Potato Puffs

2 T. onion, chopped
2 T. parsley, chopped
2 T. butter
2 cups mashed potatoes
1 cup gravy or milk
salt and pepper, to taste
3 eggs, separated and beaten
1 pound ground beef

Sauce:

3 cups cooked tomatoes
1 bay leaf
¼ tsp. salt
3 whole cloves
3 slices onion
1½ tsp. sugar
dash of pepper
2 T. all-purpose flour
2 T. butter

Cook the chopped onion and parsley for a few minutes in two tablespoons butter, then mix thoroughly with the meat, potatoes and gravy or milk. Season to taste. Add the beaten egg yolks and then the beaten whites. Pile lightly into an oiled baking dish.

Bake in a 350 degree oven for one hour.

Prepare the sauce by cooking tomatoes, bay leaf, salt, cloves, onion, sugar, and pepper for 10 minutes. Strain through a sieve and stir gradually into the blended flour and butter. Cook the sauce for a few minutes, stirring constantly until smooth and thickened. Remove bay leaf.

To serve, pour piping hot sauce over hot beef and potato puffs.
4 servings
April 16, 1955

Cranberry Meat Loaf

1 pound ground chuck
1½ cups cooked rice
½ cup tomato juice
1 T. horseradish
1 egg
¼ cup onion, chopped
1½ tsp. salt
1 pound can whole cranberry sauce
⅓ cup brown sugar

Mix together ground chuck, rice, tomato juice, horseradish, egg, onion, and salt. Place in loaf pan. Mash and mix cranberry sauce and sugar, and spoon over loaf.

Bake in a 350 degree oven for one hour.
6 servings
November 1, 1968

Good Fortune Beef Loaves

1 can (8 ounces) tomato sauce
⅓ cup sweet and sour sauce
2 T. soy sauce
2 pounds ground beef
2 eggs, beaten
1 tsp. dry mustard
2 tsp. onion powder
1 can (3 ounces) chow mein noodles, finely crushed
1 can (1 pound) Chinese mixed vegetables, rinsed and drained
¼ tsp. pepper
1½ tsp. salt

Combine tomato sauce, sweet and sour sauce, and soy sauce; reserve one-quarter cup of the mixture for baste. Combine remaining sauce, ground beef, eggs, mustard, onion powder, noodles, vegetables, pepper, and salt. Shape into eight loaves. Place in shallow baking pan.

Bake in a 350 degree oven for 50 minutes, basting occasionally with sauce.
8 servings
May 12, 1973

Meat Loaf Ring

Meat Ring:

¾ cup onion, chopped
¼ cup butter or margarine
1 egg, beaten
1 cup prepared seasoned dry bread crumbs
½ tsp. oregano
½ tsp. basil
1 tsp. salt
dash pepper
2 cups canned applesauce
2 pounds ground chuck

Green Bean Succotash:

1 package (9 ounces) frozen French green beans
1 package (10 ounces) frozen whole kernel corn
¼ cup butter or margarine
2 T. sugar
½ tsp. salt
few grains pepper

Preheat oven to 375 degrees.

Saute onion in butter or margarine until a delicate brown. Combine egg, seasoned crumbs, oregano, basil, salt, pepper, and applesauce; mix thoroughly. Add meat and browned onion; blend well. Put meat in an oiled one and one-half quart ring mold or form into ring on baking pan.

Bake in oven for 60 minutes.

Meanwhile, prepare succotash. Cook green beans and corn according to package directions. Drain. Add butter, sugar, salt, and pepper. Stir until well mixed.

To serve, place meat ring on a platter. Fill center with succotash.
February 7, 1970

Blanketed Beef Loaf

2 pounds ground beef
1½ cups soft bread crumbs
1 egg
¼ cup, plus 2 T. catsup
⅓ cup salad olives
1 T. prepared mustard
1 tsp. salt
½ tsp. rubbed sage
⅛ tsp. pepper
pastry for double-crust pie
all-purpose flour, as needed

Preheat oven to 375 degrees.

Combine ground beef, bread crumbs, egg, one-quarter cup catsup, olives, mustard, salt, sage, and pepper lightly but thoroughly. Place in a 9x5-inch loaf pan, pressing lightly to fill evenly, and chill in refrigerator while preparing pastry.

Turn loaf out of pan onto rack in roasting pan and spread top with remaining catsup. Roll out pastry on a lightly floured board into a rectangle approximately 10x15 inches, one-eighth to one-quarter inch thick. Cut into eight strips one inch wide and 10 inches long. Place pastry strips crosswise over loaf to cover top and sides, pressing them to loaf. (Leave ends open.) Cut eight strips from remaining pastry, twist, and use to decorate loaf.

Bake for 50 minutes or until meat loaf is done and pastry lightly browned. Let stand 10 minutes before slicing.
8 servings
January 22, 1977

Loaf in a Loaf

1 loaf Vienna bread
2 pounds lean ground beef
1 egg
¼ cup chili sauce
3 T. instant minced onion
3 T. green pepper, chopped
2 tsp. salt
⅛ tsp. pepper
4 slices (3 ounces) American cheese
parsley, as needed for garnish

Cut a shallow slice, two and one-half-inches wide, from top of loaf of bread. Remove bread to hollow out inside of loaf until sides and bottom are one-half-inch thick. Make one cup crumbs from removed bread and combine with ground beef, egg, chili sauce, onion, green pepper, salt and pepper. Line bottom of inside of loaf with slices of cheese. Add the meat mixture, a portion at a time, pressing lightly to fill loaf. Place top on loaf and wrap in foil, sealing top and ends.

Place on rack in jelly roll pan or large roasting pan and bake in a 350 degree oven for two hours. Let stand 10 minutes before slicing.

To serve, garnish with parsley as desired.
8 servings
May 22, 1976

Savory Meat Loaf

1½ cups dry bread crumbs
⅔ cups milk
¼ cup tomato juice
1 tsp. salt
½ tsp. celery salt
¼ tsp. pepper
1 T. onion, grated
1 tsp. parsley, minced
3 eggs, beaten
2 T. chili sauce
2 cups (1 pound) ground beef, pork,
    veal, or lamb

Preheat oven to 375 degrees.

Combine bread crumbs, milk, tomato juice, salt, celery salt, pepper, onion, parsley, eggs, and chili sauce. Add meat and mix well.

Bake in a greased 4x9-inch loaf pan for one hour.
6 servings
December 18, 1948

Gourmet Beef Loaf

Meatloaf:

1 can (16 ounces) tomatoes
2 pounds ground beef
1½ tsp. salt
⅛ tsp. pepper
¼ tsp. sage
2 eggs, beaten
1 cup cracker crumbs (about 24
  crackers)
1 medium-sized onion, finely chopped
1 beef bouillon cube
½ tsp. Worcestershire sauce
2 T. catsup
2 T. ripe olives, sliced
½ cup sour cream

Drain one-quarter cup tomato juice from tomatoes; reserve for sauce. Combine ground beef, salt, pepper, sage, eggs, crumbs, tomatoes and onion. Shape mixture on an open roasting pan into a 9x5-inch loaf. Alternatively, you can pack mixture into a 9x5-inch loaf pan.

Place in a 325 degree oven. Bake mixture on the baking pan for one and one-quarter hours; allow 15 minutes longer for the mixture in the loaf pan.

While the meat is cooking, prepare the sauce. Dissolve bouillon cube in one-quarter cup tomato juice. Add Worcestershire sauce, catsup and olives. Bring to a boil; stir well. Reduce heat below boiling. Stir in sour cream slowly.

To serve, spoon warm sauce over meatloaf.
8 servings
September 9, 1972

Father's Favorite Meat Loaf

An all-meat loaf, like the following, is nice either hot or cold, and its basting sauce adds a flavor you'll not soon forget.

Mix two pounds each of ground round steak and veal steak, a pound of ground pork steak, four beaten eggs, one-fourth cup of milk, one and one-half teaspoons of salt, one-fourth teaspoon of pepper and a pinch of red pepper. Place half of this in a long, narrow pan and press well into corners. Press three shelled, hard-cooked eggs into the center and top with the remaining mixture.

Bake for 90 minutes in a 350 degree oven. Baste frequently with a sauce made by blending one-half cup of melted butter or thick sour cream, one teaspoon each of salt, pepper, paprika and prepared mustard, one-fourth cup of lemon juice or tomato catsup, two teaspoons of brown sugar, a dash of Worcestershire and one-fourth cup of hot water.
July 18, 1936

Remember how you watched grownups cook and bake when you were a child? You wondered how long it would be until you could make fluffy, white frosting and spread it all over a cake. You were sure you'd leave more frosting in the bowl for kids than these grownups did. If you begged to help, a few of you were brushed aside with "You're too little," but many of you will remember the wonderful days with your mother or father in that big kitchen. You helped in so many ways—you oiled the cookie tins, beat the eggs, poured the chips into the batter. And maybe that's why you enjoy cooking and baking today.

Here's a meal a child can make, from meat loaf with baked potatoes, to a gelatin salad, to a chocolate pudding dessert.

Easy-to-Make Meat Loaves

1 egg, beaten
1½ tsp. salt
⅛ tsp. pepper
2 tsp. onion, chopped
1 cup bread crumbs
1 cup milk
1½ pounds ground beef
12 slices bacon

Preheat oven to 400 degrees.

In a bowl, combine egg, salt, pepper, onion, bread crumbs, and milk. Mix and let stand a few minutes. Add to the ground meat and mix well with hand or a fork. Form meat into 12 little loaves. Wrap a strip of bacon around the edge and fasten with a toothpick. Place in a shallow pan in the oven and bake for 15 minutes, then reduce heat to 350 degrees and bake for 20 to 30 minutes longer.
6 servings

Baked Potatoes

6 baking potatoes

Wash potatoes and bake in the oven alongside the meat loaves.
6 servings

Orange Cottage Cheese Salad

2 oranges, peeled and cut into pieces
2 pkgs. orange gelatin
1 pint creamed cottage cheese
12 large lettuce leaves

Rinse a pudding mold or glass baking dish in cold water. Oil lightly. Arrange oranges in bottom of dish. Prepare gelatin. When cold, pour half of it over the oranges. Chill, and when firm, spread with a layer of cottage cheese. Pour remaining gelatin over cottage cheese. Chill.

To serve, arrange chilled orange mixture on lettuce leaves.
6 servings

Chocolate Pudding

2½ cups milk
¾ cup sugar
6 T. cocoa
6 T. cornstarch
pinch of salt
½ cup cold milk
1½ tsp. vanilla
1 cup chilled heavy cream
pinch sugar, to taste

In a double boiler or heavy pan heat two and a half cups milk. Combine sugar, cocoa, cornstarch, and salt. Blend with cold milk. Add this mixture to the hot milk and cook until thickened, stirring constantly with a wooden spoon. Cook two minutes longer, still stirring constantly, then remove from heat. Add vanilla and pour into 6 small dessert dishes.

Whip cream with a beater until thick. Add sugar and continue beating until mixture is firm enough to mound from a spoon.

To serve, spoon a dollop of whipped cream over each dish of pudding.
6 servings
May 5, 1956

We're Not Sure We Would Wholeheartedly Recommend This One

A strong washing solution, though harmless, is made from equal parts of clear limewater, kerosene and turpentine, shaken together until creamy. A small cupful of this mixture added to a boilerful of clothes will be sufficient. Keep them over the fire half an hour, but do not allow them to boil.
February 3, 1910

Any host or hostess is on the lookout for a good and convenient cocktail party recipe. Cocktail Meat Balls can be prepared ahead of time and frozen until the day of the party. Just pack sauce and meat balls in moisture vapor-proof containers leaving a head space. Freeze and store at 0 degrees or below for four to six months. Reheat over boiling water in a chafing dish or slow cooker.

Cocktail Meat Balls

Meatballs:

2 pounds ground beef
1 T. parsley flakes
1 tsp. monosodium glutamate
2 tsp. salt
¼ tsp. pepper
¼ cup onion, finely chopped
1 cup bread or cracker crumbs
1 egg
½ cup milk

Sauce:

½ cup vinegar
¾ cup brown sugar
¼ cup soy sauce
1 cup catsup
¼ cup water
1 tsp. prepared mustard
¼ tsp. garlic salt

Prepare meatballs by mixing ground beef, parsley flakes, monosodium glutamate, salt, pepper, onion, cracker crumbs, and egg, and shape into one to one and a half-inch balls. Place in shallow pan and bake at 350 degrees for about 25 minutes or until done.

Prepare sauce by mixing together vinegar, brown sugar, soy sauce, catsup, water, mustard, and garlic salt in a saucepan. Bring to a boil. Add meat balls.

Serve hot.
7 to 8 dozen meat balls
December, 1977

With your microwave, this appetizer can be ready for unexpected guests or a take-along hors d'oeuvre in less than ten minutes.

Ginger Meatballs

1 pound lean ground beef
¼ cup bread crumbs
¼ cup teriyaki sauce
1 tsp. ground ginger

Mix all ingredients well. Shape into one-inch balls. Place on a round rack, with microwave-safe casserole underneath. Cover with paper towels. Microwave on HIGH (100 percent power) five to seven minutes. Drain meatballs. Serve immediately.
3 dozen appetizers
California Beef Council

Oriental Meat Balls

Oriental Sauce:

2 T. cornstarch
1 tsp. ginger
½ cup brown sugar
½ cup soy sauce
⅔ cup tarragon vinegar
1 cup pineapple juice

Meatballs:

1 pound ground beef
1 pound ground pork
½ cup dry bread crumbs
½ cup almonds or pecans, finely
* chopped*
½ tsp. ginger
dash of salt
⅓ cup cornstarch
3 T. lard or shortening

To prepare sauce, combine cornstarch, ginger, and brown sugar. Add soy sauce and mix to a smooth paste. Add vinegar and pineapple juice and cook until thick and glossy. Set aside.

Combine ground beef, ground pork, bread crumbs, nuts, ginger, and salt. Form into balls the size of walnuts.

Marinate meat balls in oriental sauce for two hours. When ready to serve, roll in cornstarch and brown on all sides in lard or shortening.
November 11, 1967

Swedish Meat Balls

Meatballs:

¾ pound ground beef
¼ pound ground veal
¼ pound ground lean pork
⅔ cup milk
½ cup dry bread crumbs (fine)
2 T. onion, chopped
2 tsp. salt
½ tsp. pepper
½ tsp. allspice
all-purpose flour, as needed
¼ cup butter
½ cup hot water

Mushroom Gravy:

1 4-ounce can sliced mushrooms,
* drain with liquid reserved*
2 T. all-purpose flour
½ cup milk
water, as needed

To prepare meatballs, have the meat ground together three times. Mix lightly together with milk, crumbs, onion, salt, pepper, and allspice. Form into balls and roll in flour. Melt butter in skillet and brown meat balls slowly on all sides. Add water and simmer 10 minutes. Remove meat balls to a warm platter and keep warm.

Prepare gravy by adding enough water to mushroom liquid to measure one cup. Stir flour into drippings where meat balls have been browned. Add liquid and milk. Cook over low heat until thickened. Add mushrooms; cook two additional minutes and pour over meatballs.
6 servings
May 13, 1967

Meat Balls in Tomato Cream Sauce

Meatballs:

1 pound ground beef
½ cup dry bread crumbs
1 egg, slightly beaten
½ cup milk
1¼ tsp. grated lemon rind
1 T. onion, chopped fine
½ tsp. garlic, chopped
1 tsp. Worcestershire sauce
½ tsp. salt
1 tsp. celery salt
½ tsp. pepper
1½ tsp. butter

Tomato Cream Sauce:

1 T. butter
½ cup green pepper, chopped
1½ T. all-purpose flour
1 8-ounce can tomato sauce
½ can water
¾ cup sour cream
salt, to taste

Prepare meatballs by combining ground beef, bread crumbs, egg, milk, lemon rind, onion, garlic, Worcestershire sauce, salt, celery salt, and pepper, and mix thoroughly. Shape into 12 balls. Heat butter in a frying pan for one minute. Add the meat balls and brown on all sides. Remove from the frying pan and place in a baking dish. Place meat balls in a 300 degree oven while making the sauce.

Prepare sauce by draining the drippings from the frying pan into another pan. Add butter and green pepper and cook for 10 minutes over low heat. Stir in the flour, and cook for a minute or two. Gradually add the tomato sauce and water, stirring constantly, until smooth. Stir in the sour cream and salt.

Remove the meat balls from the oven. Pour the sauce over them, and return to the oven to bake for 30 minutes.
4 servings
May 7, 1955

Baked Vegetables and Meat Balls

1 pound ground beef
1 cup dry bread crumbs
1 egg, beaten
1 T. onion, chopped
2 tsp. salt
¼ tsp. pepper
¼ cup plus 3 T. all-purpose flour
2 cups tomatoes
1½ cups raw potatoes, diced
1½ cups raw carrots, sliced
1 cup onion, sliced
½ cup celery, chopped
1 tsp. salt
parsley, as needed for garnish

Thoroughly mix together ground beef, bread crumbs, egg, onion, one teaspoon salt and pepper. Form into 12 small meat balls. Roll meat balls in one-quarter cup flour, then brown in fat. Arrange six meat balls in bottom of a well oiled, two-quart, heat-resistant glass casserole.

Add remaining flour to drippings in skillet in which meat balls were browned. Add tomatoes. Stir in potatoes, carrots, onion, celery, and remaining salt. Pour vegetables over meat balls in baking dish. Arrange six remaining meat balls on top of vegetables.

Cover and bake in a 350 degree oven for about one hour, or until vegetables are tender.
4 servings
October 7, 1950

Sour Cream Meat Balls on Rice

Meatballs:

1 pound ground beef
½ cup condensed tomato soup
2 T. onion, grated
1 cup bread crumbs
1 egg
1 tsp. salt
⅛ tsp. pepper
3 T. butter or margarine, melted

Sauce:

¼ cup green pepper, chopped
2 T. all-purpose flour
1 can (1 pound, 1 ounce) tomatoes
1 cup sour cream
½ tsp. salt
⅛ tsp. pepper
dash of Worcestershire sauce

3 cups hot cooked rice

Combine ground beef, soup, onion, bread crumbs, egg, salt, and pepper and mix thoroughly. Form into two-inch balls. Fry in three tablespoons butter. Remove meat balls from pan. Set aside while making sauce.

Cook green pepper in pan drippings from meatballs. Stir in flour and cook until browned. Break up tomatoes by stirring with fork and add to green pepper mixture; blend thoroughly. Add sour cream, salt, pepper, and Worcestershire sauce. Return meat balls to sauce and heat.

Serve over beds of hot rice.

6 servings
June 14, 1975

Spaghetti and Meat Balls

⅓ cup hot olive oil
¾ cup onion, chopped
¾ cup green pepper, chopped
1 clove garlic
1 can tomato paste
1 No. 2 can tomatoes
dash each of sage, chili powder,
    paprika, salt, pepper
⅔ cup bread crumbs
2 eggs
salt and pepper, to taste
2 pounds ground beef
hot cooked spaghetti noodles, as
    needed
grated Parmesan cheese, as desired

To hot olive oil, add one-half cup onion, one-half cup green pepper, and garlic. Fry until brown. Add tomato paste, diluted with four parts water, and tomatoes. Season to taste with paprika, sage, chili powder, salt, and pepper. Let simmer for 30 minutes.

Add rest of onion and green pepper, bread crumbs, eggs, salt, and pepper to meat. Mix well and roll into small balls and drop into prepared tomato mixture. Simmer for three hours.

To serve, arrange meatballs around a dish of cooked spaghetti and cover with sauce. Top with cheese and serve immediately.
September 18, 1954

With all the pastas available today, whether homemade or purchased at the store, the cook needs a variety of sauces to serve with them. A classic choice is this meat sauce.

Deluxe Spaghetti Meat Sauce

1 pound ground beef
3 T. shortening
1 medium onion, chopped
1 clove garlic, minced
1 can (1 pound, 14 ounces) tomatoes
1 can tomato paste
1 3-ounce can of mushrooms, drained
1 tsp. salt
¼ tsp. pepper
1 tsp. sugar
½ tsp. chili powder
1 T. Worcestershire sauce
½ to 1 cup ripe olives, sliced

Heat shortening in a heavy deep pan and cook onion until a light brown. Push to one side, add beef, and brown thoroughly. Add garlic, tomatoes, tomato paste, mushrooms, salt, pepper, and sugar. Cook, covered, over low heat for 45 minutes, stirring occasionally. Add chili powder and Worcestershire sauce and cook another 15 minutes. Add olives and a little water if sauce has become too thick. Add extra salt if necessary.

Serve over hot cooked spaghetti.
4 servings
August 2, 1969

When you find you need a meal for a crowd—a large crowd of 100, for instance—turn to a menu of spaghetti and meat sauce, crisp carrot and celery sticks, hot French bread and butter, and, for dessert, baked apple pudding.

Family Reunion-Size Spaghetti and Meat Sauce

1½ ounces (36) garlic cloves, minced
1½ quarts onion, chopped
2 cups salad oil
20 pounds ground beef
1½ gallons tomato puree
3 quarts tomato paste
2 gallons water
2 T. sugar
1 cup salt
2 T. Worcestershire sauce
3½ pounds uncooked spaghetti

Brown garlic and onion lightly in salad oil in heavy pot. Add ground beef and cook until brown. Blend in tomato paste, tomato puree, water, sugar, salt, and Worcestershire sauce. Simmer one hour or until sauce is thick.

Cook spaghetti in boiling, salted water until tender. Drain.
100 servings

Baked Apple Pudding

5½ pounds sugar
1½ pounds (6 cups) sifted all-purpose
   flour
½ cup baking powder
3 T. salt
4 tsp. cinnamon
1 dozen eggs, beaten
½ pound butter, melted
3 gallons (16 pounds) pared, diced
   apples

Preheat oven to 375 degrees.

Sift together sugar, flour, baking powder, salt, and cinnamon. Blend in eggs and butter. Add apples and mix well.

Place in large greased pans and bake in oven for about 40 minutes, or until apples are tender.
100 servings
March 3, 1962

Here's a sauce that dresses up plain meats—try it on beef or lamb patties, veal, or lamb chops.

Sour Cream Sauce

2 T. butter
½ cup green onions, sliced
1 cup fresh mushrooms, sliced
1 cup sour cream
1 T. parsley, chopped
salt, to taste

While the meat you will be serving is cooking, melt butter in a saucepan. Add green onions and mushrooms and saute until onions are slightly transparent, but not brown. Reduce heat to very low. Add sour cream, chopped parsley and salt to taste; stirring constantly.

For variety, add a teaspoon of dill seed, marjoram, or basil to the sauce along with a tablespoon of crumbled blue cheese and a teaspoon of sherry flavoring.
1½ cups sauce to make 4 to 6 servings
May 13, 1973

Beef Vegetable Soup

3 onions, chopped
2 T. butter
1 pound ground beef
garlic powder, to taste
3 cups beef stock
2 large cans tomatoes
1 cup potatoes, diced
1 cup green beans, diced
1 cup celery, diced
1 cup carrots, diced
1 cup red wine
2 T. parsley, chopped
½ tsp. basil
¼ tsp. thyme
salt and pepper, to taste

In a soup kettle, saute onions in butter until golden and tender. Stir in ground beef and garlic powder and cook until meat is brown. Add remaining ingredients and bring to a boil. Reduce heat and simmer for one to one and a quarter hours.
4 to 6 servings
March 5, 1977

Stuffed Green Peppers

3 large green peppers or
   6 small green peppers
¾ cup ground beef, cooked
¼ cup milk or meat stock
2 cups cooked rice
½ tsp. paprika
1 T. onion, grated
1 tsp. salt
¼ tsp. pepper

Preheat oven to 400 degrees.

Boil the green peppers for five minutes. Plunge into cold water. If peppers are large, cut in half lengthwise. If peppers are small, cut off tops. Remove seeds. Mix ground beef, milk or stock, rice, paprika, onion, salt, and pepper thoroughly and stuff the peppers. Place in a pan, pour about one cup of hot water around the peppers and bake for 45 minutes, or until peppers are soft.
6 servings
September 3, 1949

Stuffed Baked Potatoes

6 baked potatoes
1 pound ground beef
1 tsp. salt
1 T. onion
2 T. steak sauce

Slice off the tops of the baked potatoes. Scoop out the inside and mash. Saute the ground beef with onion, salt, and steak sauce. To the beef add the mashed potatoes. Whip this beef-potato mixture and use to fill potato skins.

Place under a broiler until heated through.
6 servings
July 13, 1964

Stuffed Cabbage

1 large head cabbage
1 pound chopped beef
1 egg
¼ cup tomato catsup
1 T. onion, minced
dash of cayenne
salt and pepper, to taste

Cut off two or three inches from the top of the cabbage. Dig out the inside with a sharp knife, making enough room for the meat. Mix meat with egg, catsup, onion, cayenne, salt, and pepper. Pack into the hollowed-out cabbage. Replace top of cabbage, tying it securely with white string. Boil or steam one and one-half hours or until cabbage is soft when poked with a fork. Remove string and cut into wedges to serve.
4 servings
February 2, 1963

Did you know that it was once considered a crime to eat mincemeat? According to legend, the Puritans of England in the 17th century declared the eating of mince pie an abomination. And, when they finally came into power, forbade the use of it and any frivolous celebration of Christmas. It was not the pie itself that aroused their wrath, but the way it was shaped. The pies were baked oblong, representing the manger in which Jesus was born.

Regardless of threats and stern prohibitions, folks continued throughout the country to eat mince pie. When the Puritans lost their power in 1660, the English people could legally serve and eat mince pie.

Strange as it seems, while the Puritans lost their power, they did win in one way. For while the folks won the right to serve mince pies, they gradually started reshaping them. With the "new round look" the pie was brought to America, and, with civilization, spread all over the United States. The old quarrels have been forgotten and everyone may eat mince pie with nothing to fear but a stomach-ache from overeating!

While mincemeat can easily be purchased now, you may want to try making your own. Several recipes follow, along with some ideas for using it— and, of course, the recipe for mincemeat pie.

This first recipe has for many years been in the family of Elsie Looker, a contributor to the *Wisconsin Agriculturist* over 30 years ago.

Old English Mincemeat

5 pounds lean beef
2 gallons pared apples
2 pounds suet
3 pounds seedless raisins
1 quart chopped watermelon preserves
2 quarts canned sour cherries
1 pint cider vinegar
1 quart fresh apple juice
2 pounds brown sugar
2 T. cinnamon
1 tsp. ground cloves

Cook the beef in salted water until tender. Run it with the suet, apples, watermelon preserves, and raisins through the food chopper. Mix the chopped ingredients together with the cherries, vinegar, and apple juice. Stir in the sugar, cinnamon, and cloves and cook together until the apples are done, stirring often to prevent scorching. Seal at once in glass jars, and process for 25 minutes in a simmering hot water bath. Keep in a cool place.
December 19, 1953

Mincemeat 1915 Style

One quart chopped meat (three pounds of neck boil, cooked tender, makes about the proper amount), three quarts chopped apples, two pounds seeded raisins, two pounds currants (well washed), one-half pound chopped suet, one-fourth pound candied citron, sliced thin, one-half pound candied orange peel, sliced thin (if the citron and orange peel are first steamed, they will slice much easier), one orange and one lemon sliced thin and cut very fine, one-fourth pound candied cherries cut in small pieces, six cups brown sugar, one small teaspoon each of cloves, allspice, and nutmeg, two pounds almonds, blanched, and cut in small pieces, one pint grape juice, one and one-half pints each of cider vinegar and water. Mix together thoroughly and cook until the apples are tender. Seal in mason jars. Will keep indefinitely. Left-over jellies, spiced vinegar from fruit or pickles, and fruit juices of all kinds will add to the flavor of the mince.
November 18, 1915

An updated 1944 recipe for:

Mincemeat

2 pounds lean beef
3 cups water
1 pound suet
4 pounds tart apples, pared and cored
3 pounds seedless raisins
1 pound currants
1 cup candied orange peel, diced
¼ pound citron, chopped
1 T. salt
1 T. cinnamon
1 tsp. allspice
1 tsp. cloves
2 cups granulated sugar
2 cups firmly packed brown sugar
1 cup molasses
3 T. lemon juice
1 pint cider or grape juice

Use an inexpensive cut of meat; cut in small pieces, add water, bring to boil. Cover and simmer two hours or until tender. (Utility beef will require longer.) Remove meat; measure one and one-half cups stock. Put meat, suet, and apples through chopper and place in large kettle. Add raisins, currants, orange peel, citron, salt, cinnamon, allspice, cloves, granulated sugar, brown sugar, molasses and one and one-half cups meat stock. simmer one hour, stirring frequently to prevent burning; add lemon juice and cider the last five minutes of cooking. Place in earthenware jar, cover closely and keep in cool place.
8 quarts mincement
December 2, 1944

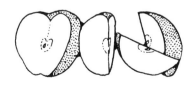

83

Holiday Mincemeat Bread

2 cups all-purpose flour, sifted
4 tsp. baking powder
1 tsp. salt
1 egg, beaten
½ cup milk
½ cup brown sugar
3 T. melted shortening
1 cup moist mincemeat

Sift flour, baking powder, and salt together. Combine beaten egg, milk, brown sugar, melted shortening, and mincemeat. Add to flour mixture, stirring only until flour is moistened.

Bake in greased loaf pan in 350 degree oven for one hour. Let stand 24 hours before slicing.

1 loaf
December, 1964

Mincemeat Mini-Muffins

1½ cups corn meal
½ cup sifted all-purpose flour
1 T. baking powder
½ tsp. salt
¼ cup sugar
½ cup prepared mincemeat
1 cup milk
¼ cup vegetable oil
1 egg, beaten

Preheat oven to 425 degrees.

Sift together corn meal, flour, baking powder, salt, and sugar into medium bowl. Stir in mincemeat. Add milk, oil, and egg. Stir only until dry ingredients are moistened. Fill oiled muffin cups three-quarters full.

Bake for 15-20 minutes or until well browned. Serve piping hot with butter.

12 servings
October 19, 1968

Mincemeat Bars

2 cups rolled oats
1¾ cups all-purpose flour
1 cup brown sugar, packed
½ tsp. soda
½ cup butter
½ cup shortening
1½ cups mincemeat

Put rolled oats through coarse food chopper to measure two cups. Add flour, sugar, and soda and mix thoroughly. Cut in the butter and shortening until the mixture is crumbly. Divide into two parts. Pack one-half firmly in the bottom of an oiled baking pan (about seven and one-half inches by 11 inches). Spread the mincemeat, prepared as for pie filling, evenly over the crust, then add rest of dough and pack with hand or spoon.

Bake in 350 degree oven for 40 minutes. Cool thoroughly and cut into strips or bars.

14 to 16 bars
December 2, 1944

Mincemeat Pie

pastry for a two crust pie, rolled thin
4 cups mincemeat
2 T. butter

Preheat oven to 375 degrees.

Line a nine-inch pieplate with half of the pastry. Add mincemeat. Cut butter into small bits and place over filling. Top with top crust. Cut slits in crust for steam to escape.

Place in oven and bake 35 minutes, or until done.

1 9-inch pie
December 19, 1953

4

What Is Ham?

Are you ready for a really basic question? What is a ham?

"In theory," answers Rosemary Mucklow from the Western States Meat Association, "the answer is simple. A ham is a product made from the hind leg of a hog. But in practice, it hasn't always been so clear, and, in fact, it took a decision of the Supreme Court to resolve the issue."

"But why," we ask her, "has it ever been an issue?"

Mucklow leans back in her chair and explains. "Up until a few years ago, whenever a processor cured a ham by adding water, salt, spices, and other curing ingredients, he was supposed to make sure that at the end of the cooking or smoking process, enough water evaporated so that the ham weighed no more than its original fresh weight, that is, what it weighed before processing. That was the intention, but the processors discovered that if they left extra moisture and spices in the ham, the ham weighed more—a benefit to them—and the product was juicier and more flavorful—a benefit to the consumer.

"But some of the pork packers," continues Mucklow, "didn't like the idea that their competitors could sell ham with added liquid and tried to get regulations preventing the ham processors

from calling their product 'ham.' The issue went all the way to the Supreme Court before it was decided that a ham can be called a ham whether it has water added or not. Still, if water is added, now the label must clearly show it."

There's more to ham lore than that. Small canned hams—those weighing about a pound—don't need refrigeration, while the big ones—they'll weigh five to eight pounds—are always sold from the fresh meat section where they're kept chilled. "The reason has to do with the heat requirements for complete sterilization," explains Mucklow.

"A small canned ham can be heated and sterilized about as easily as a can of peaches or a can of beans. The high internal temperature from the 'retorting' process makes them thoroughly shelf stable and they won't spoil. The big hams, in contrast, would require so much heat for the center of them to reach the sterilization temperature that the rest of the meat would be terribly overcooked. In fact, it would be mush."

The processors, according to Mucklow, determined that they'd be able to provide the consumer with a better product if they processed the large hams at a high enough temperature so that the meat was pasteurized but not so high or for so long that the texture would be ruined. What that means for us, as consumers, is that we need to store large canned hams in the refrigerator, even though we don't need to do so with the one pound cans.

Hams labeled "fully cooked" need no further cooking and are excellent served cold in sandwiches or hors d'oeuvres or salads. If you want to serve the fully cooked hams warm, the eating quality is at its best at 130 degrees internal temperature.

The "Cook-Before-Eating" label means that you should cook the ham to an internal temperature of 160 degrees before serving. The majority of hams sold today, however, are fully cooked. If neither term appears on the label, or if you're unsure, assume the ham should be cooked before eating.

Mucklow has a final thought for us on ham: "Get to know the labels on the cans or packages. There are four classes of products and they're ranked according to the amount of fat free meat protein they contain: Ham; Ham with Natural Juices; Ham, Water Added; and finally, Ham and Water Product. The plain ham and ham with natural juices are the most desirable products in terms of their meat protein value."

How does Mucklow like to cook ham? "Try microwaving fully-cooked ham" is her recommendation. "It's especially suited for the speed and convenience of microwave cookery."

To microwave your fully-cooked hams, use medium or 50 percent power (approximately 325 watts). For hams weighing under three pounds, you can microwave them either pre-sliced or whole. To microwave a boneless ham in one piece, follow these steps:

- Place the fully-cooked ham on a rack in a microwave-safe baking dish.

- Place plastic wrap over the cut surface of the ham and cover the edges with foil.
- Cook at medium power, turning the ham once and rotating the dish several times during cooking, until it reaches an internal temperature of 130 degrees.
- Cover it with a tent foil and let it stand 10 to 15 minutes before carving.

For a one to two pound slice, three-quarters to an inch thick, cook it for about ten minutes. A three pound slice would take 25 to 28 minutes. You can add a glaze during the last few minutes of cooking time.

Cooking a Ham for Dinner?

One of our most popular meats is cured, smoked ham. It's been a long time, however, since we had to cure, smoke, boil, and bake each ham. There are several choices for today's housewife.

With bones and much of the fat removed it is now possible to get fully cooked hams which are canned and ready for eating. Canned hams that must be cooked can be held for long periods in the refrigerator.

Freezing ham tends to reduce its smoked flavor. Refrigeration is necessary, but freezing is not recommended.

"Country style" hams are heavily cured. They usually require soaking and simmering in water before baking. They are not as common in stores today as fully cooked or "Cook-before-eating" hams.

Slow oven temperature of 325 to 350 degrees is suggested for cooking most hams. Internal temperature of 130, 160, or 170 degrees should be reached, depending on the kind of ham or picnic ham.

Ham has a tendency to dry out when it is baked. But not when you use this method of cooking in heavy foil. Follow the timetable below to estimate how long your ham will need to cook.

Ham baking timetable   (oven temperature 350 degrees F)

Fully cooked hams	Weight	Approximate total time	Meat thermometer temperature
Whole, with bone	8- 12 lb.	3 hours	130 deg. F.
Half, with bone	4- 6 lb.	1½ hours	130 deg. F.
Whole, partially boned	7- 11 lb.	3 hours	130 deg. F.
Half, partially boned	3½- 5½ lb.	1½ hours	130 deg. F.
Whole, rolled, no bone	6- 10 lb.	2½-2¾ hours	130 deg. F.
Half, rolled, no bone	3- 5 lb.	1-1½ hours	130 deg. F.
Canned Hams	3- 6 lb.	1 hour	130 deg. F.
	6- 10 lb.	1½-1¾ hours	130 deg. F.
Cook-before-eating hams			
Whole, with bone	8- 12 lb.	3½- 4 hours	160 deg. F.
Half, with bone	4- 6 lb.	1¾- 2 hours	160 deg. F.

In the first recipe below you'll find some suggested glazes for ham. In recipes following are other flavorful variations of baked ham, then recipes for using leftover or sliced ham. There is an idea for most every occasion.

Flavor Glazed Baked Ham

Arrange a large sheet of heavy duty foil wrap in a shallow roasting pan and place ham in center. Pour half the amount of one of sauces described below over ham and brush it over the ham. Bring foil up, covering ham loosely. Bake according to chart. Half an hour before baking is finished, open, and turn back foil.

Spoon out melted fat; remove skin, if any. Score ham in diamond pattern and stud with cloves, diamonds cut from orange rinds, or other fruit. Pour remaining sauce over. Insert meat thermometer, and continue baking with foil open, basting with drippings, until browned. Serve with fruit sauce.

Flavor Sauces

½ can (6 ounces) frozen orange juice
  concentrate, thawed
1 cup brown sugar
½ cup A-1® Steak Sauce
Combine orange juice concentrate, brown sugar, and A-1® sauce.

¾ cup cider or pineapple juice
1 cup brown sugar

Combine cider or juice and brown sugar. Decorate ham with pineapple slices.

2 cups sherry or madeira flavoring,
  Or 2 cups wine
brown sugar, as needed

Pour one cup of flavoring or wine over ham before baking. To brown and glaze, sprinkle ham lightly with brown sugar and baste with remaining cup of wine.

Fruit Sauce

½ can (6 ounces) frozen orange juice
  concentrate, diluted according to
  can directions, Or 1 cup cider or
  other tart fruit juice
1 T. cornstarch, as needed
2 T. water, as needed

Carefully skim the fat from drippings remaining in foil-lined pan. Add orange juice or cider. If flavoring or wine has been used in preparing ham, use equal parts wine and water. Heat this liquid with pan juice, tipping the pan from side to side to dissolve brown juices. Stir in a mixture of one tablespoon cornstarch and 2 tablespoons water for *each* cup liquid in pan. Stir and cook until slightly thickened.
February 13, 1971

87

The main entree of this Eastertime (or any-time) dinner is ham baked in foil. Along-side it serve a vegetable dish of carrots and green beans, and scalloped potatoes. A fruity molded salad, rolls and butter, and a light-as-a-cloud dessert complete the menu. And for the children, an Easter Basket Cake.

Easter Dinner

Ham Baked in Foil

½ cup pineapple juice
1 tsp. dry mustard
¼ tsp. ginger
¼ tsp. cloves

Combine juice, mustard, ginger, and cloves. Place ham on large sheet of heavy duty foil. Brush liberally with sauce. Pad bone ends with folded pieces of foil. Bring foil up, covering ham loosely. Bake according to chart on page 000.

This vegetable dish may also be chilled and used in tossed salads.

Dilly Carrots and Beans

¾ cup water
1 tsp. sugar
½ tsp. salt
½ tsp. dill seed
½ pound fresh green beans
4 carrots (medium-sized), cut into
*   thin strips, 2- to 3-inches long*
¼ cup Italian dressing

Combine water, sugar, salt, and dill seed in a saucepan. Bring to boil. Wash and trim green beans; leave whole. Add to boiling water. Simmer five minutes. Add carrots to grccn bcans. Boil until both vegetables are tender. Add Italian dressing and toss to mix well.
   Serve at once.
6 servings

Scalloped Potatoes

4 cups raw potatoes, thinly sliced
2 T. all-purpose flour
1½ tsp. salt
pepper, to taste
2 cups milk
2 T. butter
4 T. onion, minced

Put a layer of potatoes in an oiled baking dish and sprinkle with some of the flour, salt, pepper, and minced onion. Repeat until all the potatoes are used. Pour milk over potatoes and dot with butter. The milk may be heated to speed the cooking. Cover and bake in a 350-degree oven for 30 minutes. Remove cover and continue baking until potatoes are tender—about 30 more minutes. If the potatoes are not brown enough on top, place the uncovered dish under the broiler for three to five minutes.
6 to 8 servings

Pineapple Ribbon Salad

1 (6 ounce) package raspberry fla-
*   vored gelatin*
1½-cups boiling water
2 (10 ounce) packages frozen
*   raspberries*
1 (13½-ounce) can crushed pineapple
¼ tsp. salt
1 pint sour cream
crisp salad greens, as needed

Dissolve gelatin in boiling water. Add rasp-berries, undrained pineapple, and salt. Pour about one and one-half cups gelatin into an oiled six-cup ring mold. Chill quickly until firm. Let remaining gelatin stand at room temperature. Carefully spread one cup sour cream over chilled gelatin. Spoon half of remaining gelatin over top. Chill firm. Layer with remaining sour cream; then top with remaining gelatin. Chill several hours or overnight.
   To serve, unmold on serving plate and garnish as desired with crisp salad greens.
8 to 10 servings

Cherries On A Cloud

40 soda crackers, crushed
1 stick butter, melted
3 egg whites
1 cup sugar

Cherry Sauce:

1 can (1 pound) pitted cherries
1 cup sugar
2 T. cornstarch
¼ tsp. almond extract
dash salt
2 T. butter

Combine crackers and melted butter. Press into 13x9 ½-inch pan. Beat egg whites with one cup sugar until stiff. Spread over crackers. Bake in a 350-degree oven for 15 to 20 minutes. Cool.

Prepare sauce by draining cherries, reserving liquid. Combine one cup sugar and cornstarch in saucepan. Stir in cherry liquid. Add almond extract, salt, and one tablespoon butter. Cook over medium heat until thickened. Remove from heat and add cherries.

Serve over meringue base.
8 to 10 servings
March 25, 1972

Easter Basket Cake and Ice Cream Eggs

1 cake, baked in a ring mold, any
desired flavor
1 pint chocolate ice cream
1 pint vanilla ice cream
1 pint strawberry ice cream
fluffy frosting, as needed
toasted coconut, as needed

Let cake cool on rack five to 10 minutes. Remove it from the ring mold and let stand until cool. Frost top and outside with fluffy frosting and cover with colored, plain, or toasted coconut.

When ready to serve, fill center and cover top with balls of ice cream, to resemble a basket filled with eggs.
10 servings
April 3, 1971

Presenting food attractively can be fun. Ham takes to decorations well. You can use inexpensive items to create fanciful designs, such as the calla lily blossoms suggested in the following recipe. Other attractive items to use are small thin carrot slices, lightly toasted blanched whole almonds or walnut halves, green pepper strips, watercress or parsley. Use your imagination and place a selection of these items on a glazed, partially cooked ham. The glaze will hold your design in place.

Calla Lily Blossoms

Cut long (two and one-half to three inches) carrot sticks. Put in ice water. Slice large, white, peeled turnips paper thin. For each lily, fold one side of a turnip slice around one end of a carrot stick; fasten securely with wooden pick. Drop into ice water until turnip flares out calla lily style. Remove from water, store in refrigerator on damp paper towel covered with plastic film until ready to use. Decorate top and sides of ham in flowers made by arranging almonds, petal fashion, around a yellow carrot center. If stems are desired, use thin strips of green pepper. Glaze will hold flowers in place. Garnish platter with calla lily blossoms.
March 13, 1971

To restore rancid lard to its former sweetness is a simple matter. Melt the lard to a boiling heat, add thereto a couple of pieces of charcoal the size of hen eggs or larger, according to quantity to be renovated, and boil slowly for one hour. Then strain through a fine cloth. All the impurities will be absorbed by the charcoal.
December 14, 1916

Each week *The Wisconsin Farmer* published a "Tried and True Recipe" for its readers. This was the featured recipe for the week of January 14, 1926.

Baked Ham

slice of ham
vinegar
brown sugar
whole cloves
mustard
flour

Cover ham with boiling water and let stand 15 minutes. Wipe and place in pan that will just hold it. Stick five or six whole cloves in the fat of the meat. Make a thick paste of three tablespoons water, one tablespoon vinegar, and flour. Season with one-quarter teaspoon mustard and three tablespoons brown sugar. Spread this paste on top of the ham and put ham in top of the oven. When paste has hardened, put in enough hot water down one side of the pan, to almost come up to the top of the meat. Cover and bake till done—30 minutes to one hour. Remove cover and brown crust before removing from oven. Your home-canned green beans will go splendidly with this ham. If you have a whole ham, cover with a paste made like the above after the par-boiling period is over and bake as per above directions. When cold, the crust gives the meat a delicious flavor that will be much appreciated in sandwiches.
January 14, 1926

While most of the holiday menus from the pages of *The Prairie Farmer* feature traditional dishes, an article in a 1961 issue suggested that the cook "plan a new Christmas Menu." It featured a glazed ham as "The Star Attraction," a green bean and onion casserole, sweet potato puffs, Sally Lunn bread and butter, and for dessert—and here the traditional returned to the menu—a steamed plum pudding.

Applesauce Glazed Ham

1 canned ham (6-11 pounds)
whole cloves, as needed
1 cup applesauce
¼ cup brown sugar
1 T. grated orange rind
1 T. orange juice

Remove ham from can and place on a rack in a shallow roasting pan. Bake in a 325-degree oven, 10 minutes per pound. (Weight of ham will be given on the label.) One-half hour before end of cooking time remove ham from oven. Pour off juices. Cut shallow diagonal gashes across ham fat to form a diamond pattern and stick each diamond with a whole clove. Combine applesauce, brown sugar, orange rind, and juice, and spread on top and sides of ham. Return to oven to glaze for 30 minutes.

Request Green Beans

1 can (1 pound) cut green beans,
  with liquid reserved
1 can (3½ ounces) French-fried onions
1 can condensed cream of mushroom
  soup
1 can (3 to 4 ounces) mushrooms
2 T. toasted almonds or sliced water
  chestnuts
½ cup grated cheddar cheese

Preheat oven to 375 degrees.
  Put alternate layers of drained beans and onions in a casserole. Mix soup and mushrooms with bean liquid and almonds. Pour over beans and onions. Sprinkle cheese over top. Bake for 30 minutes.
6 servings

Sweet Potato Puffs

shortening or oil, as needed for deep
  frying
2 cups sweet potatoes, mashed
1 tsp. salt
dash pepper
8 marshmallows
1¼ cups dry bread crumbs
1 egg, beaten
2 T. water

Preheat deep fat fryer to 365 degrees.

Combine sweet potatoes, salt, and pepper; form into eight balls. Insert a marshmallow into center of each ball. Roll in bread crumbs. Combine egg and water; dip balls in mixture and roll again in bread crumbs.

Deep fry in heated fat for approximately four minutes.

6 to 8 servings

Sally Lunn Bread

1 cup milk
¼ cup sugar
2 tsp. salt
¼ cup margarine or butter
½ cup warm, not hot, water
1 package of cake yeast, active dry
  or compressed
3 eggs, well-beaten
4 cups sifted all-purpose flour

Scald milk. Add and stir in sugar, salt, and margarine or butter. Cool to lukewarm. Measure water into a large mixing bowl (warm, not hot, water for active yeast; lukewarm water for compressed yeast). Sprinkle or crumble in yeast; stir until dissolved. Add lukewarm milk mixture. Stir in eggs and flour. Beat until smooth. Cover with a cloth and let rise in a warm place until doubled in bulk, about 50 minutes. Stir and pour into an oiled eight-inch pan. Cover and let rise in a warm place fo 45 minutes.

Preheat oven to 400 degrees.

Place pan in oven and bake for 30 minutes.

1 round or square loaf

Steamed Plum Pudding

⅓ cup butter
1 cup brown sugar, packed
2 eggs, beaten
½ cup milk
1 cup seedless raisins
1 cup currants
⅓ cup sliced citron
⅓ cup diced candied pineapple
⅓ cup sliced candied cherries
½ cup blanched slivered almonds
2 cups sifted all-purpose flour
1 tsp. salt
1 tsp. baking soda
1 tsp. cinnamon
½ tsp. nutmeg
1 quart vanilla ice cream

Cream butter, add brown sugar, blend. Stir in eggs and milk. Mix fruits with one-half cup of the flour. Sift flour, salt, baking soda, cinnamon and nutmeg; add with fruit to butter mixture, and stir to blend. Turn into well-oiled quart mold. Cover and steam two and one-half hours. Unmold.

Serve hot or cold with ice cream.

December 16, 1961

An excellent sauce to serve on slices of baked ham. You can adjust the hotness depending on the mustard you use—anything goes, from the mild to the spicy, hot!

Butter Mustard Sauce for Ham

2 T. butter
1 T. all-purpose flour
1 tsp. salt
1 T. prepared mustard
dash of pepper
1 cup milk

Melt butter in saucepan over low heat. Blend in flour, salt, mustard, and pepper; cook until smooth. Remove from heat. Stir in milk. Heat to boiling, stirring constantly, boil one minute.

Serve hot over ham slices.

4 servings

February 5, 1972

Ham with Best Ever Glaze

1 can pineapple slices, drained;
reserve syrup
½ cup currant or other red jelly
½ tsp. ground cloves
½ tsp. dry mustard
½ tsp. black pepper

Bake a ham according to your favorite method and remove from oven 15 minutes before done.

Set oven temperature up to 400 degrees.

Whip jelly with one tablespoon reserved pineapple syrup; add cloves, mustard and black pepper. Score ham, then cover with glaze mixture. Top with some of the pineapple slices and return to oven for 15 minutes.

February 17, 1968

For a 1934 buffet, the following recipe for serving ham to a group was popular, but first note the advice given to the planner of the buffet:

There are a few things to know and plan beforehand in giving a buffet supper. The buffet, if a long one, may be used for the food, with the dishes and silverware placed on the dining-table, or the table may be lengthened, the food set on one end and the dishes and silverware on the other. This is a little more convenient, as guests may circle the table and have easy access to the food. The silverware should be laid out in rows, the forks and spoons being separated and easily acquired. Some of us are sticklers for paper napkins for group eating occasions, although etiquette frowns. But there are such attractive designs now and the napkins are so large and thick that it is no longer necessary for large-handed husbands to wrestle with a flimsy little square of white paper spread over the knee, which the least little puff will send scooting under the piano or into the darkest corner of the room. Dainty chintz and plaid designs lend dignity and beauty to any meal, especially an informal one such as this buffet supper, so let's use paper napkins.

Ham with Lemon

A portion of the liquid that is left in the pan after the ham is removed should be thinned with lemon juice until quite tart. Slice the ham and arrange the slices in a flat baking pan or something else that is large enough to allow turning the slices without tearing them. Slice the ham a little thick—men like it that way. Now, about an hour before you plan to serve, start a very slow oven and place the ham and lemon mixture in to simmer, so that the ham will become saturated with the tartness of the lemon. When ready to take to the table, arrange in neat rows on a warmed platter and garnish with very thin slices of lemon.

March 17, 1934

If you have a barbecue with a spit, ham is a perfect meat to cook on it.

Barbecued Ham on a Spit

8 pound ready-to-eat whole ham
1 cup brown sugar
½ cup thick apricot or peach preserves
¼ cup water

Place a meat thermometer in the thickest part of the ham. Balance ham on spit, placing so that it just clears coil. Roast for about two hours, or until about 145 degrees on the meat thermometer. Combine brown sugar, preserves, and water and heat. Brush roast with glaze during last 20 minutes of cooking.

10 to 12 servings
August 15, 1964

Ham Hock Dinner

2 pounds smoked ham hocks
4 medium carrots, sliced
4 medium onions, sliced
4 medium potatoes, unpeeled and
*   quartered*
1 small head green cabbage, quartered

Cover ham hocks with water. Cover pan and simmer about two hours. When meat has cooked one and one-half hours, remove skins from hocks. Return hocks to cooking liquid and add carrots, onions, and potatoes. Cook 20 minutes and add cabbage. Cook 15 minutes longer or until meat and vegetables are done. Arrange ham hocks and vegetables on a platter.
4 servings
January 7, 1950

Ham Slices with Orange Stuffing

2 ham slices, about ½-inch thick
1 medium orange
1 quart day-old bread cubes
½ cup diced celery
¼ cup butter or margarine, melted
2 eggs, slightly beaten
½ tsp. salt
⅛ tsp. pepper
1 T. brown sugar
¼ tsp. marjoram

Place one ham slice in bottom of a shallow baking pan. For stuffing, grate orange rind, then remove peel and white membrane, and cut pulp into cubes, discarding seeds. Combine grated orange rind with fruit pulp, bread, celery, butter, eggs, salt, pepper, marjoram, and brown sugar. Spoon on top of ham slice, and cover with remaining slice. Cover pan, using foil if no cover is available, and bake in a 325-degree oven for one hour. Uncover, spoon drippings over top slice, and broil five to 10 minutes, or until top slice is browned and edges crisp. Serve immediately.
6 servings
March 21, 1970

Another for the outdoor barbecue.

Ham and Vegetables

1 2-pound ham steak
¾ cup chili sauce
3 T. light brown sugar, firmly
*   packed*
2 tsp. prepared mustard
2 tsp. horseradish
2 tsp. Worcestershire sauce
zucchini, as needed, cut in ½-inch
*   slices*
cherry tomatoes, as needed
small canned onions or potatoes, as
*   needed*
Italian dressing, as needed for
*   basting*
small orange wedges, as desired for
*   garnish*

Prepare barbecue grill.
   Slash edge of ham steak. Stir together chili sauce, brown sugar, mustard, horseradish, and Worcestershire sauce. Brush ham with some of the sauce. Thread zucchini, tomatoes and onions, or potatoes alternately on six skewers. Brush with dressing.
   Grill or broil ham about 15 minutes, turning once and brushing with more sauce. Grill or broil vegetable kabobs the same length of time, turning once and brushing with more dressing.
   To serve, garnish with orange wedges.
6 servings
May 28, 1977

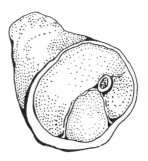

Cranberry Ham Rolls

4 T. butter or margarine
4 T. onion, finely chopped
4 T. celery, chopped
2 cups rice, cooked
salt and pepper, to taste
8 slices (⅛-inch thick) boned boiled
    ham
1 pound jellied cranberry sauce
½ cup brown sugar

Melt butter in small saucepan. Add onion and celery. Cook until soft. Remove from heat. Add rice, salt, and pepper. Spread on each ham slice. Roll up. Fasten with toothpick. Place in an oiled shallow pan.

Prepare cranberry glaze by crushing cranberry sauce and adding brown sugar. Spoon over ham rolls.

Bake in a 350-degree oven 15 to 20 minutes.
8 servings
October 21, 1967

The section of *The Wisconsin Farmer* called "Other Good Things" yielded this good thing back in 1915.

Fricassee Ham

Have the slice of fresh ham cut an inch and a half thick. Cut into small pieces and parboil for ten minutes in salted water. Drain and dip first in beaten egg and then in cracker crumbs. Fry in deep, hot fat until a golden brown. Make a thick, brown gravy by thickening a tablespoonful of the fat with two of flour, and adding two cupfuls of milk. Arrange the ham on a platter and pour the brown gravy over the meat, serving hot and well seasoned.
October 28, 1915

Scalloped Potatoes and Ham

4 T. butter
3 T. all-purpose flour
2 cups milk
1 tsp. salt
¼ tsp. pepper
4 cups raw potato, peeled and sliced
½ pound or more smoked ham

Melt butter; blend in flour. Add milk, salt and pepper. Cook slowly until thickened. While the white sauce is cooking, peel and slice potatoes into a one-quart measure. Butter a casserole, and arrange a layer of potatoes on the bottom. Cut the ham in bite-sized pieces or small serving sized pieces, and lay on top of the potatoes. Add the rest of the potatoes, and pour the hot white sauce over them. Work it through with a fork so every piece of potato is coated with white sauce.

Bake uncovered in a 325-degree oven for about two hours.
4 to 6 servings
February 4, 1956

Ham Cheese Scallop

4 T. butter
3 T. all-purpose flour
2 cups milk
2 cups American cheese, shredded
3 cups cooked elbow macaroni
½ tsp. salt
1½ cups cooked ham, chopped
2 T. horseradish
2 tsp. prepared mustard

Melt butter in saucepan. Stir in flour. Add milk slowly. Cook over low heat, stirring constantly until sauce is smooth and thick. Add cheese and macaroni and salt. Pour into the buttered casserole.

Combine ham, horseradish, and mustard and mix. Sprinkle over top of macaroni mixture, pressing down slightly. Bake in a 350-degree oven for 20 to 25 minutes or until heated through and lightly browned on top.
6 servings
August 20, 1955

Ham-Green Bean Casserole

1 pound green beans, cut into 2-inch
   pieces
1 pound fresh mushrooms, cut into
   small pieces
¼ cup butter
⅓ cup sifted all-purpose flour
2 cups milk
1 cup cream
1 tsp. salt
dash of white pepper
3 cups cooked ham, cut in strips
⅓ cup pimiento, cut in strips
grated cheese, as needed for topping

Cook beans until tender. Saute mushrooms in butter for five minutes. Gradually blend flour into butter and mushrooms; add milk, cream, salt and pepper; cook until thickened. Add ham, beans, and pimiento to mushroom sauce; mix and pour into two-quart casserole. Sprinkle with grated cheese. Bake in a 350-degree oven for 20 minutes.
6 to 8 servings
April 4, 1964

Ham Mustard-Roni

2 T. onion, finely chopped
2 T. butter or margarine
6 T. all-purpose flour
2 cups milk
2 T. prepared mustard
1 cup cheddar cheese, shredded
2 cups cooked ham, cubed
3 cups cooked macaroni

Pan fry onion in butter. Stir in flour. Slowly add milk and mustard. Cook until thickened. Stir in one-half cup cheese. Continue heating until cheese melts and sauce is smooth. Combine ham, macaroni, and sauce in a two-quart casserole. Sprinkle remaining cheese on top.
    Bake in a 350-degree oven for 20 minutes.
4 to 6 servings
April 2, 1966

Ham á la King Deluxe

1 small green pepper, minced
½ pound fresh mushrooms, sliced
5 T. butter, divided
2 T. all-purpose flour
1 cup milk
1 cup thin cream
2 egg yolks, lightly beaten
2 cups cooked ham, diced
½ cup pimiento, diced
1 tsp. lemon juice
2 T. cooking sherry
salt and pepper, to taste
4 to 6 slices hot toast

Cook green pepper and mushrooms in two tablespoons butter until soft but not brown. Make cream sauce by blending flour and remaining butter in top of double boiler; gradually add milk and cream. Cook over direct heat, stirring constantly until thickened. Mix a little sauce with egg yolks, then combine with rest of sauce. Place top of double boiler over boiling water. Add ham, pimiento, lemon juice, sherry, salt, and pepper. Stir until sauce reaches right consistency and is hot.
    Serve on toast.
4 to 6 servings
April 2, 1966

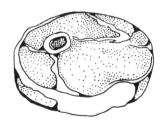

Undercover Ham Casserole

2 T. butter or margarine
¼ cup onion, chopped
2 cups cooked ham, cubed
1 (10½-ounces) can cream of
    mushroom soup
½ cup milk
¼ tsp. pepper
¼ tsp. paprika
1 tsp. Worcestershire sauce
1 cup cheddar cheese, shredded
2 cups hot mashed potatoes

Melt butter in a saucepan. Add onion and cook for about five minutes. Add ham, then blend in mushroom soup and milk. Stir in pepper, paprika, and Worcestershire sauce. Blend in cheese. Pour ham mixture into a one and one-half-quart casserole which has been rubbed with butter. Spoon mashed potatoes over ham mixture. Bake in a 350-degree oven about 15 to 20 minutes or until potatoes are lightly browned. Serve hot.
4 to 6 servings
April 2, 1966

The following make-ahead recipe freezes extremely well, serves a large group and can be table-ready in an hour or less. If this dish is frozen, plan to serve it within two weeks for optimum flavor.

Ham and Bean Scallop

1¾ quarts (3 pounds) dry pea beans
3 quarts boiling water
½ cup ham fat
1½ cups onion, finely chopped
½ cup sifted all-purpose flour
2 T. Worcestershire sauce
2 tsp. powdered dry mustard
2 tsp. salt
2 quarts hot milk
3 cups cheese, grated
5 cups cooked ham, diced

Add beans to boiling water and boil two minutes. Remove from heat and soak in the hot water one hour. Or, if more convenient, soak overnight after the two-minute boil. Discard the soaking water; cook beans in an equivalent amount of fresh water about one and one-half hours (slightly underdone). Heat the fat, add onion, and cook until golden brown. Add flour, Worcestershire sauce, mustard, and salt, blending to a smooth paste. Stir into the hot milk. Cook until thickened, stirring constantly. Combine cheese, ham, and beans with the sauce. Remove from heat. Cool quickly. Pack in freezer containers, leaving head space. Seal and freeze immediately.

To serve, preheat oven to 400 degrees.
Reheat in the top of a double boiler, stirring occasionally to speed thawing. Or, if food is frozen in an ovenproof container, uncover, top with fine dry bread crumbs and bake about 45 minutes for pints, one hour for quarts.
25 servings
August 15, 1964

Company Casserole

8 hard-cooked eggs
¼ cup butter, melted
½ tsp. Worcestershire sauce
¼ tsp. prepared mustard
¼ tsp. parsley, finely chopped
1 tsp. chopped chives
⅓ cup finely chopped cooked ham
1 cup process American cheese,
    shredded

Sauce:
3 T. butter
3 T. all-purpose flour
1 cup chicken broth
¾ cup milk
dash of salt and pepper

Cut hard-cooked eggs in half lengthwise; remove and mash yolks. Mix yolks with melted butter, Worcestershire sauce, mustard, parsley, chives, and ham. Fill whites with this mixture. Arrange filled egg halves in an oiled flat one and one-half to two-quart baking dish.

For white sauce: melt butter in saucepan. Blend in flour and cook until bubbly. Add chicken broth, milk, salt, and pepper. Cook over low heat, stirring constantly until mixture is smooth and thickened throughout. Pour sauce over egg halves. Sprinkle with cheese.

Bake in a 350-degree oven for 20 minutes or until cheese is melted.

4 to 6 servings
March 6, 1971

Ham Tetrazzini

¼ cup onion, finely chopped
½ cup butter, melted
½ pound fresh mushrooms, sliced
⅓ cup all-purpose flour
2 cups milk
2 cups half and half
3 T. cooking sherry, optional
¼ tsp. salt
dash garlic salt
dash pepper
¾ cup Parmesan cheese, shredded
1 7-ounce package spaghetti, cooked
2 cups cooked ham pieces, thinly sliced

Preheat oven to 375 degrees.

Saute onion in butter until transparent; add mushrooms and cook until tender. Blend in flour. Stir in milk and half and half; continue stirring until mixture is smooth and thickened. Add sherry, salt, garlic salt, and pepper. Mix together one-half cup Parmesan cheese and spaghetti in the bottom of a two-quart shallow baking dish. Cover with alternate layers of sauce and ham, ending with sauce. Sprinkle remaining cheese over top.

Bake until bubbly around edges of dish and brown on top, about 20 to 25 minutes.

6 to 8 servings
March 20, 1971

With the conciseness typical of the early recipes in this collection, this scalloped ham recipe from the 1920s reminds us that simple foods still taste good.

Scalloped Ham and Peas

Add one cup of finely chopped boiled ham and one can of peas to two cups of thin white sauce. Add two teaspoons of Worcestershire sauce to this and pour the mixture in a baking dish. Cover with finely grated cheese, and bake until cheese is melted.

June 23, 1927

Ham Creole

¼ cup butter or margarine
1 cup onion, sliced
2 cups cooked ham, cut in strips
1 medium green pepper, coarsely
    diced
½ tsp. salt
⅛ tsp. ground cloves
1 can (16 ounces) tomatoes,
    undrained
1 can (3 to 4 ounces) mushrooms,
    undrained
¼ cup dark molasses
2 T. cornstarch
5 T. water

Heat butter or margarine in a saucepan; saute onions until tender. Add ham, green pepper, salt, cloves, tomatoes, mushrooms, and molasses. Cover and simmer 30 minutes, stirring occasionally. Blend cornstarch with water until smooth; stir into ham mixture. Cook, stirring occasionally until thickened.

4 to 6 servings
March 21, 1970

Half the fun of cooking with curry is the assortment of easy condiments you can serve with it. The condiment tray that accompanies this recipe could include chutney, salted whole or chopped peanuts or almonds, preserved kumquats, toasted coconut, seedless raisins, mixed sweet pickles, mangoes, and bananas.

Curried Ham And Rice

½ cup onion, chopped
2 T. butter or margarine
2 T. flour
4 bouillon cubes
2 cups boiling water
½ cup sliced fresh mushrooms
¾ cup half and half
1 T. lemon juice
2 tsp. curry powder, or to taste
1 pound (3 cups) fully cooked ham
 cubes (¾ inch)
4 cups hot cooked seasoned rice

Saute onion in butter or margarine. Stir in flour. In a saucepan, dissolve bouillon cubes in boiling water; add mushrooms and simmer for seven minutes. Combine with onion and flour mixture and cook til thickened. Add half and half, lemon juice, and curry powder; mix and heat. Stir in ham.

To serve, mound rice in center of heated serving dish. Spoon ham mixture around rice. Serve with some of the curry condiments suggested above.
6 servings
March 13, 1971

Get out the barbecue and try an exotic Hawaiian version of ham on a skewer. An easy way to entertain eight guests, serve with lots of fresh vegetables, hot buttered rice, and fruit for dessert.

Ham Teriyaki Hawaiian

1 can (1 pound, 4½ ounces)
 pineapple chunks
2 T. soy sauce
½ tsp. ground ginger
½ tsp. sugar
½ tsp. garlic salt
2 pounds ham, cut into 48 1-inch
 cubes

Prepare barbecue grill.

Drain pineapple and retain syrup. Make marinade by combining pineapple syrup, soy sauce, ginger, sugar, and garlic salt in a shallow dish large enough to hold the ham. Marinate ham for 10 minutes at room temperature, turn, and let stand another 10 minutes. Drain ham and thread on skewers, alternating with pineapple, three of each to an eight-inch skewer.

Cook and turn over coals until brown, about three to five minutes on each side.
16 skewers, 8 servings
June 1, 1968

The good flavor combination of ham and eggs needn't be confined to breakfast—main dishes for lunch and dinner often are based on these two nourishing and delicious food items. The following recipes show how versatile this combination can be.

Swiss Cheese and Ham Pie

pastry for single crust 9-inch pie
2 T. butter
2 T. all-purpose flour
½ tsp. salt
⅛ tsp. nutmeg
1½ cups milk
1 cup Swiss cheese, shredded
3 eggs, beaten slightly
1 cup cooked ham, diced
grated Swiss cheese, chopped chives,
*   or broiled tomato slices as desired*
*   for garnish*

Preheat oven to 425 degrees.

Line nine-inch pie pan with pastry, fluting the edges. Chill in refrigerator. Melt butter in saucepan over low heat, blend in flour, salt, and nutmeg. Add milk, stirring constantly, and cook until sauce is smooth and thickened. Add Swiss cheese gradually and stir until melted. Cool slightly and stir a small amount of mixture into beaten eggs, then stir eggs into sauce and add ham.

Bake pie shell for 15 minutes. Lower heat to 300 degrees, and pour filling into pie shell. Bake until filling sets, or until knife blade inserted in middle comes out clean, about 40 minutes. If desired, garnish top with additional Swiss cheese, chopped chives, or broiled tomato slices.

5 to 6 servings
March 6, 1971

Creamed Ham and Eggs

½ cup butter or margarine
½ cup all-purpose flour
1 tsp. salt
1 tsp. sugar
2 T. prepared mustard
½ cup strong coffee
few drops Tabasco®
1 quart milk or half and half
1 dozen eggs, hard-cooked and
*   sliced*
2 pounds cooked ham, cut 1-inch
*   thick and cubed*

Melt butter or margarine. Smoothly blend in flour, salt, sugar, mustard, coffee, and Tabasco®. Add milk; cook and stir over medium heat until smooth and thickened. Add eggs and ham. Heat to serve.

8 servings
April 5, 1969

99

Ham Ball with Sweet Potatoes

3 T. brown sugar
2 tsp. cornstarch
½ tsp. dry mustard
½ cup canned apricot nectar
3 T. corn syrup
1 T. vinegar
1½ pounds ground lean ham
½ pound ground lean fresh pork
1 cup crushed cornflakes
1 T. brown sugar
¼ tsp. ground cloves
1 egg, beaten
½ cup milk
1 can sweet potatoes or yams, drained

Combine three tablespoons brown sugar, cornstarch, and dry mustard; add nectar, corn syrup, and vinegar. Set aside.

Mix ham, pork, cornflakes, one tablespoon brown sugar, cloves, egg, and milk together until well blended. Shape into balls the size of large walnuts. Brown slowly on all sides in small amount of shortening in preheated skillet. Allow about 15 to 20 minutes to brown. Drain sweet potatoes and place in skillet with ham balls and apricot/mustard glaze. Cover; let cook over lowest heat until sauce is thickened and potatoes are done.

6 servings
October, 1953

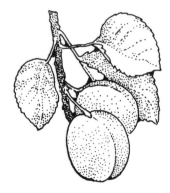

Ham Balls with Cranberry Sauce

1 pound cooked ham, ground
½ cup bread crumbs
⅛ tsp. pepper
2 eggs, beaten
¼ cup water
3 T. shortening
8 ounces broad noodles
2 T. salt
3 quarts boiling water
¼ cup sugar
¼ cup brown sugar
1 cup water
1 cup raw cranberries
2 T. cornstarch
2 T. water
1 tsp. orange rind, grated
½ cup butter, melted

Combine ham, crumbs, and pepper. Mix eggs and one-quarter cup water; add to ham mixture and mix thoroughly. Shape mixture into balls. Melt shortening in large skillet. Add ham balls and cook until browned on all sides, about 20 minutes.

Meanwhile, cook noodles. Add salt and noodles to boiling water. Boil rapidly, stirring constantly, for two minutes. Cover, remove from heat, and let stand 10 minutes.

To make sauce, combine sugar and brown sugar and one cup water; bring to boil. Add cranberries and cook until skins pop, about five minutes. Combine cornstarch and two tablespoons water and stir into cranberry mixture. Add orange rind and cook sauce until thickened, stirring constantly.

Rinse noodles with hot water and drain well. Add noodles to butter and toss lightly to coat.

To serve, top noodles with ham balls and cranberry sauce.

6 servings
February 21, 1959

Buffet Ham Balls

⅔ cup milk
¾ cup dry bread crumbs
½ tsp. dry mustard
1 egg
2 cups ground ham
3 T. butter
¼ cup water

Sauce:

2 T. all-purpose flour
2 T. ham drippings
1 cup sour cream
1 T. sugar
1 tsp. dill weed
½ tsp. salt

Combine milk and crumbs: allow to stand until moisture is absorbed. Add mustard, egg, and ham; blend thoroughly. Form into balls about one and one-half-inch in diameter. There should be about two dozen. Melt butter in heavy skillet, add ham balls, and brown lightly. Add water, cover, and cook over low heat for 15 minutes if ham is precooked, 25 minutes for uncooked ham.

To make sauce blend flour into ham drippings, then add sour cream, sugar, dill weed, and salt. Cook over low heat and stir until smooth and slightly thickened.

Serve ham balls with sauce.
2 dozen ham balls and sauce
April 3, 1971

Ham 'N' Loaf with Horseradish-Whipped Cream Sauce

6 slices bread
¼ cup milk
4 cups ground cooked ham
¼ to ¾ cup ground onion
¼ tsp. celery seed
4 hard-cooked eggs, sliced

Sauce:

3 T. horseradish, grated
¼ tsp. salt
1 T. lemon juice
1 tsp. prepared mustard
½ cup whipping cream, whipped

Break bread into small pieces. Add milk and whip with a fork until bread is soft and dough-like. Add ham, onion, and celery seed. Pack half of meat mixture into bottom of oiled loaf pan, 10x5x3-inch size. Arrange eggs on top. Pack remaining meat mixture on top of sliced eggs. Bake loaf in a 350-degree oven for one hour.

To make sauce, fold horseradish, salt, lemon juice, and mustard into whipped cream. Keep chilled.

To serve, cut loaf in slices or squares and top with horseradish sauce.
4 to 6 servings
March 6, 1971

Ham Loaf Ring with Creamed Vegetables

1 pound ground ham
1 pound ground beef
⅔ cup fine crumbs
1 cup undiluted evaporated milk
¼ tsp. salt
¼ tsp. pepper
¼ tsp. celery salt
¼ cup onion, chopped
¼ cup green pepper, chopped
2 cups well-drained cooked vegetables
2 T. all-purpose flour
2 T. butter
1 tsp. salt
1⅔ cups (large can) undiluted
evaporated milk

Blend ham, ground beef, crumbs, one cup milk, one-quarter teaspoon salt, pepper, celery salt, onion, and green pepper thoroughly. Be sure to use undiluted milk. It's this double-richness that makes the loaf so moist and juicy. After blending, place in eight or nine-inch ring mold. Bake in a 350-degree oven about one hour. Allow to stand about 10 minutes.

Meanwhile, prepare creamed vegetables by blending flour and butter with one teaspoon salt over low heat. Slowly add one and two-thirds cup undiluted milk. Stir until thickened and smooth. Pour sauce over vegetables.

Turn ring out on a serving plate. Fill center with creamed vegetables.
6 to 8 servings
August 1, 1953

Ham and Cheese Loaf

2 envelopes unflavored gelatin
1 cup cold water
1 tsp. salt
2 T. lemon juice
1½ cups salad dressing
1 T. lemon rind, grated
1½ cups celery, finely diced
½ cup green pepper, finely diced
1½ cups ground cooked ham
½ cup cheese, grated

Soften the gelatin in cold water. Place over boiling water, and stir until gelatin is dissolved. Add salt and lemon juice, and cool. Gradually stir in the salad dressing. Mix in lemon rind, celery, pepper, ground ham, and cheese. Turn into a loaf pan, and chill until firm.
4 servings
April 4, 1953

Ham and Corn Fritters

2 cups sifted all-purpose flour
3 tsp. baking powder
1 tsp. salt, approximately
1 cup milk
¼ cup light molasses
1 egg
1 cup minced ham
1 cup canned whole-kernel corn,
well-drained

Heat deep fat fryer to 360 degrees.

Sift flour, baking powder, and salt into bowl. Combine milk, molasses, and egg; add to dry ingredients. Stir in ham and corn; mix well.

Drop batter by tablespoons into hot deep fat; fry four to five minutes, until richly browned on both sides.
4 servings
March 21, 1970

Ham Salad in Tomato Cups

2 cups ham, diced
1 cup celery, finely diced
French dressing, as needed
2 tsp. sweet pickle relish
2 hard cooked eggs, coarsely
*   chopped*
mayonnaise, as needed
salt and pepper, to taste
4 large ripe tomatoes
parsley or watercress, if desired for
*   garnish*

Combine ham and celery; add enough French dressing to moisten. Refrigerate for one-half hour, stirring occasionally. Add relish, eggs and enough mayonnaise to moisten slightly. Season with salt and pepper. Peel tomatoes and cut almost through into six sections so they will open like flowers. Place ham salad in center of each tomato. Garnish with parsley or watercress.
4 servings
July 8, 1967

A meal-in-itself salad.

Hearty Supper Salad

1 cup elbow macaroni
2 cups cooked ham or lunchmeat,
*   diced*
1½ cups sharp cheddar cheese, diced
1 cup celery, chopped
1 small onion, chopped
½ cup sweet pickle, chopped
½ cup sour cream
2 T. prepared mustard

Cook macaroni in boiling salted water until tender, according to package directions. Rinse and drain. Put in mixing bowl with ham, cheese, celery, onion, and pickle. Blend together sour cream and mustard. Add to macaroni mixture. Toss until well blended. Chill thoroughly before serving.
4 servings
July, 1959

This suggestion from 1911 reminds us that picnics have always been favorite occasions.

Ham Filling for Sandwiches

Roll the ham the day before it is needed and allow it to become cold. Put it through the food chopper and add enough sweet cream to make it moist and good. At the picnic grounds spread the bread very thinly with butter and add a layer of the chipped ham. For a change save out some of the ham and mix with it chopped cucumber pickles and mayonnaise dressing. This is also nice used between lettuce leaves in sandwiches.
August 31, 1911

The McIntosh

12 slices enriched white sandwich
*   bread*
mayonnaise or salad dressing, as
*   needed*
mustard, as needed
12 1-ounce slices baked ham
48 slices McIntosh apple (6 small
*   apples)*
24 1-ounce slices American cheese

Spread bread with mayonnaise or salad dressing, then with mustard. Cover each slice with one slice ham, four apple slices, and two slices cheese. Arrange sandwiches on baking sheet. Broil until cheese melts and is slightly brown.
12 open-faced sandwiches
August 7, 1965

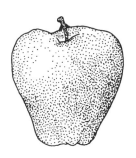

You can make a meal out of this sandwich and a crisp green salad.

Ham and Cheese Barbecue

½ cup mayonnaise
1 T. mustard with horseradish
2 T. chili sauce
6 hamburger buns
6 slices baked ham
6 slices cheese

Combine mayonnaise, mustard, and chili sauce. Split the buns, and spread all halves with mayonnaise mixture. Cover the bottom half of each bun with a slice of ham, then a slice of cheese. Place all halves under low broiler heat until the cheese is melted. Put the bun halves together and serve hot.
6 servings
March 21, 1953

When you tire of plain sliced ham and mustard sandwiches, try this hearty (and healthy!) filling.

Ham Sandwich Filling

⅓ cup light or dark raisins
2 cups cooked ham, finely chopped
½ tsp. dry mustard
1 tsp. lemon juice
½ cup mayonnaise
½ cup carrots, finely grated
¼ cup peanuts, chopped

Rinse and dry raisins; chop coarsely. Combine with ham, mustard, lemon juice, and mayonnaise. Add carrots and peanuts, and additional mayonnaise if desired.
    Store in covered jar in refrigerator.
2 cups filling
April 22, 1967

Hot Ham Sandwiches

½ cup sweet pickle, chopped
½ cup dill pickle, chopped
3 T. pimientos
1 cup American cheese, grated
⅓ cup mayonnaise
4 slices bread
4 thin slices baked ham

Mix the pickles, pimientos, cheese, and mayonnaise together. Butter the bread, and place buttered side down in hot skillet until lightly browned. Turn browned side up, and place a slice of ham on each piece of bread. Top with the pickle-cheese mixture. Place under broiler until cheese melts. Serve immediately.
4 servings
September 15, 1956

Ham 'N' Cheese Snack Sandwiches

3 ounces ham, thinly sliced
¾ cup (3 ounces) Swiss cheese, shredded
1 T. green onion, finely chopped
1½ tsp. prepared mustard
8 ounce can refrigerated crescent dinner rolls
1 T. water
1 egg, slightly beaten
¼ tsp. poppy seed

Preheat oven to 375 degrees.
    Oil eight muffin cups. In small bowl, combine ham, Swiss cheese, green onion and mustard. Separate crescent dough into eight triangles. Spoon meat mixture on wide end of each triangle. Wrap dough around ham mixture; completely cover mixture and seal edges of dough tightly to prevent leakage during baking. Place in muffin cups. Combine water with egg and brush on tops of crescents. Sprinkle with poppy seed.
    Bake for 20 to 25 minutes until golden brown.
8 sandwiches
September 8, 1973

5
You and Dachshund Sausages

If you were a hot dog maker, you, like the rest of us, would have loved the Centennial Celebration with the Tall Ships in New York Harbor. You would have been moved by the majesty and the symbolism of the event—but you'd also have liked it for a different reason. Never before in all of history had so many hot dogs sold in such a short space of time. In fact, spectators consumed 10 million hot dogs that day!

The Tall Ships were special, but summertime is also important to hot dog makers. Americans consume more than five billion hot dogs between Memorial Day and Labor Day, and—here's a thought to delight the hot dog people—if you laid all of those hot dogs end to end, they'd be long enough to circle the globe more than 15 times.

Hot dogs are America's favorite sausage, but if sports cartoonist Tad Dorgan had been a better speller, none of us would be eating them today.

Why?

Well, it has to do with one Harry Stevens, a concessionaire at the New York Polo Grounds back in April of 1901. When Stevens found that he was losing money with his ice cream and sodas, he sent his salesmen out to buy all the then popular "dachshund" or "little dog" sausages they could find. In less than an hour, his vendors were hawking these popular German sausages from portable hot water tanks, crying, "They're red hot! Get your dachshund sausages while they're red hot!"

Meanwhile, Tad Dorgan, a sports cartoonist, was facing a deadline and desperately looking for an idea. Hearing the vendors, he quickly sketched a cartoon of a little barking dachshund sausage nestled in its roll. Not sure how to spell the correct name of the sausage, he simply wrote, "hot dog!" The cartoon was a success and the name "hot dog" was launched.

Hot dogs are popular, but what exactly *are* they? The traditional hot dog is a pre-cooked, smoked sausage made of selected chopped meats and seasonings, sold in links. Products may also contain up to three and one-half percent non-meat binders such as non-fat dry milk, cereal, or dried whole milk, or two percent soy protein. These binders, which actually add to the nutritive value, must be distinctly labeled. Hot dogs are made from skeletal meat unless they are clearly labeled otherwise. For example, if the label says, "Frankfurters with By-product," it contains organ meats.

Another ingredient is more controversial. Manufacturers add up to 200 parts per million of sodium nitrite to prevent the growth of food poisoning bacteria, specifically, *C. botulinum.* However, this represents only 4 percent of the amount of nitrite that our bodies are exposed to from sources such as drinking water or fresh vegetables. Diet contributes a total of about 13 percent of our average nitrite load; our bodies' salivary glands are responsible for the other 87 percent.

Manufacturers, well aware of the controversy surrounding preservatives, wish we all knew that the level of sodium nitrite they use is well below the natural level found in many vegetables. Beets, spinach, lettuce, broccoli, and radishes all contain 500 to 1900 parts per million of sodium nitrite.

The average (10 to the pound) hot dog contains 150 calories—about the same as three ounces of lean hamburger or tuna fish, or a cup of whole milk, a scoop of ice cream, one hard roll, or 10 french fried potatoes. A hot dog also has five to seven grams of protein, which is about the same as one egg, but with only about $\frac{1}{10}$th the amount of cholesterol.

As for fat, the average hot dog contains approximately 15 grams, compared with 17 grams in a three-ounce hamburger, and 34 grams of fat in the same amount of rib roast.

With all that nutrition, coupled with good flavor and ease of preparation, no wonder we eat so many of them.

How does Sara Lilygren from the American Meat Institute recommend serving hot dogs? "Try Bagel Barkers," is her suggestion. "You'll hear howls of amazement and delight as children watch the hot dogs magically curl into fanciful circles." By simply making 10 to 12 cuts down each wiener, the hot dogs will curl as they heat through. You'll find them on page 000.

Corn dogs are as American as apple pie. And like apple pie, every cook has his or her favorite way of preparing them. Two follow.

Saucy Corn Dogs

½ cup cornmeal
½ cup all-purpose flour
1 tsp. salt
½ tsp. oregano
dash garlic powder
½ cup milk
1 egg, beaten
2 T. vegetable oil
1 pound wieners
wooden skewers, as needed
½ cup grated Parmesan cheese
6 T. mayonnaise
2 tsp. mustard

Heat oil in a deep fat fryer to 375 degrees.

Combine cornmeal, flour, salt, oregano, and garlic powder. Add milk, egg, and oil; mix well. Lightly roll each wiener in seasoned flour, then coat evenly with batter; drain off excess.

Combine Parmesan cheese, mayonnaise, and mustard to make a thick sauce.

Fry corn dogs in hot deep fat until golden brown. Drain on absorbent paper. Insert skewers. Serve with sauce.
10 to 12 corn dogs
February 12, 1972

Prairie Dogs

4 to 6 crusty French rolls, 6 to 8
inches long, about 3 ounces each
1 can (10 to 11 ounces) condensed
cream-style soup (choose from
cream of tomato, chicken, potato,
celery, mushroom) or Cheddar soup
2 eggs, beaten
8 ounces shredded cheese (choose
Swiss, brick, Cheddar, hot pepper,
process American or mozzarella)
½ pound frankfurters
½ can fried onion rings (2.8 ounces)

Preheat oven to 400 degrees.

Slice off top one inch of each roll. Remove center, leaving shells with bottom and sides about three-quarters of an inch thick. Place shells in shallow baking pan. Bake for about six minutes, until golden.

Meanwhile, combine soup and eggs; stir in cheese. Fill each shell with soup mixture. Reduce heat to 375 degrees and return filled shells to oven for 25 minutes.

For S-shaped weiners, cut 10 crosswise slits (five on one side and five on the other) on each frankfurter, cutting about one-half through. (See diagram.)

Top each shell with one frankfurter and bake about six minutes longer, until frank is heated through and curled. Sprinkle each Prairie Dog with onion rings and return to oven for one to two minutes.

4 to 6 servings

National Hot Dog & Sausage Council

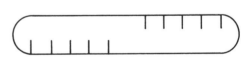

Bagel Barkers

4 frankfurters
2 bagels, split
8 slices process American cheese
4 slices pineapple

Make 10 to 12 cuts down one side of each frankfurter without cutting completely through, as shown on diagram. Heat franks in simmering water for about five minutes until curled. Place bagel halves, cut sides up, on baking sheet or toaster oven tray. Top each half with a slice of cheese. On one bagel half, top cheese slice with curled frankfurter; on the other half, place pineapple slice.

Bake until cheese is bubbly, about three minutes. Or broil, about five inches from heat, for two to three minutes.
4 servings
The National Hot Dog & Sausage Council

Baked Potato Salad and Frankfurters

1 egg
4 cups cooked, mashed potatoes
1 T. prepared mustard
2 T. vinegar
4 T. butter, melted
½ cup celery, chopped
¼ cup onion, chopped
salt and pepper, to taste
¾ pound frankfurters

Beat egg and add to potatoes. Add mustard, vinegar, butter, celery, onion, salt, and pepper and mix thoroughly. Pour into a casserole.

Place in a 350 degree oven and bake for 30 minutes. Top with frankfurters and bake for 10 minutes longer to heat franks.
4 servings
August 16, 1947

Frankfurters Deluxe

8 frankfurters
¼ pound liverwurst
⅓ cup mayonnaise
2 T. pickle, chopped
1 T. onion, chopped
8 slices bacon
8 toasted frankfurter buns

Split frankfurters lengthwise, cutting only part way through. Mash liverwurst; mix in mayonnaise, pickle and onion. Stuff into frankfurters. Press together and wrap each in a bacon slice. Fasten with toothpick.

Broil three inches from heat until bacon is crisp—eight minutes. Serve on toasted buns.
8 servings
October 8, 1966

Rice-Frankfurter Casserole

¼ cup salad oil
2 T. vinegar
2 T. prepared mustard
1½ tsp. salt
dash of pepper
4½ cups hot cooked rice (1½ cups rice cooked in 3 cups chicken broth)
2 hard cooked eggs, diced
1¼ cups ripe olives, sliced
1 cup celery, diced
¾ cup green onions, chopped
½ cup sour pickle, chopped
½ cup crisp bacon, crumbled
1 T. celery seed
1½ pounds frankfurters

Preheat oven to 450 degrees.

Blend together salad oil, vinegar, mustard, salt and pepper. Pour over hot rice; mix well. Add eggs, olives, celery, green onions, sour pickle, bacon, and celery seed; toss.

Cut frankfurters in half, stand them on end in a casserole to form a crown. Fill with rice mixture. Cover and bake for 15 minutes.
8 servings
January 4, 1964

Hot dogs are a traditional part of the American barbecue scene. But you can serve them in more unusual ways than the traditional plain hot-dog-with-relish. Here is an example.

Franks and Cabbage Wrap-Ups

1½ cups cabbage, shredded
2 T. green pepper, chopped
1 T. pimiento, chopped
½ cup American cheese, shredded
2 tsp. prepared mustard
3 T. mayonnaise
¼ tsp. Worcestershire sauce
salt, as needed
10 frank buns
butter, as needed
1 pound franks

Prepare barbecue grill.

Combine cabbage, green pepper, pimiento, cheese, mustard, mayonnaise, Worcestershire sauce, and salt. Cut the buns and spread with butter. Spoon about three tablespoons of the cabbage mixture on each bun. Cut franks in half, lengthwise. Place frank halves on top of cabbage. Add top of bun. Wrap each bun in aluminum foil.

Cook on grill for 25 to 30 minutes, or until warmed through.
10 filled buns
June 17, 1961

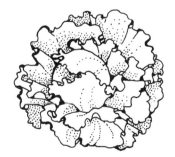

Frankfurters with Barbecue Sauce

1 pint canned tomatoes
½ small clove garlic, finely minced, or ½ tsp. garlic salt
1 onion, minced
1 carrot, minced
1 tsp. chili powder
¼ tsp. curry powder
¼ tsp. ground mustard
salt, to taste
cayenne, to taste
2 T. butter
1 dozen frankfurters

Simmer together tomatoes, garlic, onion, carrot, chili powder, curry powder, mustard, and salt for 30 minutes. Add cayenne. Melt butter in large heavy frying pan. Add frankfurters and saute to delicate brown. Spread prepared barbecue sauce over top.

Cover; cook over low heat about 25 minutes.
6 servings
January 5, 1946

Bean 'N' Frank Casserole

1 pound wieners, sliced
1 16-ounce can pork and beans
½ cup catsup
½ cup onion, chopped
3 T. brown sugar
1 8-ounce can refrigerated buttermilk or country style biscuits
1 cup cheddar cheese, shredded

Preheat oven to 400 degrees.

In medium saucepan, combine wieners, pork and beans, catsup, onion, and sugar. Bring to boil and simmer five minutes. Spoon hot meat mixture into ungreased eight or nine-inch square pan. Separate biscuit dough into 10 biscuits; arrange over hot meat mixture. Sprinkle with cheese.

Place in oven and bake for 20 to 25 minutes until biscuits are golden brown and no longer doughy.
5 to 6 servings
April, 1955

A meal-in-a-skillet does more than blend flavors—it saves work at dish-washing time. Prepare this in a heavy cast-iron skillet, or any other heavy skillet on your kitchen shelf.

Frankfurter Noodle Skillet

1 can tomatoes
1 can tomato paste
1 quart water
4 beef bouillon cubes
1 medium onion, chopped
2 cloves garlic
2 tsp. salt
⅛ tsp. pepper
¼ tsp. crushed oregano
¼ tsp. crushed basil
8 ounces medium egg noodles
    (about 4 cups)
¼ cup pimiento-stuffed olives, sliced
1 pound frankfurters, cut in 1-inch
    pieces
grated Parmesan cheese, as needed

Combine tomatoes, tomato paste, water, bouillon cubes, onion, garlic, salt, pepper, oregano, and basil in large skillet. Cover and cook over low heat for one hour, stirring occasionally. Discard garlic. Gradually add noodles; cover and cook 20 minutes, or until noodles are tender, stirring frequently. Mix in olives and frankfurters, heat thoroughly.

Serve with Parmesan cheese.
4 to 6 servings
November, 1969

Cheese Filled Franks

1 cup American cheese, shredded
⅓ cup pickle relish
1 tsp. prepared mustard
1 tsp. chili sauce
3 T. salad dressing
1 pound franks

Have cheese at room temperature. Mix cheese with a fork until it has a smooth, buttery consistency. Add pickle relish, mustard, chili sauce, and salad dressing. Mix ingredients well. Split franks almost through lengthwise. Fill franks with deviled cheese mixture.

Grill or broil until franks are hot and cheese is slightly melted.
6 servings
June 6, 1964

Hot Dog 'N' Eggwiches

1 hot dog, thinly sliced
2 tsp. butter
2 eggs
2 T. milk
¼ tsp. salt
dash pepper
2 buttered hot dog buns

Lightly brown hot dog in butter. Mix eggs, milk, salt, and pepper. Pour egg mixture over frankfurter. As mixture begins to set at bottom and sides, gently lift cooked portions with a spatula so that the thin, uncooked part can flow to the bottom. Avoid constant stirring.

Cook until eggs are thickened throughout but still moist, about three to five minutes. Spoon onto buns.
2 servings
September 22, 1954

Bacon and Frank Roll-Ups

6 frankfurters
6 hard rolls
½ cup sharp cheddar cheese, shredded
6 T. pickle relish
2 T. salad dressing
1 tsp. prepared mustard
1 T. chili sauce
¼ tsp. Worcestershire sauce
dash of salt and pepper
12 slices bacon

Preheat oven to 425 degrees.
Split frankfurters and rolls lengthwise. Combine cheese, relish, salad dressing, mustard, chili sauce, Worcestershire sauce, salt, and pepper. Spread cheese mixture on top half of rolls. Place split franks on bottom halves; sandwich together. Lay end of each roll in center of bacon strip, bringing ends of bacon up and across end of roll, spiral fashion. Wrap opposite end of roll with bacon in same manner; secure with wooden picks. Place on broiler rack.
Place in oven and bake 12 to 15 minutes, turning once to cook bacon thoroughly.
6 servings
March 25, 1967

Crunchy Cheese Franks

2½ cups bite size toasted corn cereal
½ cup cheddar cheese, shredded
5 frankfurters, finely chopped or ground
2 T. pickle relish
1 T. mustard
3 T. catsup
2 T. salad oil
¼ tsp. salt
4 hot dog buns, split

Crush cereal to make one cup. Mix thoroughly crumbs and cheese. Combine half of cereal mixture with chopped frankfurters, relish, mustard, catsup, oil, and salt. Spread frank mixture over bun halves. Sprinkle remaining crumb and cheese mixture over top. Place in shallow baking dish.
Bake in a 325 degree oven for 15 minutes or until crumbs are crisp.
8 open-faced sandwiches
October 3, 1964

In 1946, this recipe recommended, "A hearty meat salad as the main dish of a meal often is a welcome change from the usual meat 'n' gravy."

Frankfurter Supper Salad

2 cups frankfurters, thinly sliced
French dressing, as needed
2 cups cooked macaroni (1 cup uncooked)
1 cup celery, sliced
½ cup cucumbers, diced
2 hard cooked eggs, diced
3 T. green pepper, finely chopped
2 T. onion, grated
2 T. parsley chopped
½ tsp. celery seed
salad dressing or mayonnaise, as needed to moisten
salt and pepper, to taste
endive or chicory, radish, carrot slice and parsley, for garnish

Marinate frankfurters in French dressing for about one half hour. Add macaroni, celery, cucumbers, eggs, green pepper, onion, parsley, celery seed, and enough salad dressing or mayonnaise to moisten, and salt and pepper to suit the taste.
Serve in a salad bowl lined with endive or chicory and center with a radish rose, carrot slice, and parsley garnish.
4 servings
August 3, 1946

Here's a hearty salad that features vegetables, meat, and cheese, in addition to the usual greens. Practically a meal in itself, it is ideal to take along on a picnic.

Hearty Tossed Salad

Zesty French Dressing:

1 cup salad oil
½ cup tarragon vinegar
2 T. light corn syrup
2 T. catsup
1 T. lemon juice
1 tsp. Worcestershire sauce
1½ tsp. salt
½ tsp. paprika
½ tsp. dry mustard
1 clove garlic

Salad:

½ pound frankfurters, thinly sliced
1 T. salad oil
1 green pepper, cut in narrow strips
½ cup celery, thinly sliced
2 cooked potatoes, diced
½ cup onion, finely chopped
1 tsp. salt
¼ tsp. pepper
1 head lettuce, shredded
¼ cup Swiss or American cheese,
   cut in thin strips
2 tomatoes, cut in thin wedges

Prepare dressing by combining one cup salad oil, vinegar, corn syrup, catsup, lemon juice, Worcestershire, one and one-half teaspoons salt, paprika, mustard, and garlic in a bottle or a jar. Cover tightly and shake well. Chill several hours, then remove garlic. Shake thoroughly before serving.

This makes approximately one and a half cups dressing.

To prepare salad, saute sliced frankfurters in salad oil until lightly browned. Remove from heat. Combine frankfurters, green peppers, celery, potatoes, onions, salt, and pepper. Add one-half cup salad dressing. Cover and chill.

Just before serving add lettuce, cheese, and tomato wedges. Toss gently.
6 servings
August 5, 1967

Hot Spaghetti Salad

6 slices bacon
½ cup onion, chopped
2 T. all-purpose flour
2 T. brown sugar
2 tsp. salt
1 tsp. dry mustard
¾ cup water
¼ cup vinegar
1 pound frankfurters, sliced
8 ounces elbow spaghetti
4 tsp. salt
1 cup celery, diced
2 hard cooked eggs

Cut bacon into small pieces and fry in a large skillet until crisp. Remove bacon from skillet. Add onion to drippings and cook about five minutes, stirring occasionally. Stir in flour, brown sugar, two teaspoons salt, and mustard. Combine water and vinegar and add gradually to skillet. Cook until thickened, stirring constantly. Add frankfurters to sauce. Cover, reduce heat and cook for 15 minutes.

Meanwhile, cook spaghetti in one and one-half quarts boiling water. Add four teaspoons salt to water. Boil rapidly, stirring constantly, for two minutes. Cover, remove from heat and let stand for 10 minutes. Rinse spaghetti with hot water and drain well.

Combine spaghetti, eggs, bacon, and celery in a large bowl. Pour frankfurters and sauce over it and toss lightly. Serve warm.
May 2, 1959

Frankfurter-Macaroni Loaf

1 T. salt
3 quarts boiling water
2 cups elbow macaroni
6 frankfurters, cooked
½ cup carrots, grated
2 T. green pepper, chopped
½ tsp. salt
1 cup mayonnaise
1½ tsp. onion, finely minced
1½ T. prepared mustard
½ tsp. Worcestershire sauce
(optional)
crisp salad greens and hard-cooked
eggs, if desired

Add one tablespoon salt to rapidly boiling water. Gradually add macaroni so that water continues to boil. Cook uncovered, stirring occasionally until tender. Drain. Rinse with cold water, drain.

Reserve three frankfurters for garnish, chop the remaining frankfurters and mix well with macaroni. Add carrots, green pepper, one-half teaspoon salt, mayonnaise, onion, prepared mustard and Worcestershire sauce. Turn into a loaf pan and pack firmly. Chill.

Unmold and garnish with reserved frankfurters. Surround with crisp salad greens and hard-cooked eggs, if desired.
4 servings
November 7, 1959

Hot Dog Relish

5 cups cucumbers, peeled and
coarsely ground (remove seeds)
2 cups sweet green peppers, coarsely
ground
1 cup sweet red peppers, coarsely
ground
3 cups celery, coarsely ground
3 cups onions, coarsely ground
¾ cup salt
¾ cup water
1 quart white vinegar
3 cups sugar
2 T. mustard seed

Combine cucumbers, green peppers, red peppers, celery, onions, salt, and water. Let stand overnight. Drain well and transfer to large saucepan or kettle. Add vinegar, sugar, and mustard seed. Bring to a boil and simmer 10 minutes. Seal in canning jars. Process for 10 minutes in a simmering hot water bath.
6 to 8 pints
August 7, 1965

6

Lamb—Tips from the World's Second Oldest Profession

Most of what you read in this book comes from the eight generations of *Prairie Farmer* tips and recipes. For lamb, though, how about a change of pace? Shepherds think of themselves as belonging to the World's Second Oldest Profession—sheep have been providing us with food and fiber for at least 8,000 years so it's only fitting we use a recipe that goes back a little farther than the *Prairie Farmer*'s first appearance. The recipe you'll be reading about shortly pre-dates the beginning of recorded history. You'll probably never read it anywhere else.

You'll also have virtually no chance of ever using it—unless you can somehow work the information into your own game of Trivial Pursuit®. Except for the inconsequential little detail of its being of no practical use whatsoever, you may enjoy it a lot. But if you want to skip ahead to more practical information on selecting, storing, and serving lamb, turn to page 000.

To start with a question, how long do you think lamb can be kept out of the refrigerator during a summer heat wave and still be safe to eat?

Would you guess three hours? Twelve? Maybe a full day?

If you answered, "two weeks," Jean Etchamendy would give you a gold star. (On the other hand, your friendly neighborhood home economist would flunk you for that answer.) Jean is a shepherd and for months at a time he has no access to refrigeration. Nevertheless, he routinely keeps freshly butchered lamb in safe and edible condition for a full two weeks.

"With proper management," he says, "it's possible to store meat safely, without refrigeration, and in 36 years I've never lost a single piece."

He does it without preservatives and without drying it or turning it into jerky. Instead he feasts on fresh lamb that's more tender and flavorful than the lamb you'd find in the best restaurants. He does it using techniques that are as old as civilization and that are now becoming a lost art in our modern world.

He's happy to share his secrets, but his wife, Louisa, warns, "He can tell you how, but unless you know what you're doing, you can make a bad mistake. Even when experienced shepherds use these techniques, I wouldn't trust their results for more than ten days." Turning toward her husband, she adds "He's the only one *I'd* trust with unrefrigerated lamb."

Just how does he do it? "The first step," he answers, "is to slaughter the animal at dusk." There are two reasons for this. First, there won't be any flies out, and second, the temperature will be turning cooler. "Next, make sure that no water touches the carcass.

Some people recommend washing it, but the more moisture, the more risk of spoilage."

He goes on to explain that there's a fairly strict order for eating the meat. "In the morning," he says, "when it's cool, before the sun comes up, cut off the piece you'll be eating. The liver, heart, and sweetbreads are the first parts to use, since they're the most perishable. The next meals will be the head and neck."

But what happens with the meat that won't be eaten in the first couple of days? How does he keep it fresh? "At night," he answers, "mountain temperatures drop to forty degrees even if they're above 100 degrees during the day." (Forty degrees, by the way, is the usual temperature of most refrigerators.) "Before the sun comes up and takes the chill away, we put the food in a heavy twill 100 percent cotton meat sack. Then we wrap burlap around this, and put the whole package in the shade, covered with a sheepskin. Sheepskin is the best insulation there is, and with it, the meat inside stays just as cold as if it were in the refrigerator."

Every night and every day, Etchamendy goes through the process of chilling and then insulating the meat until it's used up. "The amazing thing," remarks his wife, "is that as the meat ages, it gets more and more tender."

The last cut Jean and his fellow shepherds eat is leg of lamb. It happens to last best, and because of the aging, it's the most tender and flavorful of all.

That's how shepherds have been preserving their meat for countless generations. But fortunately for us, we have some easier methods to keep our meat at its best, methods that food scientists and home economists can recommend. (No one recommends Jean Etchamendy's methods to you, unless you happen to have spent a dozen or so years mastering the art.)

For home storage of lamb, put it in the coldest part of your refrigerator as soon after buying it as you can. You can store it in its original wrapping and for most cuts, it should maintain its quality for three to five days. Ground lamb is an exception, however, and you should either plan to use it within a day or two, or you should freeze it. Cooked lamb can be refrigerated, wrapped or covered, for four to five days. Try to get it into the refrigerator within an hour after cooking.

For longer storage, freeze the meat. To keep the best quality, guard against freezer burn by rewrapping or over-wrapping the meat closely and sealing tightly in moisture-proof wrap such as freezer paper, aluminum foil, or heavy plastic wrap. "You're doing this," explains Becky Berg, from the National Livestock and Meat Board, "to keep the moisture in. Any time you freeze meat you gradually lose some of the moisture and the longer it's frozen the more moisture you're losing. That's one reason why it's really important to wrap it well."

Frozen lamb should last in good condition for six to nine months, with the exception of ground lamb or cooked lamb, which should not be frozen for much longer than three or four months. Incidentally, it's not that your meat is bad after the recommended storage time; it's just that it will be getting drier and less palatable, which means you won't be getting the most for your money.

Frozen lamb can be defrosted in the refrigerator or in the microwave oven on low power. Defrosting at room temperature isn't recommended since spoilage organisms may grow at these temperatures.

Roasting Schedule
Leg of Lamb

Meats roasted from refrigerator temperature in an open pan in a 325-degree oven.

Weight	Approximate Roasting Time	Internal Temperature
6 pounds	3 hours	160 degrees (medium)
	3½ hours	170 degrees (well done)
8 pounds	4 hours	160 degrees (medium)
	4½ hours	170 degrees (well done)

February 13, 1964

Lamb can also be defrosted successfully during cooking—something worthwhile knowing on days when you're in a hurry or have unexpected guests. To broil frozen lamb chops, place farther from the heat and broil one and a half to two times the required time for unfrozen chops. Frozen cuts to be braised, such as shanks or neck slices, will require about the same time as comparable defrosted cuts.

When it comes to cooking the lamb, you'll find recipes here for old familiar dishes, and some new combinations that you may never have considered. But one recipe that the shepherds who taught Jean Etchamendy how to preserve lamb never dreamed of, is microwaved lamb.

For the most tender, juicy, and flavorful results, use medium-low power, approximately 30 percent or 200 watts, and follow these steps:

- Place roast on rack in microwave-safe dish or roaster.
- Do not add liquid.
- Place waxed paper over top of roast.
- Invert roast during cooking, starting with the fat side down, and turning later so the fat side is up.
- Rotate dish during cooking, for uniformity of doneness.

- Shield specific areas such as edges of ends, with small pieces of foil.
- Use a quick recovery or regular meat thermometer for determining doneness after you've removed the roast from the oven.
- Allow about 10 minutes resting time out of the oven before carving, and remember, the internal temperature of the roast will rise approximately five degrees during this time. If you want rare lamb, remove the roast at 135 degrees internal temperature, and it will reach 140 degrees, or rare, at the end of the resting period. For medium lamb, remove it at 155 degrees so it can come to 160 degrees, or medium done, and for well-done, remove your roast at 165 degrees and you'll find that ten minutes later, the internal temperature will be 170 degrees, or well done.

Try lamb soon. As Stan Kooyumjian, from the American Lamb Council says, "Because of improved genetics and better farm and flock management, it's leaner and more nutritious than ever before. A three-ounce serving of cooked lean American lamb has an average of only 176 calories, making it perfect for today's active and healthful lifestyles."

Stuffed Lamb Chops—Mushroom Dressing

3 lamb shoulder chops, 1½ to
    2-inches thick
2 cups fine dry bread crumbs
½ cup mushrooms, chopped
1 small onion, grated
salt and pepper, to taste
2 T. bacon drippings or butter
½ cup meat broth or mushroom
    stock

Remove shoulder bones from chops and cut a pocket each way from the center of the cavity. Combine bread crumbs with mushrooms and onion. Season with salt and pepper and moisten with bacon drippings and meat broth or mushroom stock. Fill cavity in chops with dressing. Place in a baking pan and cook covered in a 300-degree oven until done, about one and one-half hours. Remove cover for last 15 minutes to brown chops.
3 servings
January 6, 1962

Let a jelly-glazed roast leg of lamb be your family feast. Choose either a whole leg or half for a delicious meal at any time during the year.

Jelly-Glazed Roast Leg of Lamb

leg of lamb
salt and pepper, as needed to season
½ cup plum jelly
1 cup hot water

Place the meat, fat side up, on a rack in a shallow roasting pan. Season with salt and pepper. Insert a meat thermometer into the thickest part of the meat, making sure the point does not rest on fat or bone. Place in a 325-degree oven and allow 30 to 35 minutes per pound, and an internal temperature of 160 degrees for a medium-done roast. Thirty minutes before roast is done, combine plum jelly and water. Pour over roast and baste with this mixture at 10-minute intervals.
January 6, 1962

118

Lamb En Brochette

2 pounds lamb shoulder, cut into
    1-inch cubes
4 small onions, sliced
8 mushroom caps
8 slices bacon
salt and pepper, as needed to season

Place lamb cubes on eight skewers, alternately with onion slices. Put a mushroom cap on each end. Wrap lengthwise with bacon slices. Place meat in broiler oven three inches from heat source. When one side is browned, season and turn. Let brown on all sides. These require about 15 minutes for broiling.
4 servings
January 6, 1962

Lamb Fricassee

2 T. salad oil
2 pounds lamb shoulder, cut in
    2-inch cubes
1½ cups water
1½ cups carrots, sliced
3 medium-sized onions, sliced
2 tsp. salt
½ tsp. pepper
1 tsp. dried mint flakes
1½ T. all-purpose flour
1½ T. cold water
hot cooked rice, as needed for 4
    servings

Heat oil; add lamb and cook until lightly browned on all sides. Drain off drippings. Add one and one-half cups water, carrots, onions, salt, pepper, and mint. Cover and cook over low heat two hours. Blend flour and one and one-half tablespoons water; add to lamb mixture. Stir constantly over low heat until thickened. Serve over rice.
4 servings
March 1, 1958

Get out your slow cooker (or improvise with a very slow oven) and try an easy, flavorful recipe for lamb.

Teriyaki Lamb

4 pounds rolled shoulder of lamb
¾ cup hot water
2 tsp. prepared mustard
2 tsp. beef-flavored instant bouillon
¼ cup soy sauce
2 cloves garlic, minced
3 T. apple, mint, cherry, or currant
*   jelly*
2 T. lemon juice
cooked rice, as needed for 8
*   servings*

Remove as much cartilage and fat from lamb as possible. Line baking pan or dish with aluminum foil. Place lamb on foil. Broil about four inches from source of heat, turning to brown all sides. Place lamb in slow cooker. In small mixing bowl, combine water, mustard, bouillon, soy sauce, garlic, jelly, and lemon juice. Pour over meat. Cover and cook about eight hours on low, or on high for four hours.

Thinly slice lamb and serve over cooked rice with thickened or unthickened liquids left from cooking.
8 servings
November 27, 1976

This is a crowd pleaser that can be prepared ahead of time and frozen. The recipe makes enough for 25 servings, or plenty to freeze for use later. As you prepare to freeze, remember that since liquid expands as it freezes, allow ample head space when packing liquid and semi-liquid foods. Most freezer containers have a mark or line to show how much head space to leave. For a tall, straight, or slightly flared container and for bags, one-half inch is generally recommended for pints and one inch for quarts. For low, broad containers less head space is needed, about one-quarter inch for pints and one-half inch for quarts. To assure good closure, keep sealing edges free from moisture or food. When packaging foods with freezer sheet material, wrap them as tightly as possible.

Lamb Pie

3 pounds boneless lamb (or beef),
*   cut into 1-inch cubes*
1 quart water
1 T. salt
1½ cups chopped celery
3 cups cubed potatoes
3½ cups quartered onions
½ cup peas, fresh or frozen
½ cup sifted all-purpose flour
pastry, to cover pie(s)

Brown lamb in its own fat. Add water and one-half of the salt. Simmer until meat is almost tender. Add celery, potatoes, onions, peas, and the remaining salt. Simmer until vegetables are almost tender. Drain the broth from the meat and vegetables and add water to the broth, if needed, to make one quart. Add a little of the broth to the flour and stir until smooth. Slowly add the mixture to the rest of the broth and cook until thickened, stirring constantly. Combine the thickened broth with the meat and vegetables. Cool meat mixture quickly. Place in ovenproof baking dish(es) and top with pastry. Wrap in freezer packaging material. Or package in freezer containers, leaving head space. Seal and freeze.

To prepare for serving, bake meat pies frozen with pastry topping at 400 degrees about 45 minutes for pints, one hour for quarts, or until stew is piping hot and crust is golden brown. If stew is frozen without pastry topping, transfer it to an oiled baking dish and place in hot oven. After stew is almost heated through (about 30 minutes to an hour), top with pastry crust. Bake until crust is golden brown.
25 servings
August 15, 1964

A good recipe for the microwave.

Holiday Leg of Lamb

5 to 9-pound leg of lamb
1 cup jellied cranberry sauce
¼ cup Russian salad dressing
2 T. lemon juice
1 tsp. ground coriander
½ cup white wine

Dressing:

4 cups coarsely crumbled dried bread
  (combine white, wheat, or corn
  bread)
½ tsp. celery salt
¼ tsp. dried thyme
¼ tsp. ground coriander
1 tsp. salt
1 egg
2 cups chicken broth
¼ cup butter, melted

Place lamb, fat side up, on a microwave roasting rack in a shallow, 12x8-inch casserole. In a four-cup measuring cup or bowl combine cranberry sauce, salad dressing, lemon juice, one teaspoon coriander, and wine. Cover with waxed paper. Microwave at HIGH two to three minutes, or until well heated. Stir to combine well. Thoroughly brush surface of lamb with heated sauce. Cover lamb with waxed paper. Microwave at MEDIUM nine to 10 minutes per pound for medium-rare (145 degrees), 10 to 11 minutes per pound for medium (160 degrees) or 11 to 12 minutes per pound for well-done (170 degrees). Brush lamb with sauce several times during roasting. Remove lamb from microwave oven. Allow to stand, covered, 10 to 15 minutes before serving.

Meanwhile, prepare dressing. In a large bowl, combine bread crumbs, celery salt, thyme, one-quarter teaspoon coriander, and salt. Stir or toss to mix well. In a medium bowl, beat egg. Stir in broth and butter. Combine and stir into bread mixture. Mix well. Pour mixture into a nine-inch round microwave casserole. Cover with waxed paper. Microwave at HIGH 9 to 10 minutes. Let stand, covered, three to five minutes.

Slice lamb and serve with dressing and remaining sauce.
6 to 8 servings
Lamb Education Center

Cooking a leg of lamb on an electric rotisserie is easy, and the result is delicious.

Roast Leg of Lamb on a Spit

4 to 6 pound leg of lamb
salt, pepper, and all-purpose flour,
  as needed to season roast
2 cloves garlic, slivered
½ cup tomato catsup
¼ cup salad oil
3 T. bottled meat sauce
1 T. sugar
1 tsp. salt
1 T. instant minced onion
2 T. vinegar

Wipe leg of lamb with damp cloth; rub with mixture of salt, pepper, and flour. Use sharp pointed knife to make deep slits all over meat; insert sliver of garlic in each one. Insert a meat thermometer in the thickest part of the leg, being careful not to touch the bone. Balance lamb on spit, allowing meat to revolve as close to coil as possible. Combine catsup, salad oil, meat sauce, sugar, salt, onion, and vinegar and brush over lamb at frequent intervals. Roast about three hours, or until 160 degrees by meat thermometer (meat will be slightly pink). If well done roast is desired, roast an additional 45 minutes.
4 to 6 servings
August 15, 1964

Andalusian Lamb Mechada

1 tsp. salt
1 T. parsley, minced
⅛ tsp. black pepper
1 small clove of garlic, crushed
2 T. olive oil
1 large, thin slice cooked ham (2 ounces boiled ham), cut into ¼x1-inch slivers
1 6-pound leg of lamb

Preheat oven to 400 degrees.

Mix salt, parsley, pepper, garlic, and oil; roll ham slivers in mixture. Cut deep gashes in leg of lamb with thin bladed sharp knife. Insert seasoned ham slivers in gashes. Place in roasting pan. Insert a meat thermometer in the thickest part of the leg, being careful not to touch the bone. Roast in oven for one and one-half hours for rare (meat thermometer will register 140 degrees); one and three-quarters to two hours for medium rare (155 degrees on meat thermometer). Or roast in a 450-degree oven for 10 minutes, then reduce to a 325-degree oven; continue roasting two hours for rare, two and one-quarter to two and one-half hours for medium rare.
6 to 8 servings
February 15, 1964

Coated Leg of Lamb

1 (5 to 6 pound) leg of lamb
1¼ cups corn cereal, crushed
1 T. seasoned salt
¼ tsp. ground rosemary
½ cup sherry or fruit juice

Remove skin from lamb. Insert a meat thermometer in the thickest part of the leg, being careful not to touch the bone. Place lamb on rack in shallow pan. Roast three to three and one-half hours or to 170 degrees on meat thermometer.

Combine cereal, salt, rosemary, and sherry or fruit juice. Mix well. Remove lamb from oven about 30 minutes before it is done. Spread coating in a thin layer. Roast until thermometer registers well done.
6 servings
February 15, 1964

This attractive rolled roast is easy and tasty. For variety, you might like to spread the lamb breast with any savory bread dressing, then proceed as directed below.

Lamb Pin-Wheel Roll

boned lamb breast
¾ pound bulk pork sausage
salt and pepper, to taste
3 T. lard
½ cup water

Spread lamb breast with sausage, roll and tie or skewer into shape. Season with salt and pepper. Brown well on all sides in hot lard. Add water. Cover tightly and reduce temperature. Simmer for one and one-half hours.
February 13, 1964

Spicy Lamb Pilaf

3 T. onion, chopped
1 T. shortening
2 cups cooked lamb, cubed
1 can (4½ ounces) mushrooms, drained; reserve liquid
2 cups water
1 cup rice
½ cup chili sauce
1 clove garlic, crushed
1½ tsp. salt
½ tsp. black pepper

Cook onion in shortening until transparent. Add cooked lamb, liquid from mushrooms, water, rice, chili sauce, garlic, salt, and pepper. Simmer 45 to 60 minutes or until rice is tender. Add mushrooms and cook an additional five minutes.
4 to 6 servings
February 15, 1964

California Lamb Casserole

2 T. butter or margarine
3 T. all-purpose flour
1 tsp. salt
1¼ cups milk
2 tsp. prepared mustard
1½ cups cooked lamb, cubed
½ cup processed American cheese,
  cubed
2 T. pimiento, chopped
1½ cups cooked rice
1 tsp. mint leaves, crumbled
½ cup ripe olives, chopped

Preheat oven to 425 degrees.

Melt butter in skillet and blend in flour and salt. Gradually add the milk, stirring constantly until sauce is thickened. Stir in mustard. Place the lamb, cheese, pimiento, rice, mint leaves, and olives in a one-quart casserole. Fold in the sauce.

Bake for 20 minutes. Serve hot.
4 to 6 servings
February 15, 1964

East Indian Lamb Curry

1½ pounds boned lamb shoulder,
  cubed
3 T. butter
1 cup onion, chopped
1 clove garlic, minced
2 tsp. curry powder, or more to taste*
1 can (20 ounces) chunk pineapple
  in juice, drained, reserving juice
¾ cup water
1½ tsp. salt
2 tsp. cornstarch
hot cooked rice, as needed for 4
  servings
peanuts, chopped, as desired
raisins, as desired
green onion, chopped, as desired
hard cooked eggs, chopped, as desired

Brown lamb well in butter. Remove. Saute onion, garlic, and curry powder until onion is soft. Return lamb to skillet. Stir in reserved pineapple juice, water, and salt. Cover, simmer 30 minutes. Combine small amount of pan juices with cornstarch. Stir back into pan juices. Cook, stirring constantly, until mixture boils and thickens. Stir in pineapple until heated through.

Serve over rice. Pass peanuts, raisins, green onion, and eggs as condiments.

*This makes a mild curry. Use two tablespoons for a pungent curry.
4 servings
November 27, 1976

Cheesy Lamb Skillet

3 pounds lamb cubes, 1-inch size
3 T. shortening
2 cans (10¾ ounces each) condensed
  cheddar cheese soup
1 cup onion, chopped
½ cup canned tomatoes, drained
  and chopped
2 medium cloves garlic, minced
¼ tsp. rosemary leaves, crushed
2 pounds fresh peas, shelled, Or
  comparable amount of frozen peas
1 pound medium mushrooms,
  quartered

In large heavy pan, brown lamb in shortening; pour off fat. Stir in soup, onion, tomatoes, garlic, and rosemary. Cover, cook over low heat for 40 minutes. Stir now and then. Add peas and mushrooms. Cook 20 minutes longer or until lamb is tender. Stir now and then. Uncover, cook to desired sauce consistency.
8 servings
April 1, 1972

Armenian Casserole

1 pound ground lamb
2 T. oil
1 (1 pound) can solid pack tomatoes
1 (1 pound) can green beans, undrained
½ cup raw rice
2 T. instant minced onion
⅛ tsp. garlic powder
½ tsp. dry mustard
1 tsp. Worcestershire sauce
1 T. sugar
1½ tsp. salt
⅛ tsp. pepper

Brown lamb in hot oil. Combine lamb with tomatoes, green beans, rice, onion, garlic powder, mustard, Worcestershire sauce, sugar, salt, and pepper in a one and one-half quart casserole. Cover and bake in a 350-degree oven, one hour, or until rice is tender.
5 to 6 servings
November 3, 1962

Jelly Glazed Lamb Chops

4 arm or blade chops, cut ¾ to
1-inch thick
3 T. all-purpose flour
1 tsp. salt
¼ tsp. pepper
1½ tsp. dry mustard
3 T. lard or drippings
¼ cup apple, currant, or mint jelly
¼ cup lemon juice
1 T. Worcestershire sauce

Combine flour, salt, pepper, and mustard. Dredge lamb chops in seasoned flour. Brown in lard or drippings. Cover tightly and cook slowly 30 minutes, turning occasionally. Pour off drippings.

Mix jelly, lemon juice, and Worcestershire sauce and pour over chops. Cover and continue to cook, turning occasionally until chops are coated in jelly glaze, approximately 20 minutes.
4 servings
October 20, 1962

Lamb Roll with Vegetables

5 to 6 pound shoulder of lamb
1 clove garlic, cut in slivers
1 envelope onion soup mix
1 envelope cream of mushroom soup
½ cup water
1 cup potatoes, cubed
1 cup carrots, cubed
1 cup onion, chopped
all-purpose flour, as needed to make
gravy

Have the lamb boned and rolled at the market, after the excess fat is trimmed off. Place a large sheet of heavy duty aluminum in a shallow pan and place the lamb in the center. Insert garlic slivers in little pockets cut in the meat. Combine the two packages of soup with water and spread over lamb. Close the foil, place in a 350-degree oven and roast for three hours.

About an hour and a quarter before the lamb is finished, open the foil and add the vegetables. To serve, open foil at one end and pour juices into a saucepan. Skim off excess fat and thicken with flour for gravy.
8 servings
February 1, 1964

Preparing the food for the family is a matter of grave importance, and while we do not believe in a woman spending valuable time in getting up rich or indigestible pastry and compounds, or too many fancy desserts, we do think it the wife's duty to see that the food for the household is pure, wholesome and well cooked, and that the husband has his favorite dish often enough, at least to not forget how it tastes.
March 28, 1901

Lamb Deluxe

2 pounds boneless lamb, cut in
   2-inch pieces
2 T. drippings
½ tsp. salt
½ tsp. dill seed
1½ cups water
1 cup celery, sliced into ½-inch pieces
1 cup carrots, thinly sliced
2 T. all-purpose flour
1 cup sour cream

Brown lamb in lard or drippings. Pour off drippings. Add salt, dill seed, and one cup water. Cover tightly and simmer for one hour. Add celery and carrots. Cover and continue cooking for 30 minutes or until meat and vegetables are done. Combine flour and remaining water for gravy. Add to meat and cook until thickened. Add sour cream and cook just until heated through.
4 to 6 servings
January 6, 1962

Individual Lamb Pies

3 T. butter
1 cup plus 3 T. all-purpose flour
1½ cups lamb stock or bouillon
1½ tsp. salt
¼ tsp. pepper
¼ tsp. rosemary
2 cups cooked lamb, diced
1½ cups cooked carrots, sliced
1½ cups cooked peas
⅓ cup shortening
¼ cup milk

Preheat oven to 450 degrees.
   Melt butter; add three tablespoons flour and blend. Gradually add stock or bouillon and cook over low heat, stirring constantly, until thickened. Add one teaspoon salt, pepper, rosemary, lamb, carrots, and peas; mix well. Turn into four individual baking dishes. Combine one cup flour and one-half teaspoon salt. Cut in shortening. Add milk and mix lightly; press into ball; roll out on lightly floured board to one-eighth-inch thickness. Cut into four rounds; place on lamb mixture. Seal edges; prick tops. Bake for 15 minutes or until lightly browned.
4 servings
December 19, 1964

Lamb Croquette

¼ cup butter
¼ cup all-purpose flour
1 cup milk
2 cups cooked lamb, ground
1 tsp. salt
⅛ tsp. pepper
⅛ tsp. marjoram
½ tsp. Worcestershire sauce
½ cup carrot, grated
2 tsp. onion, grated
1 egg, beaten
⅓ cup corn meal
¼ cup lard or drippings

Melt butter; blend in flour. Add milk and cook, stirring constantly, until sauce is thick. Add lamb, salt, pepper, marjoram, Worcestershire sauce, carrot, and onion. Mix well. Chill. Shape mixture into eight oblong croquettes; dip in beaten egg; roll in corn meal. Brown slowly on all sides in melted lard or drippings.
4 servings
August 12, 1967

Don't think that outdoor cooking is limited to steaks and hot dogs. Lamb, too, develops a wonderful flavor when cooked over a charcoal grill.

Sirloin Lamb Chops En Brochette

1 package (1 ounce) dry onion gravy
* mix*
½ cup salad oil
½ cup water
⅓ cup vinegar
2 T. sugar
1 tsp. hickory smoked salt
6 sirloin lamb chops, 1½- to
* 2-inches thick*
6 ears of corn, each cut in 4 pieces
6 plum tomatoes or 2 regular
* tomatoes, each cut into 6 wedges*
2 green peppers, each cut in 6 pieces

Mix together gravy mix, oil, water, vinegar, sugar, and smoked salt. Pour over lamb; marinate several hours or overnight, turning now and then. Place chops on skewers. Grill five to six inches from coals, 12 to 15 minutes per side, or until done as desired. Brush often with marinade. Place vegetables alternately on skewers, grill 10 to 15 minutes, or until done, brushing with marinade often.
6 servings
June 1, 1968

Lamb Patties

2 cups cooked lamb, ground
½ tsp. salt
1 tsp. onion, minced
1 tsp. vinegar
1 egg
½ cup thick gravy or white sauce
1 T. parsley, chopped
¼ cup fine cracker or bread crumbs
½ cup drippings
mint jelly, as desired

Combine lamb, salt, onion, vinegar, egg, gravy, and parsley. Shape into patties one inch thick. Roll in cracker crumbs. Pan brown in hot drippings. Drain on soft paper.
    Serve with mint jelly.
4 servings
February 17, 1968

Lamb in Patty Shells

¼ cup scallions, sliced
¼ pound mushrooms, sliced
¼ cup butter
¼ cup all-purpose flour
1½ tsp. salt
¼ tsp. rosemary leaves
⅛ tsp. pepper
¾ cup milk
1 cup light cream
2 cups cooked lamb, diced
2 T. pimiento, diced
1 package frozen patty shells, prepared

Saute scallions and mushrooms in butter until tender. Stir in flour, salt, rosemary leaves, and pepper. Gradually add milk and cream; cook, stirring constantly until sauce thickens and boils. Add lamb and pimiento; mix and heat thoroughly. Spoon into hot patty shells. Garnish as desired.
6 servings
February 8, 1969

Barbecued Lamb Shanks

4 lamb shanks
2 T. lard
1 cup onions, sliced
1 cup catsup
1 cup water
2 tsp. salt
2 T. Worcestershire sauce
½ cup vinegar
¼ cup brown sugar
2 tsp. dry mustard

Brown shanks in hot lard in a heavy kettle. Combine onions, catsup, water, salt, Worcestershire sauce, vinegar, brown sugar, and mustard. Add onions and catsup mixture to shanks; cover and cook over low heat or in a 325-degree oven until tender, one and one-half to two hours. Uncover and continue cooking for 15 minutes.
4 servings
April 16, 1966

Lamb Chops with Blue Cheese Topping

6 lamb shoulder chops, cut ¾ to
*   1-inch thick*
½ cup American blue cheese, crumbled
2 T. green onion, minced
⅛ tsp. salt
dash pepper
¼ cup softened butter

Place chops on broiler rack. Insert broiler pan and rack so the top of the chops is three inches from the heat. Broil first side until browned, about eight minutes. Turn and brown second side about four minutes. Combine blue cheese, onion, salt, pepper, and butter. Spread about two tablespoons of cheese mixture evenly over each chop. Continue broiling two minutes or until cheese is lightly browned.
6 servings
April 16, 1966

One for the rotisserie.

Lamb Shoulder Roast

1 can (8 ounces) tomato sauce
1 tsp. garlic salt
1 tsp. onion salt
2 tsp. Worcestershire sauce
¼ tsp. pepper
¼ cup molasses (or honey)
1 5- to 6-pound shoulder of lamb,
*   boned, rolled, and tied*

Combine tomato sauce, garlic salt, onion salt, Worcestershire sauce, pepper, and molasses; mix well. Insert a meat thermometer in thickest part of meat. Place lamb on spit. Brush lamb with molasses mixture. Cook on rotisserie or on outdoor grill two hours or until meat thermometer registers 160-170 degrees (depending upon desired degree of doneness). Brush lamb frequently with molasses mixture during cooking period.
6 to 8 servings
April 16, 1966

Lamb-Stuffed Green Peppers

3 large green peppers
1 pound ground lamb
1 cup onion, chopped
1 clove garlic, minced
1 T. dried mint leaves, crumbled
2 tsp. salt
2 beef bouillon cubes
1 cup boiling water
1½ cups dry bread crumbs
½ cup currants or raisins
½ cup nuts, chopped
1 medium tomato, cut in 6 wedges

Cut peppers in half, remove seeds, and stems. Cook in boiling, salted water until almost tender, about five minutes. Drain and arrange hollow side up in nine-inch square baking dish. Combine lamb, onion, garlic, mint leaves, and salt in skillet and cook until lamb is browned and onion is tender. Dissolve bouillon cubes in water and stir into lamb mixture.

Remove lamb from heat and stir in bread crumbs, currants or raisins, and nuts. Stuff pepper halves with lamb mixture. Press tomato wedge into center of each stuffed pepper half. Cover pan with lid or aluminum foil. Bake in a 350-degree oven for 45 minutes; uncover and bake an additional 15 minutes.
6 servings
April 16, 1966

Lamb Chops with Minted Pea Stuffing

1½ quarts soft bread cubes
½ tsp. salt
½ tsp. savory
2 tsp. dried mint leaves
¼ cup butter, melted
1 package (10 ounces) frozen peas
6 lamb chops or patties

Combine bread cubes, salt, savory, mint leaves, and butter and mix with frozen peas. Place in a baking dish and arrange lamb chops or patties on top. Bake in a 350-degree oven for 30 minutes.
6 servings
April 16, 1966

Irish stew is a wonderfully hearty meal for any time of the year. Serve a warm loaf of Irish Soda bread and butter with it, along with a crisp salad, and you'll have a complete meal.

Irish Stew

2 pounds boneless lamb
3 T. all-purpose flour
1½ tsp. salt
¼ tsp. pepper
3 T. lard or drippings
¼ tsp. marjoram
1 bay leaf
1 T. parsley, chopped
12 small white onions
4 white turnips, quartered
4 carrots, cut in 2-inch pieces
3 celery stalks, cut in 2-inch pieces

Cut lamb in 1½-inch cubes, dredge in flour seasoned with salt and pepper. Brown meat in lard; pour off drippings. Add marjoram, bay leaf, parsley, and enough water to cover meat. Cover tightly; simmer one and one-half hours. Add onions, turnips, carrots, and celery; continue cooking about 30 minutes or until vegetables are done. Discard bay leaf. Thicken cooking liquid with flour for gravy, if desired.
4 to 6 servings

Irish Soda Bread

3 cups sifted all-purpose flour
⅔ cup sugar
1 T. baking powder
1 tsp. baking soda
1 tsp. salt
1½ cups dark seedless raisins
2 eggs, beaten
1¾ to 2 cups buttermilk
2 T. melted shortening

Sift together into a large bowl the flour, sugar, baking powder, baking soda, and salt. Stir in raisins. Combine eggs, buttermilk, and shortening. Add liquid mixture to dry ingredients; mix only until flour is moistened. Turn batter into a greased 9½ by 5¼-inch loaf pan.

Bake in a 350 degree oven for about one hour. Remove from pan immediately. Allow to cool thoroughly before slicing.
1 loaf
March 9, 1968

Leg of Lamb with Apricot Stuffing

1⅓ cups packaged precooked rice
1⅓ cups dried apricots, sliced
⅔ cup celery, chopped
¼ cup parsley, chopped
2 tsp. salt
¼ tsp. pepper
½ tsp. instant minced onion
½ tsp. rosemary leaves, crushed
1 cup chicken bouillon
5 pound boned leg of lamb

Mix together rice, apricots, celery, parsley, salt and pepper, onion, rosemary, and bouillon; let stand 10 minutes for liquid to absorb. Stuff lamb with one-half the mixture; wrap remainder in aluminum foil. Secure lamb with string and skewers. Place on rack in shallow roasting pan. Insert meat thermometer in the thickest part of the meat.

Bake in a 325-degree oven for three hours, or until meat thermometer registers 160 degrees for medium doneness. Bake foil wrapped stuffing for last hour.

Serve lamb on platter with extra stuffing. Prepare gravy, if desired.
8 to 10 servings
January 13, 1968

7

America Can *Lean* on Pork

"A pork chop a day keeps the psychiatrist away!"

Iowa Organization of Women for Agriculture Secretary, Sandy Greiner, is only partly joking when she says this. As a pork producer, she knows that one of pork's nutritional strong points is that it contains three times as much vitamin B1 (thiamine) as other meats. It is this vitamin that's crucial for keeping our nervous systems healthy. It also helps prevent irritability.

"The B vitamins," she points out, "can't be stored in the body, so we have to get a new supply each day."

Besides the possibility of keeping psychiatrists at bay, pork has other virtues. "Pork is much leaner than it has been in the past," she emphasizes. "Everyone is calorie conscious today, and I wish they all knew that pork has less than half the fat that it did 30 years ago. A three-ounce serving of cooked pork has only 197 calories, and that's only about 8 percent of the average daily caloric intake of an adult male."

She goes on to point out that the cholesterol level of pork, at 77 milligrams per three-ounce serving, is just about the same amount as in three ounces of dark meat roast chicken without the skin. It's less than half the cholesterol of a similar serving of shrimp.

But how much cholesterol is 77 milligrams? The USDA estimates that the average daily U.S. consumption is about 500 milligrams. The American Health Association recommends a diet of 300 milligrams of dietary cholesterol a day. The cholesterol in a three-ounce serving of pork amounts to only 26 percent of this recommendation.

Today's lean pork is quite different from the pork grandmother used to cook. Thirty years ago, animals were grown for lard as well as meat, and often were brought to market at a big, fat 1,000 pound weight. Today's pork weighs closer to 220 pounds. "In fact," points out Greiner, "if we bring an overweight animal to the packer, we'll get docked, that is, we won't get as good a price for it. The market place is telling us to select our breeding stock from the leanest animals with the smallest amount of fat possible."

We ased Sandy Greiner her favorite way to fix pork. "If it were a Sunday evening and I were having family or friends over, I'd probably grill some center-cut pork chops, each about an inch and a half thick. I'd grill them very slowly over medium heat and I wouldn't salt the meat until I was ready to serve it. But I would baste it now and then with Italian dressing, to give it a special, different flavor. The rest of the menu would be baked potatoes, tossed salad, French bread and home-made ice cream."

Another favorite, if there's a big crowd expected, is ham balls. "Take one and a half pounds of hamburger and an equal amount of ground ham and mix it up with two eggs and two cups of crushed graham crackers. Then add one-half cup of milk. Mix it like meatloaf and then form the mixture into meatballs, each one bigger than a golf ball, but smaller than a baseball. Those on low sodium diets can substi-tute lean ground pork for the ground ham. You do give up some flavor, but this, too, is very good.

"Now, make a sauce using two cans of condensed tomato soup and a cup of brown sugar. Do not add water. Microwave until bubbling, then pour over the ham balls, spooning the sauce carefully, if necessary, to coat each lit-tle ball. Then bake for one hour and fifteen minutes at 375 degrees. You can prepare them ahead of time and bake just before serving. Guests always love them."

Try Sandy Greiner's favorite recipes, or some of the others you'll find in this chapter. And when you do, think of all the vitamin B1 you're getting and how good it is for maintaining a healthy ner-vous system. Then, make Sandy happy by remembering her favorite saying, the one about "A pork chop a day keeps the psychiatrist away!"

There's more than one way to roast a pig— many, in fact. In the first recipe below, we'll show you how to stuff and roast a whole pig in the oven. Directions in the second recipe show you how to cook the pig out-of-doors.

Roast Suckling Pig

1 suckling pig, dressed, about 10 to 15 pounds

Onion stuffing:

8 cups bread crumbs
1 cup butter or margarine, melted
1 tsp. salt
¼ tsp. pepper
1 dozen onions
1 egg, slightly beaten
melted butter, as needed
salt and all-purpose flour, as needed
2 cups water, boiling

Stuff dressed pig with onion stuffing pre-pared as follows: Combine crumbs, butter or margarine, salt and pepper. Parboil onions 10 minutes; drain and chop fine. Add to crumb mixture with egg. After pig is stuffed, skewer legs in position, hind legs backward, forelegs forward. Make four parallel gashes, three inches long, through skin on each side of backbone. Place on rack in shallow pan. Brush surface with melted butter; sprinkle with salt and flour. Pour two cups boiling water around pig; cover with buttered paper.

Roast in a 350-degree oven for 30 minutes per pound or until done, basting every 15 minutes with liquid in pan. After cooking two and one-half hours, remove paper, brush with fat, continue roasting until tender.

10 servings

Suckling Pig Roasted Outdoors

1 suckling pig, dressed
stuffing, as needed
apple or pineapple juice, as needed

Prepare barbecue with a spit.

Clean and dress suckling pig. Stuff with dressing (your favorite, or the onion stuffing given above) while dressing is hot. Sew shut; place stone or block of wood to hold mouth open. Fasten skewer so pig is balanced and secure. Cook slowly, turning constantly. Baste with marinade of equal parts drippings, hot water, and apple or pineapple juice. Catch drippings in pan. Use only drippings for basting during last hour of cooking. Baste about every 15 minutes. Plan on roasting pig about 30 minutes per pound, or until done.
October 22, 1966

Herbed Roast of Pork

1 T. all-purpose flour
4 pounds center cut pork loin
¼ tsp. each marjoram, rosemary
*   and thyme*
dash of pepper
1½ tsp. salt
1 or 2 medium onions, sliced
½ cup cider, apple juice, or dry
*   white wine*

Shake flour in small size (10x16-inches) cooking bag, and place in two-inch deep roasting pan. Trim excess fat from roast. Sprinkle with herbs, pepper, and salt; pat in firmly. Place in pan. Place onion slices in bag. Slide in roast; add liquid. Close bag with twist tie and puncture six half-inch slits in top. Insert meat thermometer.

Place in a 325 degree oven and cook two to two and one-half hours or until thermometer registers 170 degrees.
6 to 8 servings
February 8, 1969

An easy-to-cook main dish that you can proudly serve is a real find. With this pork roast, which bakes in a Brown-In-Bag in a fairly slow oven, you can bake potatoes or winter squash. Serve it with rolls and butter, a salad, and a simple green vegetable. For dessert, a traditional winner—Orange Carrot Cake.

Marinated Pork Roast

1 T. all-purpose flour
1 T. dry mustard
1 tsp. ground ginger
1 tsp. dried thyme, crushed
1 clove garlic, minced
½ cup soy sauce
½ cup orange juice
3 pounds pork loin roast, boned,
*   rolled, and tied*

Sauce:

1 10-ounce jar currant jelly
2 T. orange juice
1 T. soy sauce

Shake flour in family-size (14x20 inches) browning bag and place in two-inch deep roasting pan. Fold bag back for easy handling. Add mustard, ginger, thyme, garlic, one-half cup soy sauce and one-half cup orange juice. Trim excess fat from pork; place meat in bag. Close bag with twist tie. Gently turn bag several times to mix ingredients well and moisten meat. Marinate two to three hours at room temperature or overnight in refrigerator. Turn once or twice. Make six one-half inch slits in top of bag; if using meat thermometer, insert through bag into meatiest portion of roast.

Bake in a 325-degree oven one and one-half hours or until meat thermometer reads 170 degrees, or until tested tender.

Meanwhile, prepare sauce by heating currant jelly until melted; add two tablespoons orange juice and one tablespoon soy sauce. Stir and simmer two minutes. Serve with pork roast.
4 to 6 servings

Orange Carrot Cake

1 orange
2 cups all-purpose flour
2 cups sugar
2 tsp. baking powder
2 tsp. baking soda
2 tsp. cinnamon
2 tsp. nutmeg
1 tsp. salt
1¼ cups vegetable oil
4 eggs
2 cups carrots (approximately 3
* medium carrots), grated*
½ cup nuts, chopped

Trim a thin slice from both ends of orange; cut in half lengthwise. With a shallow V-shaped cut, remove white center core. Cut halves into wedges, removing any seeds. Cut into chunks and place in electric blender; puree. Reserve one tablespoon puree for use in frosting. Sift together flour, sugar, baking powder, baking soda, cinnamon, nutmeg, and salt. Add oil, then orange puree, mixing well. Add eggs and combine thoroughly. Stir in carrots and nuts. Line two nine-inch cake pans with waxed paper. Pour batter into pans and bake in a 350-degree oven for one hour or until cake tester inserted into cake comes out clean. Let cool in pans for 10-15 minutes. Remove from pans and cool completely before frosting with Orange Carrot Cake Frosting.

Orange Carrot Cake Frosting

1 package (8 ounces) cream cheese
¼ cup margarine
1 pound powdered sugar
1 T. orange puree

Beat cream cheese and margarine until just blended. Add powdered sugar and puree.
  Frosting for 9-inch two-layer cake.
November 2, 1974

The early recipes—like this one from 1904—assumed the cook knew *All* the basics about cooking.

Roasted Pork Tenderloin

Take two tenderloins and split lengthwise. Place two together and fill with dressing made of bread, onion, egg, sage, and seasoning. Wind a string around to keep them together. Season on the outside and tack on with toothpicks three slices of bacon. Roast as you would any other roast, about forty-five minutes. This will make a nice cold meat dish sliced.
April 28, 1904

Pork loin roasts to tender and juicy perfection easily on a rotisserie. The boneless roll will delight diners and the carver as well as the carefree chef.

Boneless Pork Loin Roast

3 to 6 pound boneless pork loin roast
commercial barbecue sauce Or glaze
* given below*

Insert rotisserie rod through exact center of roast. Use prongs to hold meat in place. Test for balance by rotating in palms of hands. Insert roast meat thermometer, angling it so bulb is centered in roast, but not resting in fat or on rod. Place on rotisserie and cook at low temperature to about 170 degrees, or to well done. Cook two to three hours. Allow 35 to 40 minutes per pound for a three to four pound roast, 30 to 35 minutes per pound for a four to six pound roast. During last 30 minutes, brush roast with commercial barbecue sauce or glaze.

Pork Loin Roast Glaze:

1 cup honey
¼ cup orange juice
2 T. soy sauce

Combine honey, orange juice, and soy sauce. Mix well and brush roast during last 30 minutes of roasting.
May 3, 1975

132

This is a delicious roast to serve with cooked vegetables such as baby carrots, green beans, and white onions.

Apple-Stuffed Roast Pork

1 pork roast, about 5 pounds
salt, pepper, garlic powder, to taste
¼ cup butter or margarine
1 large onion, chopped
2 apples, cored and diced
1 cup celery, chopped
1 package (8 ounces) herb stuffing mix
1 cup pineapple juice
¼ cup steak sauce
parsley, as needed for garnish

Sprinkle pork roast with salt, pepper, and garlic powder. In a skillet, heat butter and saute onion, apples, and celery for five minutes or until wilted. Stir in stuffing mixture, pineapple juice and steak sauce. Place pork, ribs side down, on an open roaster. Cut six deep slashes in meat, cutting down to the bone, and stuff.

Insert a meat thermometer into the thickest portion of the muscle and roast in a 325-degree oven for three hours or until meat thermometer registers 170 degrees.

To serve, divide portions between slashes so that each serving gets some stuffing. Garnish with parsley.
6 to 8 servings
May 21, 1977

To Smoke the Pickled Pork

The first two days, have very little fire; use green alder or vine or hard maple (the subscriber who sent in this recipe uses apple tree branches etc., cut at the time of pruning) and smoke for 10 to 12 days, and you will have a good article. If you want to keep your meat through the summer, pack it in corn or oats, layer by layer, and keep well covered.
January 28, 1926

Fresh Pork Shoulder with Savory Stuffing

Stuffing:

¼ cup celery and leaves, chopped
1 T. onion, chopped
1 T. parsley, chopped
2 T. butter or margarine
2 cups soft bread crumbs
¼ tsp. savory seasoning
salt and pepper, to taste

5 or 6 pounds fresh pork shoulder,
    boned
salt and pepper, to taste
all-purpose flour, if needed

Cook celery, onion, and parsley in butter or margarine for a few minutes. Add bread crumbs, savory seasoning, salt and pepper, and stir until well mixed.

Sprinkle meat on the inside with salt and pepper, and pile in the stuffing. Sew, or skewer and lace edges of shoulder together to make a pocket and hold dressing.

Sprinkle outside of stuffed shoulder with salt and pepper and if desired, with flour also.

Place the roast, fat side up, on a rack in a shallow pan. Insert a meat thermometer in the thickest portion of muscle. Do not add water or cover. Cook until tender in a 350-degree oven. Allow about three hours for a five-pound picnic shoulder of pork. Cook until thermometer registers 170 degrees.

Make gravy, if desired, with pan drippings. Remove lacings before serving. Slice across the grain, serving slices of meat with stuffing.
10 to 12 servings
August 18, 1956

This recipe for Dandelions with Pork was popular two generations before it was published in 1901.

Dandelions with Pork

The pork and greens of our grandmothers. Put over the fire, in three quarts of cold water, one pound of pork selecting a piece in which the fat and lean are about equal. Allow three hours to cook, adding more water, as it evaporates. Pick over and wash a large panful of dandelions, drain all the water from them, and add to the pork. Peel and wash six medium-sized potatoes, place on top of the dandelions, cover closely, and cook for one hour. When done, dish the potatoes, and drain the dandelions, pressing out all the water. Heat one-half cupful vinegar in a saucepan. Chop the greens, add the vinegar, toss a moment and dish. Slice the pork thin, and send all to the table.

Should there be any of this dish left over, it may be served for tea, prepared in the following manner: Place the greens in the center of a platter, slice the cold potatoes around the dandelions, cut the cold pork into very small pieces, strewing over the dandelions, and pour over all a mayonnaise dressing.
June 6, 1901

In 1913, this was the advice to the cook on how to prepare spareribs.

Roasted Spare Ribs

Hack the ribs down the center, just enough so they may be bent together. Prepare any desired dressing; the old-time bread dressing is a general favorite, seasoned with either sage or finely minced onion. Spread thickly on one-half of the ribs and bend the other side over, fastening with a skewer or twine. Place in the oven and baste frequently. When done, remove from pan and pour a little cold water into the stock that the fat may be easily removed. Thicken with flour stirred smoothly into a small quantity of water.
October 30, 1913

Baked Spareribs with Barbecue Sauce

Barbecue Sauce:

2 T. brown sugar
1 tsp. paprika
1 tsp. salt
1 tsp. dry mustard
¼ tsp. chili powder
⅛ tsp. cayenne pepper (optional)
2 T. Worcestershire sauce
¼ cup vinegar
1 cup tomato juice
¼ cup catsup
½ cup water

3 pounds spare or loin ribs
1 lemon sliced
½ cup onion, chopped

Mix brown sugar, paprika, salt, mustard, chili powder, cayenne pepper, Worcestershire sauce, vinegar, tomato juice, catsup, and water in a saucepan and simmer for about 15 minutes or until slightly thickened.

Preheat oven to 450 degrees.

Cut spareribs in serving size pieces and place on a rack in a shallow baking pan. Place the lemon slices on top of each piece and sprinkle the onion over all.

Place in oven and bake for 30 minutes. Lower heat to 350 degrees and pour the barbecue sauce over the ribs; continue baking for one and one-half hours. Baste with the sauce every 15 minutes. If sauce thickens add hot water. Cover ribs the last 30 minutes of baking.
3 to 4 servings
January 7, 1961

If you have the time, marinate these ribs overnight before cooking. The flavor of the sauce will be worth the planning ahead.

Hawaiian Spareribs

2½ cups pinapple chunks with syrup (No. 2 can)
¼ cup vinegar
¼ cup chili sauce
½ cup brown sugar
¼ cup water
1 tsp. soy sauce
1 tsp. ginger
¼ tsp. garlic powder
3 pounds spareribs

Combine pineapple chunks with syrup, vinegar, chili sauce, brown sugar, water, soy sauce, ginger, and garlic powder. Simmer gently about 30 minutes. Cut each rack of ribs into serving size pieces. Cover with sauce and marinate at least four hours, preferably overnight, in refrigerator.

Transfer ribs to broiler rack; spoon on remaining marinade. Bake in a 250-degree oven for three hours.
4 servings
January 28, 1967

Turn an ordinary meal into a special meal with Oriental food. By adding a couple of touches to an inexpensive main dish you have a real treat for the whole family. Start with any clear soup, but substitute chow mein noodles for crackers, and garnish with scallions. Try Chinese-Style Pork Ribs for your main dish, along with hot cooked rice and Broccoli with Bamboo Shoots. Finish the meal with fortune cookies, almond cookies, or ice cream or sherbet topped with mandarin oranges.

Chinese Style Pork Ribs

4 to 5 pound country-style pork spareribs
½ cup soy sauce
4 cloves garlic
1 T. salt
pepper, to taste
1 small can pineapple chunks, drained
1 can (10½ ounces) chicken broth
½ cup catsup
1 onion, diced
hot rice, as needed for 4 to 5 servings

Sauce:

2 T. cornstarch
⅓ cup sherry or water

Line broiler pan with heavy-duty foil. Cut spareribs into serving portions, removing fat that can be trimmed easily. Place under broiler and brown, turning once. Brush with the soy sauce while browning. Turn off broiler and set oven at 300 degrees. Remove broiler pan.

Crush garlic and salt with the tip of a heavy knife and sprinkle over ribs. Add any remaining soy sauce, drained pineapple chunks, chicken broth, catsup and onion. Cover with a second sheet of foil, crimping it to the liner foil. Place in oven and bake for two hours or until fork tender. Remove foil cover. Remove from oven and tip pan so juice runs to the corner. Skim off fat.

If a thickened sauce is desired, combine cornstarch with sherry or water and stir into the juice. Pour sauce over all and serve with rice.
4 to 5 servings
August 21, 1976

In the 1920s meat pies were a frequent item in recipe collections. Here is one from 1927.

English Pork Pie

Make a pie crust, not very rich, and line sides of deep baking dish. Fill with layers of thinly sliced bacon, potatoes, onions and lean fresh pork, cut into small pieces. Season with salt, pepper, and sage. Pour over gravy left from a roast or stock thickened with browned flour. Cover with crust and bake for an hour and a half.
September 29, 1927

Pork Goulash

1½ pounds lean pork cubes
¼ cup all-purpose flour
½ tsp. garlic salt
dash pepper
2 T. shortening
1 can (10½ ounces) condensed onion
  soup
½ cup water
1 cup cooked tomatoes
½ medium green pepper, cut into strips
¼ cup celery, chopped
⅛ tsp. ground thyme
2 cups cooked noodles

Trim fat from pork cubes. Combine flour, garlic salt, and pepper; roll meat in this mixture. In large skillet, brown meat in shortening; pour off any excess drippings. Add soup, water, tomatoes, green pepper, celery, and thyme. Sprinkle remaining flour over mixture. Cover; simmer about one hour or until meat is tender, stirring now and then. Remove cover; cook about 15 minutes longer to thicken sauce.
    Serve over noodles.
6 servings
September 2, 1969

Just for fun, celebrate St. Patrick's Day with a complete Irish menu from Dublin Stew to dessert with Irish coffee. Everything's comin' up shamrocks!

Dublin Stew

1 pound pork shoulder, cubed
1 T. shortening
½ cup onion, chopped
½ cup celery, chopped
1 clove garlic, minced
1½ tsp. salt
3 cups water
3 beef bouillon cubes
6 medium carrots, quartered
1½ cups mixed vegetables
¼ cup all-purpose flour
½ cup water

Brown meat in shortening in heavy skillet. Add onion, celery, garlic, and salt. Cook until vegetables are tender. Add three cups water and bouillon cubes. Heat to boiling. Cover, reduce heat, and simmer 45 minutes. Add carrots; simmer 10 minutes longer. Add mixed vegetables and cook until tender, about 10 minutes. Mix flour with one-half cup water. Stir into meat-vegetable mixture, and cook until thickened.
4 servings

Brine for Pork

For one hundred pounds trimmed meat use 8 pounds fine salt, 2 pounds brown sugar, 1½ ounces black pepper, and 1 teaspoon pulverized saltpeter; mix together well. If hams and shoulders are large, run a butcher's steel through the thick parts in three or four places. Then rub the salt mixture in well and place on a shelf or table or in a barrel for 20 to 25 days. Wash off in very warm water and hang up to dry 24 hours, then begin to smoke.
January 28, 1926

St. Patrick's Green Rice

¾ cup green onion, minced
3 T. shortening
½ cup green pepper, minced
1 cup uncooked rice
2 cups chicken broth
1 tsp. salt
¼ tsp. pepper
¼ cup minced parsley

Cook onions in shortening until soft but not brown, using tops as well as bottoms. Add green pepper, rice, chicken broth, salt and pepper, and cook about 15 minutes. Fluff with fork, then press into shamrock mold and let stand one minute. Unmold and garnish with parsley in shamrock design. To color the rice mold, add two drops green vegetable food coloring to chicken stock. Rice mixture may be baked in a covered casserole or one-quart shamrock mold, if desired.

Bake about 45 minutes in a 350-degree oven, or until set.
4 to 6 servings

Irish Raspberry Buns (Cookies)

½ cup butter
¾ cup sugar
1 egg yolk
¼ cup milk
3 cups sifted cake flour
1 tsp. baking powder
½ cup raspberry jam
1 egg white, slightly beaten

Preheat oven to 400 degrees.

Cream butter and sugar together until light and fluffy. Add egg yolk and milk; mix well. Sift together flour, baking powder; add in two additions, beating well after each addition. Make one-inch balls from dough; flatten to one-quarter-inch thickness. Drop one-quarter teaspoon jam in center of each; fold in half; pinch edges to seal. Brush with egg white. Place on cookie sheet covered with aluminum foil.

Bake for 15 to 20 minutes.
2 dozen cookies

Irish Coffee

sugar, as needed
3 cups hot strong coffee
½ cup whipping cream, whipped
4 mugs

Combine four teaspoons sugar and three-quarters cup hot coffee in each mug; stir until sugar dissolves. Top coffee with about two tablespoons whipped cream, allowing it to float on top of coffee (don't stir).
4 servings
March 7, 1964

Pickled Pigs' Feet

Put the clean feet in enough boiling water to cover them and cook till the meat is about to drop from the bones. Do not add more water, but be careful not to scorch them. There should be a quart or more liquid when finished. Take out the feet and set the liquor aside to cool. When the grease is hard on top remove it and return the jelly—for it will be jelly by this time—to the fire. Add one quart of good vinegar to the hot broth and pour the whole over the feet. If they were not salted and peppered when put on to boil, add the seasoning to the hot liquor. A small bag of mixed spices (about one tablespoon tied in a thin cloth) may be added if the flavor is liked.

Boneless Pickled Pigs' Feet:

Proceed as above, but, when the feet are cooling, remove all the bones. When preparing boneless pigs' feet, only about one-half as much broth and vinegar should be used as for the others or there will be too much jelly. Pack in a crock or dish and when cold cut in thin slices.
March 7, 1912

Flemish Pork Stew

*3 pounds lean boneless pork, cut
   into 1½-inch cubes*
1 T. shortening
1½ cups onion, coarsely chopped
1 clove garlic, minced
2 T. all-purpose flour
3 tsp. salt
¼ tsp. pepper
¼ tsp. allspice
dash of nutmeg (optional)
1 cup water
1 small bay leaf
2 cups celery, cut in 1-inch slices
2 cups carrots, cut in 1-inch slices
8 to 10 small white potatoes
2 T. parsley, chopped

Brown pork cubes well in shortening in
heavy Dutch oven or skillet with close-
fitting cover. Add onion and garlic. Cook
over moderate heat until onion is tender.
Combine flour, two teaspoons salt, pepper,
allspice, and nutmeg, if used; mix. Sprinkle over meat. Add water and bay leaf.
Cover and cook slowly 35 minutes. Add
vegetables and remaining salt. Cook slowly
until both vegetables and meat are tender,
about 25 to 30 minutes.
8 to 10 servings
October 28, 1972

Pork and Kraut Casserole

*1½ pounds pork shoulder, cut in
   1-inch cubes*
½ cup onion, sliced
2 T. shortening
1 can (10¾ ounces) chicken gravy
1 cup green pepper, sliced
½ tsp. caraway seed
½ tsp. paprika
1 can (1 pound) sauerkraut

In skillet, brown meat and onion in shortening; pour off drippings. Stir in gravy,
green pepper, caraway, and paprika. Transfer to a one and one-half quart casserole.
Bake in a 350-degree oven for one and one-
half hours. Place drained sauerkraut around
edge of casserole for the last five minutes.
4 servings
January 15, 1966

Sweet and Sour Pork

*1 pound lean pork, cut into 1-inch
   cubes*
1 tsp. sugar
3 tsp. salt
1 tsp. soy sauce
2 eggs, beaten
¼ cup plus 1 T. water
½ cup cornstarch
½ cup corn oil
½ cup onion, chopped
¼ cup green pepper, chopped
¼ cup preserved ginger, chopped
2 cloves garlic, minced
¾ cup cider vinegar
¼ cup light corn syrup
*hot cooked rice, as needed for 4
   servings*

Sprinkle pork with sugar, one teaspoon salt,
and soy sauce. Toss; let stand one-half hour.
Stir eggs with one tablespoon water. Dip
pork into egg; coat with cornstarch. Then
dip again in egg. Heat one-half the corn oil
in skillet. Saute pork about 15 minutes,
turning frequently, until browned. Remove
meat from pan. Pour in remaining corn oil.
Add onion, green pepper, ginger, and garlic.
Cook, stirring frequently, until onion has
browned lightly. Mix together four
teaspoons cornstarch, remaining salt, and
water. Add with vinegar and corn syrup to
mixture in skillet. Cook, stirring constantly,
until sauce thickens. Add pork. Simmer 15
minutes. Serve with rice.
4 servings
February 16, 1974

Chop Suey

1 pound lean pork, cut in thin strips
2 T. shortening
½ cup onion, sliced
1 cup celery, cut in strips
½ cup green pepper, cut in thin strips
1½ cups water
1 bouillon cube
1 T. cornstarch
1 can bean sprouts
½ tsp. salt
2 T. soy sauce

Cook pork in the hot shortening until thoroughly done. Add onions, celery, and green peppers, and cook three minutes. Add one cup water and the bouillon cube. Mix cornstarch with remaining water. Add to vegetable mixture, and cook until thick. Add bean sprouts, salt, and soy sauce. Vegetables will be crisp.
4 servings
October 1, 1955

Here is a prepare-now-cook-later dinner which is quick and easy to assemble and a snap to serve at those busy times when you can't spend much time in the kitchen. The recipe is expandable for large families or large appetites.

Pork Chop Dinner

Pork chops
Acorn squash
Pineapple slices, drained
Brown sugar
Salt and pepper

Brown pork chops in a skillet. Split small squashes or slice large ones in thick rings, removing seeds. For each dinner serving, place on a large square of heavy duty foil one pork chop, a slice of pineapple, and a serving portion of the squash. Sprinkle brown sugar over the pineapple and squash. Season all with salt and pepper. Bring two sides of foil up over food, and double-fold edges tightly on top of package. Double-fold both ends. Store in refrigerator or freezer.

Preheat oven to 375 degrees.

To cook place on a cookie sheet and bake or grill one hour for one-half-inch chops; one and one-quarter to one and one-half hours for thicker chops. Do not turn.
June, 1970

Pork Chops and Vegetables

5 slices bacon, cut into pieces
½ cup onion, chopped
8 pork chops, thinly sliced
½ tsp. salt
¼ tsp. ground pepper
1 can (17 ounces) lima beans,
    drained
1 can (17 ounces) whole kernel corn,
    drained, reserving ⅓ cup liquid
½ cup milk
1 cup sharp cheddar cheese, shredded
1 egg, beaten
1 cup saltines, coarsely crushed

Cook bacon according to package directions until crisp. Remove and drain on paper towel. Saute onion in bacon drippings until transparent, about five minutes. Remove and drain on paper towel. Season chops with salt and pepper. Brown in bacon drippings on both sides. Meanwhile, combine lima beans, corn and liquid, milk, cheese, egg, and saltines in bowl. Blend well. Pour into a shallow one and one-half quart baking dish. Arrange pork chops on top.

Bake in a 350-degree oven for 30 minutes.
4 servings
April 23, 1965

Piquant Pears and Chops

4 pork chops
4 thin slices lemon
4 thin slices onion
2 Anjou or Bosc pears, halved and
    cored
¼ cup lemon juice
¼ cup water
2 T. brown sugar
2 T. soy sauce
¼ tsp. powdered ginger

Brown chops on both sides in heavy skillet. Drain off any accumulated fat. Place lemon and onion slices on each chop. Place pear halves, cut side down, around chops. Combine lemon juice, water, brown sugar, soy sauce, and ginger. Pour over pears and chops. Cover, steam for 30 to 45 minutes. Halfway through, turn pears, and baste.
4 servings
March 26, 1977

Peachy Pork Chops

6 ribs or loin pork chops, cut ½- to
    ¾-inch thick
2 T. lard or drippings
1 tsp. salt
⅛ tsp. pepper
1 can (16 ounces) sliced peaches,
    drained, reserving ½ cup liquid
1 tsp. lemon juice
¼ tsp. ginger
⅛ tsp. cinnamon
2 T. honey
all-purpose flour, as needed for gravy

Brown the pork chops in lard or drippings. Pour off drippings, season with salt and pepper. Combine reserved liquid with lemon juice, ginger, cinnamon, and honey. Pour over pork chops. Cover tightly and cook slowly 45 minutes or until done. Add peach slices and cook until heated through. Remove chops. Thicken liquid with flour for gravy and spoon over chops.
6 servings
April 18, 1964

Pork Chop-Potato Casserole

6 medium potatoes, peeled and
    sliced thin
¼ cup butter
¼ cup onion, minced
2 T. all-purpose flour
2 cups milk
1 tsp. salt
⅛ tsp. pepper
1 tsp. Worcestershire sauce
¼ cup catsup
2 cups sharp American cheese,
    shredded
6 large pork chops

Place potatoes in a 9x12-inch baking dish. Melt butter in saucepan over low heat. Cook onion in butter until transparent. Blend in flour. Add milk, stirring constantly and cook until sauce is smooth and thickened. Add salt, pepper, Worcestershire, catsup, and cheese. Pour sauce over potatoes.

Trim extra fat from pork chops and use to brown chops. Place on top of potatoes. Cover and bake in a 350-degree oven for one-half hour. Remove cover and bake one-half hour longer.
6 servings
September 5, 1959

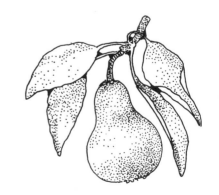

Following are six stuffed pork chop recipes which vary in ingredients or in method of cooking, but all promise delicious results.

Corn Stuffed Pork Chops

4 2-rib pork chops
1 tsp. salt
dash of pepper and sage

Stuffing:

1 cup whole kernel corn, drained
1 cup white bread crumbs
½ cup apple, finely diced
1 egg, beaten
2 T. cream
½ tsp. salt
½ tsp. sage
dash of pepper
½ cup water

Slash chops between ribs to make pocket for stuffing. Rub chops with salt, pepper, and sage.

Lightly toss corn, bread crumbs, apple, egg, cream, salt, sage, and pepper. Stuff pockets in chops. Brown on all sides in heavy skillet. Place chops in casserole having tight fitting cover. Add water to drippings in skillet, then turn over chops. Cover tightly and bake in a 350-degree oven for 45 minutes or until chops are tender. Add more liquid if needed.
4 servings
January 18, 1964

Use your slow-cooker to stew up a meal while you work.

Slow Cooker Pork Chops

4 double pork loin chops, well trimmed
salt and pepper, to taste
1 can (12 ounces) whole-kernel corn, drained
1 small onion, chopped
1 small green pepper, seeded and chopped
1 cup fresh bread crumbs
½ tsp. leaf oregano or leaf sage
⅓ cup raw long-grain converted rice
1 can (8 ounces) tomato sauce

Cut a pocket in each chop, cutting from the edge almost to the bone. Lightly season pockets with salt and pepper. In bowl, combine corn, onion, green pepper, bread crumbs, oregano or sage, and rice. Pack vegetable mixture into pockets. Secure along fat side with wooden picks. Pour any remaining vegetable mixture into slow cooker. Moisten top surface of each chop with tomato sauce. Add stuffed pork chops to slow cooker, stacking to fit if necessary. Pour any remaining tomato sauce on top. Cover and cook on low setting for seven to ten hours or until done.

To serve, remove chops to heatproof platter and mound vegetable-rice mixture in center.
4 servings
December, 1975

Fruit-Stuffed Pork Chops

1½ cups cheddar cheese, cubed
¾ cup soft bread crumbs
½ cup dried apricots, diced
¼ tsp. celery seed
¾ cup apple juice
2 T. butter
4 pork loin chops with pocket cut,
*   ¾-inch thick*
1 cup celery, chopped
1 cup carrots, thinly sliced

In a mixing bowl combine cheese, crumbs, apricots, celery seed and one-quarter cup apple juice. Stuff pockets of chops; set aside remaining stuffing. In large skillet melt butter; slowly brown chops. Place celery and carrots in bottom of casserole; arrange chops over vegetables. Top each chop with one-quarter remaining stuffing. Pour remaining apple juice over all. Cover.

Bake in a 325 degree oven 45 minutes; remove cover and bake an additional 15 to 20 minutes.
4 servings
September 24, 1966

Cheese Stuffed Pork Chops

3 T. butter or margarine
1 tsp. onion, minced
¼ cup mushrooms, finely-sliced
½ cup (about 3 ounces) crumbled
*   blue cheese*
¾ cup fine dry bread crumbs
dash salt
6 double thick pork loin chops, with
*   pockets cut*

Melt butter in skillet. Add onion and mushrooms. Cook five minutes. Remove from heat and stir in blue cheese, bread crumbs and salt. Stuff pockets in each chop with dressing. Secure with picks.

Bake in a 325-degree oven for one hour or until meat is nicely browned and cooked through.
6 servings
February 4, 1967

Stuffed Butterfly Pork Chops

1 cup apple, cored and finely
*   chopped*
⅓ cup celery, finely chopped
⅓ cup onion, finely chopped
2 T. butter
3 cups dry bread cubes
2 T. raisins
½ tsp. salt
1 tsp. poultry seasoning
2 T. water or meat stock
6 1-inch butterfly pork chops, with
*   pockets for stuffing*
2 T. lard or drippings
1 tsp. salt
⅛ tsp. pepper

Prepare stuffing by cooking apple, celery, and onion in butter until tender. Combine bread cubes, raisins, one-half teaspoon salt, poultry seasoning, and apple mixture. Add water or meat stock, mixing thoroughly. Stuff each chop with bread mixture. Brown chops in lard or drippings. Season chops with one teaspoon salt and pepper. Cover tightly and cook slowly for 45 minutes to one hour.
6 servings
February 22, 1975

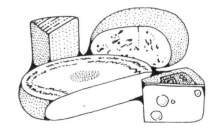

Smoked Pork Chops Flambe

*6 to 8 smoked pork chops, cut ¾ to
  1-inch thick*
6 to 8 canned cling peach halves
*6 to 8 sugar cubes, soaked in lemon
  extract*

Arrange smoked pork chops on rack of
broiling pan. Insert pan so tops of chops
are three to four inches from the heat. Broil
eight minutes on one side. Turn chops and
arrange peach halves, cut side up, on broiling rack. Broil eight to 10 minutes longer,
or until meat is heated through. Arrange
chops and peaches on hot platter. Put sugar
cube in cup of each peach and ignite.
6 to 8 servings
October 28, 1972

The title of this 1916 recipe is a real
mistake—at least to our current way of
thinking—Fruit and Spice Cake better
describes it.

Pork Cake

One pound of fat salt pork, one pint of boiling water, two cups of sugar, one cup of
molasses, one teaspoonful of soda, one
teaspoonful of cloves, two teaspoonfuls of
cinnamon, one pound of currants, one
pound of raisins, one-fourth pound of citron,
flour. Wash and dry the currants. Wash,
seed, and chop the raisins. Shred the citron.
Have the pork entirely free from lean and
rind and chop very fine or put through the
food chopper, using the finest cutter. Pour
the boiling water over the chopped pork,
add the sugar, mix the soda with the
molasses and add the molasses. Mix the
spices with part of the flour and stir into the
mixture. Add the fruit and then the rest of
the flour. No definite amount of flour is
given, but the batter should be as thick as
one can stir. It is well to try a sample cake,
as one seldom uses enough flour the first
time. Bake in a moderate oven from three
to four hours, or steam three hours and bake
one hour.
February 24, 1916

Pickled Tongue

Take four pounds of either pigs' or
calves' tongues, and four pigs' feet,
clean nicely in warm water and put
in your soup pot: add one and one-
half pints of vinegar and enough cold
water to cover; let come to a boil
quickly and remove all scum as soon
as it rises.

When the liquor is clear, add one
large onion, one tablespoonful of
whole black pepper and two
tablespoonfuls of salt, reduce the heat
and let simmer until the tongue is
tender.

Now take up all the meat, skin and
trim, but leave the tongue whole and
place in a deep earthen bowl or gal-
lon jar.

Boil down the liquor to one-half
pint and strain through a napkin,
wrung out of boiling water, and pour
over the tongue.

When cold this will be a beautiful, clear meat jelly. When serving
take out only as much as will be
required for one meal, cut in slices
and garnish with jelly.

This tongue can be kept in a cool,
dry place for two or three weeks, and
is especially nice when served for
luncheon or supper with fried
potatoes.
April 11, 1912

Bacon

Most of us think of bacon as the side-dish on the breakfast table. While plain broiled bacon is good to eat, don't stop there. Bacon is a versatile food that can find its way into meals from breakfast through dinner.

An appetizer with an exotic flavor.

Bacon-Wrapped Water Chestnuts

1 can water chestnuts, drained
¼ cup French dressing
½ tsp. curry powder
bacon slices, as needed

Combine French dressing and curry powder. Let water chestnuts stand in dressing mixture for one hour; drain. Wrap each chestnut in a half slice of bacon. Fasten with wooden pick and broil until bacon is crisp.
4 servings
November 3, 1962

Cheese Spread Sandwiches

shredded sharp American cheese, as desired
finely diced green pepper, as desired
diced, cooked bacon, as desired
chili sauce, as desired
Worcestershire sauce, as desired
6 to 8 buttered sandwich rolls or 12 to 14 thick slices French bread

Preheat oven to 425 degrees.
Combine cheese with green pepper, bacon, chili sauce, and Worcestershire sauce. Spread generously between halves of buttered rolls or bread. Placc on a baking sheet or wrap individually in pieces of aluminum foil. Place in oven until lightly browned or under broiler about five to six inches from heat.
6 to 8 sandwiches
February 13, 1971

Canadian Mushroom Sandwich

1 T. uncooked bacon, chopped
2 T. onion, chopped
6 T. canned sliced mushrooms
1 tsp. snipped parsley
butter, softened, as needed
6 enriched Kaiser rolls
18 slices Canadian-style bacon, cut ⅛-inch thick
6 slices (1 ounce each) Swiss cheese
6 thick green pepper rings
paprika, as needed
6 cherry tomatoes
6 large stuffed green olives

Saute chopped bacon, onion, mushrooms, and parsley for about five minutes. Split and butter rolls. Arrange three slices Canadian-style bacon on each bottom half of roll and top with mushroom mixture and one slice of cheese. Place one green pepper ring on each cheese slice; sprinkle paprika inside of green pepper ring. Place sandwiches on baking sheet and broil six inches from heat until cheese melts, about three to five minutes. Serve sandwich open-faced. Garnish with cherry tomato and stuffed green olive on skewer.
6 sandwiches
September 15, 1973

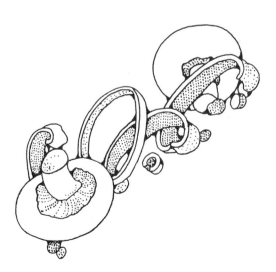

Dandelions were very popular on the menu at the turn of the century.

Dandelion Salad

Fry until crisp and brown three or four thin slices of bacon. Cut and dice. There should be about two tablespoonfuls of the bacon. Wash a quart of the whitest dandelion leaves, and season well with salt and pepper. Add these to the bacon. Take about a tablespoonful of the fat in which the bacon was fried, mix with two tablespoonfuls of vinegar, pour over the dandelion, toss, and serve.

June 20, 1901

I laughed when I read the inquiry about using mutton for something besides candles. We use it for many things: chops, roasts, stews, etc., and even use the surplus tallow with pork fat for soap. We are very fond of mutton, though I have eaten some that did not taste so well as what we prepare at home.

Some say that the wool should not touch the meat in dressing it or it will not be good. That is not true. The way to dress mutton properly is to remove the entrails first, just as soon as the animal is dead. Take your time then about skinning it. Do not rinse the carcass out with cold water as this seals the pores in the fat and does not let the animal heat out. This is important. Try this way of dressing and I am sure any one will like mutton. I have seen confirmed mutton-haters relish it when dressed this way.

May 6, 1926

Turn this tasty mixture into a large salad bowl lined with the most perfect red cabbage leaves you can find, and you'll have an eye-catching treat for your family or guests.

Confetti Salad with Bacon Sour Cream Dressing

6 strips bacon, cut in small pieces
2 tsp. all-purpose flour
2 tsp. sugar
½ tsp. salt
1 tsp. dry mustard
dash of cayenne pepper
1 egg
¼ cup vinegar
1 cup sour cream
¼ cup milk
3 cups green cabbage, finely shredded
3 cups red cabbage, finely shredded
¾ cup green onion, sliced

In a skillet, fry bacon until crisp. Remove bacon; drain. Remove skillet from heat; pour off all but about two tablespoons of bacon drippings. Blend in flour, sugar, salt, dry mustard, and pepper. Beat together egg and vinegar. Add to skillet mixture. Cook, stirring constantly, over low heat until smooth and thickened; cool. Blend together sour cream and milk; stir into thickened mixture along with bacon.

In a large bowl combine green cabbage, red cabbage, and green onion. Add dressing and gently toss.

To serve, turn into a bowl lined with cabbage leaves.

8 servings
June 5, 1965

A hot 1927 version of today's cold salad.

Spinach with Bacon

Boil the spinach as usual. Cut the bacon into small cubes and fry. Add it to the spinach when cooked and season with one-fourth cup of vinegar, salt and pepper. This may be garnished with slices of hard cooked egg, if desired.
June 23, 1927

This salad is sweet and sour, rich and delicious, and—unlike many salads—excellent on a cold day.

Hot Potato Salad

5 slices bacon, fried crisp
2 cups diced hot potatoes
¼ cup herb vinegar
½ cup sugar
¾ tsp. salt
pepper, to taste
¼ cup bacon fat
1 T. all-purpose flour
3 green onions, including tops
½ tsp. celery seed
¼ tsp. paprika

Crumble bacon over potatoes. In a saucepan add vinegar, sugar, salt, and pepper to the drippings and thicken with the flour. Cook until thick and clear. Add onions and celery seed to potatoes. Pour hot dressing over all (all dressing may not be needed) and sprinkle with paprika.
    Serve at once.
4 servings
March 17, 1973

Asparagus-Bacon Bake

8 slices Canadian bacon
½ cup cooked asparagus spears
4 eggs
½ cup Parmesan cheese, grated
parsley or paprika, if desired for
*   garnish*

Pan fry bacon lightly. Arrange asparagus in oiled shallow casserole. Place bacon over asparagus in overlapping circles. Break eggs over bacon, sprinkle with cheese, and bake in a 325-degree oven until eggs are set. Garnish with parsley or paprika, if desired. Serve piping hot.
4 servings
May 1, 1971

Barbecued Baked Beans

1 pound Canadian bacon, cut into
*   ¼-inch slices and then into large*
*   cubes*
½ cup onion, chopped
1 clove garlic, minced
2 1-pound cans pork and beans
2 T. mixed seasonings
¼ tsp. marjoram
¼ tsp. salt
1 tsp. dry mustard
½ cup molasses

Fry bacon in skillet until brown and slightly crisp. Add the onion and garlic and saute until just tender, about five minutes. Add beans, mixed seasonings, marjoram, salt, and mustard. Dribble molasses over the top and mix lightly, but well. Cover and cook over low heat for about 30 minutes. Remove cover and continue cooking 15 minutes longer, stirring occasionally.
6 servings
April 20, 1963

8

Sausage—Man's First Convenience Food

Have you heard the Ben Franklin maxim about no man should watch either laws or sausage being made? Rosemary Mucklow of the Western States Meat Association wishes that you hadn't, or at least that this saying wasn't quite so familiar. In fact it's probably one of her least favorite quotes.

"In the bad old days, sausage was made from leftover scraps," she admits, "but that's not true now. Ingredients for sausage today are specially selected for the purpose and today's stainless steel sausage-kitchens are kept as sterile as a good hospital. The sausage makers *have* to use good quality ingredients because they taste better, and therefore, sell better. The firms are interested in staying in business—something they couldn't do using scraps."

Another factor keeps the sausage makers on their toes in a way that could never have been the case in Franklin's time. The USDA spends $320 million each year on meat inspection; in fact, an army of 8,000 full-time meat inspectors insures the wholesomeness of our meat supply. Those inspectors mean that today's sausage is certifiably wholesome. But just what

exactly is sausage? It's a food product made from chopped or ground meat, including pork, beef, veal, lamb, or any combination of these, blended with spices or other seasonings. It's a product that's been around since before recorded history, and some refer to it as one of man's first convenience foods. History tells us that virtually all primitive people preserved meat for times when their food supplies were scarce. Even the word "sausage" comes from the Latin word, *salsus,* meaning "preserved" or "salted." The Babylonians made sausage 3,500 years ago, and Homer mentions sausage in the *Odyssey,* written in the nineteenth century B.C.

In America today, there are more than 200 different kinds of sausage to choose from. The major kinds are:

Fresh Sausages—made from selected cuts of fresh meats. They are neither cooked nor cured and they must be kept refrigerated. If you see the word "fresh" in front of the words Kielbasa, Italian, Bratwurst, Bockwurst, Chorizos, Thuringer, or bulk sausage, then realize that that sausage should be used within two or three days and it must be cooked thoroughly before serving.

Uncooked Smoked Sausage—sometimes includes cured meat. As its name indicates, this kind has been smoked but not fully cooked. It should be refrigerated and used within one week, and, like the fresh sausage, it must be cooked thoroughly before serving. Some of the kinds to look for are: smoked-pork sausage, Kielbasa, Mettwurst, and Smoked Country-Style.

Cooked Sausage—made from fresh meats which are cured during processing and fully cooked. These should be refrigerated and used within four to six days. They are ready to eat as is, but you can also serve them hot. Some varieties to look for are: Blood Sausage, Blood and Tongue Sausage, Bockwurst (precooked), Bratwurst (precooked), Kiszka, Liver Loaf, Yachwurst, Braunschweiger, and Liver Sausage.

Dry and/or Semi-Dry Sausages—made from fresh meats which are cured during processing. They may or may not be smoked. These are prepared by carefully controlling bacterial fermentation which acts as a preservative as well as developing flavor. Most dry sausages are salamis; most semi-dry are the summer sausage kind. The dry sausages can be stored in a cool area and the semi-dry should be refrigerated. They're ready to eat, and should be used within three to six weeks. Some of the kinds to look for are: Summer Sausage, Cervelat (Farmer), Thuringer, Salami, Genoa, German (hard), Italian, Kosher, Milano, Chorizos, Fizzes, Lebanon Bologna, Lyons, Medwurst (Swedish), Metz, Mortadella, and Pepperoni.

When it comes to cooking sausage, all sausage should be cooked at a low to moderate temperature to prevent shrinkage. Fresh sausage is fully cooked and ready to eat when the color turns from pink to gray. Fully-cooked sausage need only be heated

148

to serving temperature if it's to be served hot.

What's Rosemary Mucklow's favorite way of serving sausage? "My favorite is Bockwurst, the Swiss kind. Serve it with red cabbage sauerkraut and warm potato salad. It's fully cooked but finish it off in the frying pan, browning it until it cracks open. It's a mild sort of sausage but it's very delicious. And the sharpness of the sauerkraut gives it a little acid taste to balance the nice blandness of the sausage."

Since there are so many kinds of sausage, experiment, and maybe you'll discover a new favorite.

Butchering and sausage-making have been a family affair for generations. The following sausage-making advice and recipes come to us from a 1927 Wisconsin farm family.

Making Sausage

Trimmings and pieces of meat which otherwise might be wasted may be converted into some form of sausage. Sausage making is a trade well worth learning. Often on the farm when animals are butchered for home consumption, portions of the carcass are not utilized to the best advantage. A demand for fresh and smoked country sausage always exists, and it is just as important for every farmer to know how to make good sausage as it is to know how to make good hams and bacon.

The only equipment necessary to make sausage is a meat cutter with a stuffer attachment. A good knife, cord string, and casings or muslin bags also will be needed. Muslin bags can be made of any size, but the most convenient are 12 inches long by two inches in diameter. When sausage is stuffed in muslin bags they should be paraffined after stuffing. Sausage, stuffed in muslin bags and paraffined, keeps longer and better than in casings. When set in a cool place, sausage will keep very well in stone crocks or tin pans if a layer of hot lard or paraffin is poured over the top.

Good pork sausage may be made as follows:

65 pounds fresh lean meat
35 pounds fat
1¾ pounds salt
2 ounces fine sage
1 ounce ground nutmeg
4 ounces black pepper

Cut the meat into small pieces, mix, and add the spices, and then put through the grinder, using the small plate. After it is well ground, mix thoroughly to be sure that it is uniformly seasoned. No water should be added if the sausage is to be stored away in bulk. If it is to be stuffed in casings a little water may be necessary to soften the meat so that it will slip easily into the casings. Cook thoroughly before eating.

The following ingredients are used in making smoked or country sausage:

85 pounds lean pork
15 pounds beef
1½ or 2 pounds salt
4 ounces black pepper
1 ounce red pepper
1 ounce sweet marjoram
1 ounce mace

Cut the meat into small pieces and sprinkle seasonings over it, then run it through the grinder, using the small plate. Put it away in a cool place for 24 to 36 hours, then add a little water and stuff into hog casings and smoke in a very cool smoke until a dark mahogany color is obtained. Cook sausage well before eating.
December 22, 1927

This 1927 recipe is short on words but long on interest.

Sausage Surprise

Place an oyster in each sausage and cover each with a light pie pastry. Bake in a slow oven until the sausage and oyster are cooked and the pie crust on the outside is a golden brown.
June 23, 1927

Golden Shepherd's Pie

1 pound bulk pork sausage
½ cup onion, chopped
1 can (10½ ounces) condensed
* golden mushroom soup*
½ cup water
1 package (9 ounces) frozen cut
* green beans, cooked and drained*
½ tsp. caraway seeds
2 cups mashed potatoes

Form sausage into 16 meatballs. In skillet, brown meatballs and cook onion until tender; pour off fat. Stir in soup, water, beans and caraway seeds. Pour into one and one-half quart casserole. Bake in a 350-degree oven for 25 minutes. Stir casserole, spoon potatoes around edge. Bake five minutes more.
4 servings
Augsut 15, 1970

Egg-Sausage Burgers

1 pound pork sausage
2 T. green pepper, finely chopped
2 T. onion, finely chopped
2 T. sausage drippings for cooking
8 eggs, beaten slightly
½ tsp. salt
⅛ tsp. pepper
8 buns
relishes, as desired for garnish

Mold sausage into eight patties to fit buns and fry. Meanwhile, cook green pepper and onion in drippings until onion is transparent but not brown. Blend eggs, salt, and pepper and add to onions and green pepper. Scramble over low heat. Place one sausage patty topped with a tablespoon of eggs between halves of buns. Serve hot with relishes.
8 servings
April 5, 1969

Old China Town Pork Burger

1½ pounds pork sausage
1 cup enriched soft bread crumbs
⅓ cup green onion, finely chopped
⅓ cup green pepper, finely chopped
1 can (6½ ounces) water chestnuts,
*   drained and chopped*
1 egg
2 tsp. sherry flavoring
2 T. soy sauce
1 small clove garlic, crushed
¼ tsp. ginger
½ cup crushed pineapple, drained
⅓ cup catsup
2 T. vinegar
2 T. orange marmalade
1 T. prepared mustard
6 large enriched sesame seed
*   hamburger buns*
butter, as needed, softened
1 cup bean sprouts, rinsed, well
*   drained*

Combine sausage, bread crumbs, green onion, green pepper, water chestnuts, egg, sherry flavoring, soy sauce, garlic, and ginger; mix well. For ease of handling, chill several hours, if desired. Shape into patties and grill until done.

Prepare sweet and sour sauce by combining pineapple, catsup, vinegar, marmalade, and mustard. Heat and stir until marmalade melts.

Split and toast buns; butter. Divide bean sprouts on bun bottoms and top with patty. Spoon equal amounts of Sweet 'n' Sour Sauce over meat. Close sandwich with bun top.
6 servings
August 23, 1954

Sweet and Sour Sausage with Rice

1 pound smoked sausage links
½ cup water
1 can (20 ounces) pineapple chunks
1 large green pepper, thinly sliced
1 T. butter
⅓ cup honey
3 T. soy sauce
1 T. vinegar
2 T. cornstarch
2 tsp. ginger
½ tsp. garlic powder
3 cups hot cooked rice

Simmer sausage in water for about 10 minutes. Drain. Cut in two-inch pieces.

Drain pineapple, reserving liquid. Add water to liquid to make one and one-half cups. Saute green pepper and pineapple in butter about two minutes. Add sausage, honey, soy sauce, and vinegar. Mix cornstarch with ginger and garlic powder; blend in measured liquid. Pour over sausage. Cook and stir over medium heat until thickened. Serve over rice.
6 servings
April 23, 1977

Sausage-Mac Dinner

2 cups elbow macaroni
¼ cup butter
¼ tsp. curry powder
½ cup onion, chopped
½ cup green pepper, chopped
1 can cream of mushroom soup
½ cup milk
¾ pound sliced summer sausage,
*   cut up*
1 cup (4 ounces) Swiss cheese,
*   shredded*
4 hard cooked eggs, sliced
egg slices, for garnish

Cook macaroni according to directions on package; drain and set aside. Meanwhile, in a small skillet melt butter, stir in curry powder. Saute onion and green pepper in butter until tender. In a large bowl combine soup and milk; add sausage, cheese, eggs, sauteed onion and green pepper, and macaroni. Turn into a two and one-half quart buttered casserole.

Bake in a 350-degree oven for 45 minutes or until heated through. Garnish with egg slices.

6 to 8 servings
September 23, 1967

Oh Boy Farm Boy

¾ cup sauerkraut, well-drained and
*   chopped*
½ tsp. caraway seeds
1 tsp. butter or margarine
1½ pounds bulk country pork sausage
6 1-ounce slices Swiss cheese
6 enriched hamburger buns, toasted
18 slices pimiento-stuffed green
*   olives (3 large olives)*
12 carrot sticks
corn chips, as desired

Cook sauerkraut and caraway seeds in butter or margarine until hot, stirring frequently to prevent browning. Keep warm. Divide pork sausage into six patties. Cook on both sides, draining off drippings. Cover sausage patties with Swiss cheese. Broil until cheese melts. Place two tablespoons sauerkraut mixture on bottom half of each bun. Cover with sausage. Place three olive slices over cheese. Partially close each sandwich with top half of bun.

Serve hot, with carrot sticks and corn chips.

6 sandwiches
August 7, 1965

Egg Surprise Turnovers

Filling:

½ pound bulk pork sausage
1 tsp. chives, chopped
4 hard-cooked eggs, coarsely
*   chopped*
1 can (10½ ounces) cream of
*   mushroom soup, undiluted*

Pastry:

2 cups all-purpose flour
1 tsp. salt
⅔ cup shortening
5 to 6 T. cold water

milk, as needed for sauce

Preheat oven to 450 degrees.

Slowly brown sausage, breaking up with fork; drain. Combine sausage, chives, and eggs in mixing bowl. Blend one-third cup mushroom soup into egg mixture. Reserve remaining soup for sauce.

For pastry, combine flour and salt; cut in shortening with fork or pastry blender until pieces are size of small peas. Sprinkle water, a tablespoon at a time, over part of mixture. Gently mix with fork until all is moistened. Form into a ball. Roll out on lightly floured board or pastry cloth to one-eighth-inch thickness. Cut into eight four by four-inch squares.

Place one-quarter cup filling on lower half of each square; fold top half over to make a triangle. Seal edges by pressing together with a fork. Bake on a baking sheet for 15 to 20 minutes, or until nicely browned.

Serve with mushroom sauce made from reserved soup, heated, and blended with milk to desired consistency.
September 12, 1970

Pork Chart

WHOLESALE CUTS OF PORK AND THEIR BONE STRUCTURE

BOSTON BUTT
CLEAR PLATE
FAT BACK
LOIN
TRIMMED JOWL
HAM (LEG)
FORE FOOT
PICNIC
SPARERIBS
BACON (BELLY)
HIND FOOT

RETAIL CUTS OF PORK AND WHERE THEY COME FROM

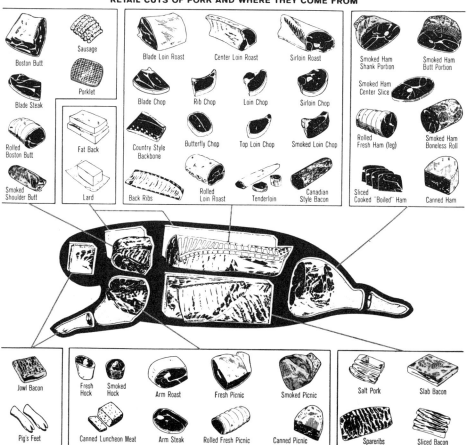

Boston Butt

Sausage

Porklet

Blade Steak

Rolled Boston Butt

Fat Back

Smoked Shoulder Butt

Lard

Blade Loin Roast

Center Loin Roast

Sirloin Roast

Blade Chop

Rib Chop

Loin Chop

Sirloin Chop

Country Style Backbone

Butterfly Chop

Top Loin Chop

Smoked Loin Chop

Back Ribs

Rolled Loin Roast

Tenderloin

Canadian Style Bacon

Smoked Ham Shank Portion

Smoked Ham Butt Portion

Smoked Ham Center Slice

Rolled Fresh Ham (leg)

Smoked Ham Boneless Roll

Sliced Cooked "Boiled" Ham

Canned Ham

Jowl Bacon

Pig's Feet

Fresh Hock

Smoked Hock

Canned Luncheon Meat

Arm Roast

Arm Steak

Fresh Picnic

Rolled Fresh Picnic

Smoked Picnic

Canned Picnic

Salt Pork

Slab Bacon

Spareribs

Sliced Bacon

Reprinted through the courtesy of
The National Live Stock and Meat Board
444 No. Michigan Avenue
Chicago, Illinois 60611

152

9
Veal—Clods Are Good Too

How about having a real clod for dinner?

Tom Houlton from Provimi Veal thinks that this would be a great idea. You'll save money, and you'll be serving something that's both delicious, and highly nutritious too.

The clod that Houlton recommends happens to be veal shoulder clod, and if you like veal scallopini, and if getting it for half price appeals to you, then take Houlton's advice and try one soon.

"Explore some of the less well known cuts from a veal's forequarters, like the shoulder clod," he suggests. "You'll find that you can make veal scallops for a half to a third of what you'd pay if you were buying the ready-made veal scallops."

Houlton has in front of him on the kitchen counter a rolled shoulder clod that's wrapped in netting and forms a cylindrical shape about six inches in diameter. "We start by removing the netting and opening up the clod. The netting is only there to make a neater presentation, like any rolled roast."

As he speaks, he takes a sharp knife and, slitting open the netting, removes the clod and places it on his cutting board. "Now we cut thin slices against the grain of the meat." He works carefully and with concentration. Each one of the scallops that he's cutting is no more than ¼-inch thick.

"It's not easy to get them this thin at home," he comments, as he works. "It takes a sharp knife—preferably a 10-inch slicing knife with a two inch wide blade—and it helps if the meat has been chilled in the freezer just long enough to form a few ice crystals."

Of course an easier way is to ask your butcher to do it for you. But whether you do it yourself or have the butcher do it, you'll end up with scallops that are just as nutritious and tender and flavorful as scallops costing twice as much.

Veal is a treat and if you do explore the less well-known cuts, like the shoulder clod or forequarter meats, you'll find it's an economical food. In fact, Houlton would argue that all the cuts are relatively inexpensive because veal is a dense meat; a small portion of veal is as satisfying as a large portion of some other meats.

Veal comes in several categories. The one you're most likely to encounter in the supermarket is "bob veal," that is, veal from calves that are usually less than one week old. It's pale in color and soft in texture. Some connoisseurs say it lacks the flavor and texture of more mature veal.

Veal from older calves fed a grain diet along with milk is quite pink, rather than the pale creamy pink of bob veal.

Milk veal—also known as "formula fed veal"—comes from calves of up to 16 weeks which have been fed a formulated milk diet. This type of veal is distinguished by a light pink color and firm texture. It's the kind that you're likely to find in some of the finest restaurants, but if you can find milk veal in your local market, try it, and you'll be pleased with the results.

Nutritionally, veal is equivalent to beef, except it's leaner. It has an abundant supply of high-quality protein, B vitamins, iron, zinc, and other minerals. Because it has less fat than beef, it has fewer calories than an equal serving of beef.

To bring out veal's tender and delicate flavor, cook most of the cuts at a low temperature for a shorter period of time than a corresponding beef cut. Since veal lacks the fat of beef, it doesn't do well with broiling. Roasting, braising, and cooking in liquid are the best cooking methods—with the exception of cutlets or scallops, which do well with sauteing. Cook all veal to well done, but avoid over-cooking since veal dries out easily and can become tough.

Veal cutlets of the kind Tom Houlton showed us, take wonderfully to breading. To achieve a thin and even breading, it's important to start with your veal at room temperature. (But, to follow the best food safety practices, avoid leaving the cutlets out of the refrigerator longer than it takes to bring it to room temperature.) Begin by wiping the veal dry and dipping it in flour, and then patting excess flour off. Make an egg mixture by adding two teaspoons of milk or water for each egg. Stir the egg mixture but don't let it get bubbly or the cutlets may not get coated evenly. Now, dip each flour-coated cutlet in the egg mixture, making sure it's covered completely, and then allow the excess to drain.

154

When drained, roll it in the breading mixture, making certain to cover the entire piece. Again pat gently to remove any excess coating. You want to do this to minimize the crumbs that fall into the oil or butter when you saute the cutlets later. Allow the cutlets with the coating to dry and set for 20 minutes, keeping them at room temperature. (Again, to follow good safety practices, don't leave the cutlets for much longer than this before cooking them.)

For pan frying the cutlets, Tom Houlton says the best flavor and color comes from using a mixture of half vegetable oil and half butter. "You'll find this works best if you'll first heat the oil over a medium high heat before adding the butter," he says.

Sauteing veal is something of an art, but once you know some of Houlton's tips, you can count on success. Keep the fat hot enough to sear the food when it's placed in the pan, but don't let the fat get so hot that it smokes; that's a sign that it's breaking down and the flavor is deteriorating. When you have the fat hot but not too hot, add the veal cutlets. Don't reduce the temperature since cooler temperatures will draw out the juices. Be sure to use only room temperature meat, so you don't cool the fat, and also, don't overcrowd the pieces; this will cause steam to form and you'll lose some of the veal's juiciness.

While the cutlets are browning, shake or agitate the pan to avoid rapid browning. Turn the cutlets only once, and only when they're browned thoroughly.

Try them. You may find that clods become a family favorite. And if not clods, try some of the other familiar or new veal recipes that follow.

Roast Veal in Herb and Cream Sauce

1 trussed, 3½ pound boneless veal
    roast
salt and freshly ground pepper, to taste
4 T. butter
2 medium onions, peeled
2 carrots, scraped and cut in thin
    rounds
1 clove garlic, peeled
1 bay leaf
6 sprigs fresh thyme or 1 tsp. dried
6 sprigs fresh tarragon or 1 tsp. dried
1 cup heavy cream
1 T. fresh tarragon, chopped, or 1
    tsp. dried

Sprinkle roast with salt and pepper. Heat half the butter in heavy skillet and, when hot, add meat. Turn meat in the butter to brown lightly on all sides.

Slice onions and scatter slices around meat. Add carrots, garlic, bay leaf, and thyme. Place meat in a 350-degree oven and bake 30 minutes. Turn meat, cover loosely with foil, and bake 45 minutes longer.

Turn meat once more and add tarragon sprigs to skillet. Cover loosely with foil and bake 45 minutes longer.

Remove roast. Add cream to skillet and place on stove. Stir to dissolve brown particles that cling to bottom and sides. If dried tarragon is used, add one teaspoon. Simmer five minutes, put sauce through fine sieve. If fresh tarragon is available, add now. Do not add dried tarragon to sauce after it is put through sieve. When ready to serve, bring sauce to boil and swirl in remaining butter. Slice veal and serve with sauce.
6 servings
Provimi, Inc.

Veal Scaloppine

8 veal rib eye slices
all-purpose flour seasoned with
    paprika, salt, and pepper
4 T. butter
olive oil, if needed
½ pound mushrooms, thinly sliced
½ clove garlic, crushed
1 cup beef broth
½ cup tomato sauce
½ green pepper, chopped
4 ounces noodles
Parmesan cheese, as desired

Pound meat until thin and dredge in seasoned flour. Brown in butter, adding a little olive oil, if necessary. Place in baking dish and add mushrooms, garlic, broth, and tomato sauce. Cover and bake in a 325-degree oven for 30 minutes; add green pepper and bake 15 minutes more, uncovered. While meat bakes, cook noodles and drain. Transfer to heated serving platter, arranging veal on top of noodles. Drizzle sauce from pan over meat and sprinkle with Parmesan cheese.
4 servings
Provimi, Inc.

Veal Cutlet Cordon Bleu

12 thin veal cutlets
salt and pepper, to taste
6 thin slices Swiss cheese
6 thin slices ham
all-purpose flour, as needed
3 eggs, beaten
¾ cup bread crumbs
¾ cup butter

Flatten the veal slices with a cleaver; sprinkle with salt and pepper. Put one slice of cheese and one slice of ham on each of six veal slices; cover with remaining veal slices. Pound edges together. Dip in flour, then eggs, then in crumbs. Fry in butter for eight minutes.
6 servings
Provimi, Inc.

French bread, spread with garlic butter and heated in the oven, makes a nice accompaniment to this Italian specialty. Also, asparagus goes well with veal parmigiana.

Veal Parmigiana

2 T. salad oil
1 green onion, finely chopped
⅔ cup (6 ounces) tomato paste
1 T. sugar
1 tsp. oregano, optional
1 tsp. sweet basil
1 tsp. salt
3 whole black peppercorns
1 cup boiling water
4 veal cutlets
1 egg, beaten
½ tsp. salt
¼ tsp. pepper
½ cup fine bread crumbs
3 T. Parmesan cheese, or aged cheese, grated
4 T. salad oil
2 slices cheddar cheese, cut in half
parsley, as needed for garnish

To make sauce, heat two tablespoons salad oil. Add and cook green onion. Add tomato paste and cook for five minutes, stirring constantly. Add sugar, oregano, basil, one teaspoon salt, peppercorns, and water. Simmer for 30 minutes.

Dip veal cutlets into egg beaten with one-half teaspoon salt and pepper. Then dip into mixture of bread crumbs and cheese. Brown on both sides in hot salad oil in a heavy skillet.

Place in a single layer in a shallow baking pan and pour sauce over meat. Bake in a 350-degree oven for 30 minutes.

Top each cutlet with a half slice of cheese. Sprinkle with more grated cheese, if desired. Continue baking for 15 minutes.

Serve hot, accompanied by sauce. Garnish with parsley.
4 servings
January 18, 1958

Stuffed Veal Birds in Sour Cream Sauce

½ cup celery, diced
¼ cup onion, chopped
½ cup butter
2 cups soft bread cubes
¾ tsp. salt
⅛ tsp. sage
dash pepper
1 T. parsley, chopped
¼ cup milk
8 boneless veal cutlets, 4 to 5 ounces each
⅓ cup all-purpose flour
¼ cup water
¼ cup white cooking wine
½ pint (1 cup) sour cream
1 can (4 ounces) mushrooms, drained

Saute celery and onion in one-quarter cup butter until onion is tender. Combine with bread cubes, one-quarter teaspoon salt, sage, pepper, parsley, and milk; toss lightly. Divide dressing evenly between cutlets, placing dressing in center of each cutlet. Roll meat around dressing and fasten with wooden picks or skewers. Roll meat in flour, saving leftover flour. Brown meat in remaining butter, turning as necessary to brown on all sides. Add water and wine; cover tightly. Cook slowly until meat is tender, about 45 minutes. Remove meat to serving platter and keep warm. Blend together leftover flour and sour cream. Stir into drippings; add mushrooms and remaining salt. Cook, stirring constantly, until gravy is heated and thickened. Serve with veal birds.
8 servings
October 24, 1970

Tarragon is a favorite salad herb and is an ideal flavoring for veal.

Veal Tarragon

2 pounds veal round steak, cut
*   1-inch thick*
¼ cup all-purpose flour
1 tsp. salt
⅛ tsp. pepper
1 T. paprika
2 T. lard
3 medium onions, sliced
½ tsp. tarragon
1 T. lemon juice or vinegar
1 cup water

Cut veal in serving-size pieces. Combine flour, salt, pepper, and paprika; rub into cut surfaces of veal. Brown meat in hot lard; add onion and brown thoroughly. Sprinkle in tarragon; add water and lemon juice or vinegar. Cook, covered, over low heat until tender, about one hour.
6 servings
October 4, 1958

Let's peek into a Wisconsin country kitchen of 1909 to see how the housewife prepared "Delicious Veal."

Delicious Veal

Take a veal steak from the round bone, cut off all the fat and cut out the bone. Cut into pieces the desired size, then dip first in crumbs, then egg, crumbs again, and then into the egg again. Fry in an iron spider till a light brown, cover, and turn a low flame for about ten minutes; then pour in enough milk to cover the meat and place in the oven for one hour. The milk will all be absorbed by the meat and the meat will be so tender only a fork will be needed in cutting it. Always season the bread crumbs before breading any meat.
August 19, 1909

Veal Provencale

1 small onion, chopped
1 carrot, peeled, chopped
1 stalk celery, chopped
1 T. butter
¼ ounce dried mushrooms, covered
*   with hot water, soaked 30*
*   minutes, drained, chopped*
⅓ cup dry white wine
⅔ cup water
4 canned plum tomatoes, drained,
*   chopped*
1 tsp. chicken stock base
1 tsp. cornstarch dissolved in 1 T. water
salt and pepper, to taste
1 T. chopped parsley
1 small clove garlic, minced
½ tsp. grated lemon rind
4 veal cube steaks
2 T. butter

Saute onion, carrot, and celery in one tablespoon butter until onion is limp. Add mushrooms and wine. Boil until liquid is almost evaporated. Add water, tomatoes, and stock base. Bring to a boil; reduce heat and simmer 10 minutes. Stir in cornstarch mixture; cook until bubbly. Add salt and pepper. Combine parsley, garlic, and lemon rind. Cook cube steaks in two tablespoons butter.

To serve, spoon sauce over cube steaks; sprinkle with parsley mixture.
4 servings
Provimi, Inc.

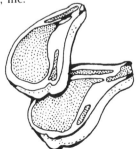

Stuffed Veal Shoulder

4 pounds boned veal shoulder
8 slices bacon
½ cup onion, medium chopped
2 packets saltine crackers, coarsely
*   crumbled*
¼ tsp. pepper
3 T. dill, finely chopped or 1 tsp.
*   dried dill*
¼ tsp. garlic powder
1 chicken bouillon cube
1 cup boiling water

Sauce:

2 T. white vinegar
2 T. dill, finely chopped
1 container of sour cream to suit
*   taste*

Have butcher cut a pocket in the meat. Fry bacon until well done. Drain on paper towels. Crumble. In same skillet, saute onion until golden. Add bacon and onion to cracker crumbs, then add pepper, three tablespoons fresh dill and garlic powder and blend. Dissolve bouillon cube in water, add to crumb mixture. Fill cavity in meat with stuffing.

Bake uncovered in a 300-degree oven at least two hours (30 minutes per pound).

Prepare sauce by adding vinegar and two tablespoons dill to sour cream; mix thoroughly.

Place veal on a serving platter. Serve with sauce.

6 to 8 servings
February 17, 1968

Veal Pot Pie

This is a comparatively inexpensive dish even with meat prices soaring skyward, while it is tasty and nourishing as well. Take for its making a pound and a half solid meat from the rump and two pounds from the shoulder or other cheap piece, that has but little fat. Cut in square pieces, dredge with salt, pepper and flour, then brown in the frying pan or shallow iron kettle, using butter or good pork drippings for the browning. When nicely browned, put into a Scotch kettle or saucepan, cover with boiling water, add a little onion for seasoning and, if desired, a little tomato (this is a matter to be decided by individual preference) with salt and pepper to taste, and simmer gently until nearly tender. It will take an hour and a half or two hours. When nearly done add three potatoes peeled and sliced. When the potatoes are about done, thicken the gravy with a little flour and butter rubbed together and add a teaspoonful minced parsley. Turn into a silver baker or earthen casserole, and lay over the top a crust of baking powder biscuits cut into shape and fitted together to form a perfect crust. Set in a hot oven long enough to bake the biscuit a crispy brown.

April 28, 1910

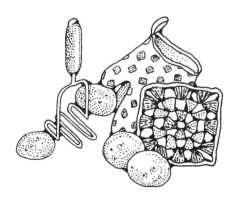

Veal and Onion Casserole with Dumplings

½ cup all-purpose flour

1 tsp. paprika

1½ pounds veal round steak, cut in 2-inch pieces

shortening, as needed for browning

½ tsp. salt

⅛ tsp. pepper

1 cup water

1¼ cups (10½ ounce can) condensed cream of chicken soup

1½ cups water

1½ cups small onions, cooked and drained

Dumplings:

1 cup sifted all-purpose flour

2 tsp. baking powder

¼ tsp. salt

½ tsp. poultry seasoning

½ tsp. celery seeds

1 tsp. onion, finely chopped

1½ tsp. poppy seeds

2 T. vegetable oil

½ cup milk

2 cups corn flakes

2 T. butter or margarine, melted

Preheat oven to 425 degrees.

Combine flour and paprika. Coat veal pieces with flour mixture. In heavy fry pan, brown meat on both sides in small amount of heated shortening. Add salt, pepper, and one cup water. Cover and simmer 30 minutes or until meat is tender. Transfer meat to a two-quart baking dish. Add chicken soup and water to drippings; stir until smooth. Cook over medium heat, stirring constantly, until mixture boils. Pour over meat. Add cooked onions.

Prepare dumplings by sifting together flour, baking powder, salt, and poultry seasoning. Mix in celery seeds, poppy seeds, and onions. Add vegetable oil and milk, stirring only until combined. Crush corn flakes into fine crumbs. Combine butter and corn flake crumbs. Drop dumplings by tablespoonfuls into buttered crumbs, rolling until well-coated. Place on top of casserole.

Bake uncovered for about 25 minutes or until golden brown. Serve immediately.

6 servings

November 17, 1962

This is a large recipe, one-half to be served immediately, the remainder to be frozen. You'll need two three-quart casseroles lined with heavy-duty aluminum foil.

Veal Marengo

3 T. olive oil
4 pounds shoulder of veal, cut in
*   1½-inch cubes*
1 clove garlic, minced
20 small white onions
1 pound mushrooms, sliced
2½ tsp. salt
½ tsp. black pepper
3 T. all-purpose flour
2 cups tomato sauce
1 cup dry white wine
2 cups chicken broth
2 herb bouquets, each containing 1
*   celery stalk with leaves, several*
*   sprigs of parsley, a bay leaf, and*
*   dash of thyme, all tied together*
*   with stem of parsley*

Heat the oil in a large skillet with the veal and the garlic, placing just enough in the skillet at a time to cover the bottom. Place veal in two casseroles lined with heavy-duty foil, dividing equally. Add a little more oil, if necessary. Brown the mushrooms and onions very quickly and lightly, and arrange over meat. Add flour, salt, and pepper to the skillet, stirring into remaining oil. Add tomato sauce, wine, and broth. Cook, stirring constantly, until thick and smooth. Pour over veal. Add to each casserole a small herb bouquet.

Cover casseroles and bake in a 325-degree oven for one and one-quarter hours. Remove bouquets.

To freeze, let the casserole cool. Remove foil containing the cooled food from the casserole dish. To reheat, fit back into original casserole, cover, and place in oven. Solidly frozen, it will take one hour at 325 degrees. It will take less time if allowed to stand at room temperature until almost thawed.

6 servings for each casserole
January 2, 1965

Veal Paprika

4 veal slices, thawed but cold
3 T. butter
2 T. oil
2 medium onions, sliced
1 red pepper, seeded, chopped
2 T. all-purpose flour
1⅔ cup whipping cream
1 tsp. chicken stock base
½ tsp. sweet paprika
⅓ cup Gruyere or Swiss cheese
3 T. Parmesan cheese, grated
1½ cups frozen peas
⅓ cup dairy sour cream
salt and white pepper, to taste
6 ounces medium noodles, cooked,
*   drained*

Prepare veal slices in butter and oil according to basic directions.* Remove from pan; keep warm. In drippings, saute onion and pepper until onion is limp over medium heat. Stir in flour; cook until bubbly. Gradually add cream, cooking and stirring until thickened and bubbly. Stir in stock base, paprika, cheeses and peas. Stir until cheese is melted. Stir in sour cream. Combine half the sauce with noodles in serving dish; arrange veal on top. Serve with remaining sauce.

*Basic Directions: Place each cold veal slice between two pieces of waxed paper and pound with flat side of mallet until about $\frac{1}{16}$th-inch thick. Sprinkle both sides with salt, white pepper, and flour. In large skillet, melt butter with oil; saute veal over medium high heat about three minutes per side until golden brown.

4 servings
Provimi, Inc.

Complete this menu by serving Osso Buco with a vegetable platter, including julienne carrots, green beans almondine, and brussel sprouts.

Osso Buco

4 slices veal shank, 1-inch thick
all-purpose flour, seasoned with salt
*   and pepper*
4 T. butter
½ cup onion, chopped
1 medium carrot, chopped
½ cup celery, chopped
1 clove garlic, finely chopped
½ cup white wine
seasoned stock, as needed
2 T. tomato puree (optional)

Roll veal rounds thoroughly in seasoned flour. Melt butter in heavy skillet and brown veal on all sides. Add butter, onion, carrot, celery, garlic, wine, enough seasoned stock to cover veal half way, and tomato puree. Bring mixture to a boil, then reduce heat. Cover and simmer gently about one and one-half hours, turning veal once while cooking. Place veal on serving platter and spoon some broth over it.
2 servings
Provimi, Inc.

Veal in Wine Casserole

2 T. vegetable oil
2 T. butter
2 pounds veal, diced
8 ounces fresh mushrooms, sliced
3 T. all-purpose flour
¾ tsp. salt
⅛ tsp. pepper
1 cup chicken broth
1 cup dry white wine
1 small bay leaf
¼ cup parsley, minced
1 pound small white onions, drained
hot, buttered noodles, as needed for
*   6 servings*

Heat oil and butter in skillet at medium high and brown meat quickly. Remove meat and set aside. Saute mushrooms, remove, and set aside. Mix flour, salt and pepper into pan juices. Add chicken broth and wine. Cook at medium heat until mixture boils and thickens. Stir constantly. Add bay leaf and parsley. Pour meat, mushrooms, and sauce into two and one-half quart casserole dish.

Cover and bake in a 325-degree oven for 30 minutes. Add onions, cover and bake for 20 more minutes. Serve with buttered noodles.
6 servings
Provimi, Inc.

This tasty loaf recipe was found in a 1901 magazine.

Veal Loaf

Three pounds of raw, chopped veal, three eggs, lump of butter the size of a walnut, three tablespoonfuls of rich, sweet cream, one tablespoonful of sifted sage, one tablespoonful of salt, and four soda crackers rolled fine. Form into a long loaf and bake about three hours, basting with hot water and butter while baking.
January 17, 1901

Pressed Veal

Two pounds veal, one-fourth can pimientos, one dozen small sweet pickles, one tablespoonful of gelatin, one tablespoonful of butter. Cook veal until tender. Put meat and pickles through food chopper. Cut pimientos into small pieces with knife. Dissolve gelatin in a cup of water. Add melted butter and salt and pepper to taste. Mix thoroughly and heat, not boil, then put into bowl and slice when cold.
May 18, 1916

Veal Logs with Blue Cheese

1 pound ground veal
¾ cup fresh bread crumbs
1 egg, slightly beaten
2 T. milk
2 T. snipped parsley
1 T. prepared mustard
1 tsp. salt
½ tsp. pepper
¼ cup onion, chopped
2 T. salad oil
1 can condensed cream of
*   mushroom soup, undiluted*
½ cup milk
¼ cup American blue cheese (about
*   1¼ ounces), crumbled*
parsley sprigs, as needed for garnish

Combine veal with bread crumbs, egg, milk, parsley, mustard, salt, and pepper. Add chopped onions. Shape into eight logs. Brown logs in hot salad oil. Remove from pan and set aside. In same pan, blend soup and milk. Return veal logs to pan and simmer, covered, for about 20 minutes. Add cheese and simmer, while stirring, until cheese is melted. Garnish with parsley sprigs.
8 servings
May 13, 1971

Veal Vittelo

2¼-inch slices bermuda onion
2¼-inch slices beefsteak tomato
2 slices American cheese
4 ground veal steaks
salt and pepper, to taste
1 can cream of mushroom soup

Place onion, tomato, and cheese on one ground veal steak and cover with second steak and press edges together to form a pocket. Bake in a 325-degree oven for 15 minutes or until veal is turning brown. Cover with heated but not diluted soup mixture.
2 servings
Provimi, Inc.

Schnitzel a la Holstein

butter and oil, as needed
12 ounces breaded ground veal
*   steaks*
4 eggs
2 green onions, thinly sliced
1 T. capers, drained
4 anchovies, drained, halved

Heat two tablepoons butter and two tablespoons oil in a large skillet. Fry patties over medium to high heat for three minutes per side until golden brown. Fry eggs in additional butter; place one on top of each patty. Sprinkle each with green onion and capers. Crisscross each with anchovies.
4 servings
Provimi, Inc.

Golden Veal Paella

salt and pepper, to taste
6 ground veal steaks
paprika, to taste
1 tsp. thyme, crushed
⅓ cup white wine or vermouth
2 garlic cloves, crushed
3 T. salad oil
1 can whole green asparagus spears
2 cups seasoned croutons
¼ cup slivered almonds
1 11-ounce can of cheddar cheese soup
6 black olives, sliced

Salt and pepper veal steaks. Sprinkle with paprika and thyme. Marinate for one-half hour in wine and garlic. Remove steaks and garlic from marinade and save. Saute garlic in oil, add steaks and saute gently until lightly browned. In a shallow casserole or pan place asparagus spears, spread croutons evenly over asparagus. Remove steaks from pan and arrange them on top of croutons. Lightly brown slivered almonds in remaining pan juice and remove almonds. Blend soup with reserved wine marinade until smooth and creamy, pour evenly over veal steaks in pan. Sprinkle almonds over veal, garnish each steak with olive slices.

Place in a 350 degree oven and bake for 30 minutes.
4 to 6 servings
Provimi, Inc.

Good advice accompanies an old recipe from around the turn of the century.

Veal Croquettes

Take one and one-third cups of cold cooked veal, chopped fine, one teaspoon of lemon juice, a dash of celery salt and one of paprika, one teaspoon of finely shredded parsley, a few drops of onion juice, and half a teaspoon of salt, mix all well together, and, if it seems too dry to mold well, add some of the gravy, or, if that is not at hand, make a white sauce from a tablespoon of butter and flour mixed and heated, and half a cup of milk stirred into it. Shape into croquettes, dip into well-beaten egg, roll in sifted crumbs, and fry in deep fat. A frying basket is convenient to have. Do not put too many in the fat at once or they will cool the grease so much that they will crack open and soak fat.
May 26, 1905

In this delicious recipe for cooked veal leftovers, you may substitute cooked beef or ham.

Veal Patties with Tomato Sauce

2 cups leftover cooked veal, ground
2 cups soft bread crumbs
1 T. onion, minced
1 T. green pepper, finely chopped
1 egg, slightly beaten
⅓ cup milk
1 tsp. salt
⅛ tsp. pepper
2 T. butter

Combine veal, bread crumbs, onion, green pepper, egg, milk, salt, and pepper; mix thoroughly. Shape into six round patties about one-inch thick. Brown in butter. Remove patties from pan while preparing sauce.

Tomato Sauce:

1 T. onion, finely chopped
1 T. green pepper, finely chopped
¼ cup butter
¼ cup all-purpose flour
1 tsp. salt
dash of pepper
1 cup milk
1 cup cooked tomatoes

Saute onion and green pepper in butter, over low heat. Blend in flour, salt, and a dash of pepper. Add milk, stirring constantly and cook until sauce is thickened. Add cooked tomatoes and heat thoroughly.

To serve, pour freshly made sauce over patties.
6 servings
February 4, 1961

Foie De Veau Saute

6 slices veal liver, cut ½ inch thick
*   (about 1½ pounds)*
salt, to taste
freshly ground black pepper, to taste
all-purpose flour, as needed
4 T. butter
2 T. vegetable oil
½ cup beef or chicken stock, fresh
*   or canned*
1 T. soft butter
few drops of lemon juice
2 T. fresh parsley, finely chopped

Season the liver slices with salt and few grindings of pepper. Dip the slices in flour, then vigorously shake off all but a fine dusting. In a heavy 12-inch skillet or saute pan, melt the butter with the oil over high heat. When the foam subsides, saute the liver quickly for two or three minutes on each side, turning the slices with kitchen tongs. Remove the liver to a heated platter and cover loosely to keep warm.

Working quickly, pour off almost all the drippings from the skillet, leaving just enough to film the bottom. Add the beef or chicken stock and cook over high heat, stirring constantly and scraping in any brown bits that cling to the pan.

Continue to cook until the stock is syrupy and has been reduced to about one-quarter cup. Remove the pan from the heat and swirl in soft butter and lemon juice. Pour the sauce over the liver, sprinkle with parsley and serve at once.
6 servings
Provimi, Inc.

About the Author

Harvard graduate and rice grower Mitzi Ayala of Davis, California, enjoys talking to the non-farm public about agriculture. She does this as the hostess and producer of "Mitzi's Country Magazine," a weekly television program, and as a professional public speaker who gives more than forty-five talks a year. In addition, as a columnist for Capitol News Service, she's the author of more than three hundred seventy-five syndicated newspaper articles. Besides the Prairie Farmer Cookbooks, she is the author of *The Farmer's Cookbook* and *Managerial Innovation*.

Index

Ham Recipes

Hotdog Recipes

Lamb Recipes

Light Meals

Menu

Main Dishes

169

Pork Recipes